This Family Catechism belongs to

_____

Baptisms

First Communions

Confirmations

Marriages

Books by Father McBride

*The Kingdom and the Glory: Commentary on Matthew
*To Love and Be Loved by Jesus: Commentary on Mark
*The Human Face of Jesus: A Commentary on Luke
*The Divine Presence of Jesus: A Commentary on John
*The Gospel of the Holy Spirit: A Commentary on Acts
*The Second Coming of Jesus: A Commentary on Apocalypse
*Essentials of the Faith
*Father McBride's Teen Catechism
*Father McBride's Family Catechism
*Millennium: End of Time or a Jubilee?
Invitation: A Catholic Learning Guide
The Seven Last Words of Jesus
A Retreat with Pope John XXIII
The Story of the Church
Catholic Evangelization
Images of Jesus
Images of Mary
Saints Are People

Other books by Father McBride

Homilies for the New Liturgy
Catechetics: A Theology of Proclamation
A Short Course on the Bible
The Human Dimensions of Catechetics
The Pearl and the Seed
Heschel: Religious Educator
Growing in Grace: Bible History
Christian Formation of Catholic Education
Year of the Lord: Cycles A,B,C
Father McBride's Homily Reflections: Cycles A,B,C
Death Shall Have No Dominion
Creative Teaching in Christian Education
The Quest For Content in Christian Education
Catechists Never Stop Learning
The Ten Commandments: Sounds of Love From Sinai
Staying Faithful

*Published by Our Sunday Visitor, Inc.

Father McBride's
FAMILY
CATECHISM

Based on the Catechism
of the Catholic Church

ALFRED McBRIDE, O.PRAEM.

Our Sunday Visitor Publishing Division
Our Sunday Visitor, Inc.
Huntington, Indiana 46750

Nihil Obstat: Rev. John J. Connelly, S.T.D.
Censor Librorum

Imprimatur: ✠ Bernard Cardinal Law, D.D.
Archbishop of Boston
October 24, 1997

The *nihil obstat* and *imprimatur* are offical declarations that a book or pamphlet is free of docrinal or moral error. No implication is contained therein that those who have granted the *nihil obstat* and the *imprimatur* agree with the content, opinions, or statements expressed.

Our Sunday Visitor Publishing Division
Our Sunday Visitor, Inc.
200 Noll Plaza
Huntington, IN 46750

ISBN:0-87973-930-4
LCCCN: 97-69273

Cover Design by Rebecca Heaston
PRINTED IN THE UNITED STATES OF AMERICA
930

Table of Contents

Chapter Three • Life in Christ

Chapter Four • Christian Prayer

The Sistine Madonna
— by Raphael

Introduction

How to Know and Love God

The whole concern of doctrine and its teaching must be directed to the love that never ends. Whether something is proposed for belief, for hope or for action, the love of our Lord must always be made accessible, so that anyone can see that all the works of perfect Christian virtue spring from love and have no other objective than to arrive at love (*Roman Catechism*, Preface, 11).

The Church in her history has published two major catechisms. The first was the catechism of the Council of Trent (or the *Roman Catechism*) published in 1566. The second was the *Catechism of the Catholic Church,* published in 1992.

Pope John Paul II said of this new *Catechism*, "I declare it [the *Catechism*] to be a sure norm of faith. . . . Therefore, I ask the Church's pastors and the Christian faithful to receive this Catechism in a spirit of communion and to use it assiduously in fulfilling their mission of proclaiming the faith and calling people to Gospel life."

The Pope also said he hoped the new *Catechism* would be helpful in preparing local catechisms. It is in that spirit that I have written this *Family Catechism*. As you will see, it is more than a collection of questions and answers. Each lesson contains several major elements:

• Resource. Here are the paragraph numbers of the *Catechism of the Catholic Church* (referred to as *CCC*) treated in each particular chapter.

• An opening story that relates to the faith teaching and situates the faith truth in a life experience.

• A "*Catechism* Reflection" that summarizes and applies to Christian living of the doctrine under consideration. Within this section there are always three questions, with answers taken from the *Catechism*. This method serves two purposes: (a) To focus attention on the actual words of the *Catechism*; and (b) to stimulate the reader to go to the *Catechism* itself for further study and prayer.

• A section titled "Connecting to Our Family" where an application of the doctrine is specifically directed to Catholic family life. This is accompanied by three sets of questions designed to help families evaluate their lives in the light of the *Catechism.*

• A family prayer. The *Catechism* should always be studied in an environment of prayer and faith.

• Glossary. Catechism language contains many technical terms that need our awareness and a precise description or definition of the terms. Knowledge of these "code words" facilitates communication about doctrines that have a history from New Testament times through twenty Ecumenical Councils and other forms of theological reflection.

Structure of the *Catechism (CCC)*

This book follows the structure of the *Catechism of the Catholic Church* which is divided into four parts:
• The Creed – Faith Professed;
• The Liturgy – The celebration of the Faith in the sacraments and the Liturgy of the Hours;
• The Moral Life – The living of the Faith through the life of virtues and the Ten Commandments;
• The Life of Prayer – Praying our Faith in the liturgy, the Our Father, and in vocal, meditative, and contemplative prayer.

Each of these four parts has two sections. The first section deals with the foundational teachings. The second concerns itself with the practice of the material. For example, part one of the Moral Life (Life in Christ) lays out the principles for Christian living, such as the Beatitudes, Christ's two laws of love, the virtues, the role of grace and the Holy Spirit, and the philosophy of the Church's social teachings. Section two explores the practical meaning of all this as found in the Ten Commandments.

Certain themes appear in every section of the *Catechism* and are reflected in the *Family Catechism*:

(1) The Trinity. The work of salvation from sin and the gift of divine life always proceed from the acts of Father, Son, and Holy Spirit working in harmony. Every doctrine ultimately reflects a Trinitarian background.

(2) Jesus Christ. In a special way, Jesus Christ embodies and achieves the divine plan of salvation from sin and the gift of divine life for us. Hence the *Catechism* is Christological in focus.

(3) The Holy Spirit and the Church. From the moment the Holy Spirit manifested the Church at Pentecost, the Spirit remains to sustain the Church throughout history as the sacrament of salvation. The teachings of the *Catechism* are always ecclesial and Spirit-guided.

(4) Revelation and Faith Dialogue. The *Catechism* follows a process found in Scripture which begins with God's self-revelation and the loving plan to save us. This revelation calls us to a faith response. Hence a living catechesis is a dialogue of salvation between God and us.

(5) Apostolic Tradition. Our religion began with Christ and the Apostles. The Apostolic Tradition has continued in the writings and witness of the Fathers, Councils, and Magisterium. Connected to this are the

witnesses of the saints, mystics, and theologians. This theme is abundantly evident in the *Catechism*.

(6) The Bible. The *Catechism* follows the Scriptures' approach of a history of salvation. God's divine plan to save us unfolds from the first pages of Genesis to the final pages of Apocalypse. The *Catechism* is filled with the texts of Scripture and the unified vision provide by Scripture. The Bible is quoted three thousand times.

Connecting to Our Family

Most people realize we are in a period of profound social change. At the end of the nineteenth century, the impact of the industrial revolution caused a revolutionary change in social life. Now at the end of the twentieth century, the technological revolution is causing a similar adjustment in our world outlook, how we earn a living, and how we raise a family in a new social setting.

The two revolutions (industrial and technological) have spawned what many call a secularistic way of life. Because of them, the world is "too much with us." This means we are so drawn, attracted, invaded, and seduced by secularity that we have lost our spiritual bearings. How are we to raise a family that has a faith perspective when everything around us seems to be going the other way?

The answer to this question may be found in understanding these Christian essentials:

(1) *The hunger of the soul for God has not changed*. No social revolutions can abolish the fundamental thirst of the human heart for God. The craving for the infinite has been in the hearts of Christians from the first moment there was a Christianity. The drive to God has persisted through the Roman persecutions, the fall of the Roman Empire, the Dark Ages, the Black Plague, the religious wars of the Reformation, the humanism of the Renaissance, the revolt against faith in the Enlightenment, two world wars, a depression, the Cold War, and now the coming of the third millenium.

The stage sets have changed, but the heart remains the same. The heart wants life, especially the most fully satisfying kind that comes from God. The religious impulse has never died. The culture claimed that God was dead. Time has shown that it was the culture that was deadly, not God. Conscientious parents have always known that religion and morality are non-negotiable for raising children and bonding a family. Indeed, never has the restless heart been more restless for God.

(2) *Learning and witnessing religion is more important than ever*. The churning storms of modern culture are both exhilarating and disorienting. Our techno-world fascinates us, frustrates us, and is here to stay. It is not designed to give us a map of life, much less walk us to the gates of paradise. We need not be hostile to this burst of technical creativity. It will

ultimately do a great deal of good for us. Religion has proven time and again that it is able to live with a new culture and to offer the riches of Christ to it.

But the intensity of modern culture is often unnerving. TV, computers, the Internet, and the other wonders of communication and transportation clamor for our attention and our inherent need to bring some order to this chaos. In a quieter time, the Catholic culture of the old ethnic neighborhoods served as kind of a cocoon in which we could safely maneuver our families into modern life. Now, what was once assumed must be created. As many say, it must be "intentional," meaning that the commitment to a faith life requires much more awareness, energy, and creative attention than before.

The family does not do this alone. The parish — centered on the liturgy and aided by religious education programs, Catholic schools, and other faith-formation services — provides an effective climate for the family's faith life. The parish community of faith is a pillar for family life. The communion of the parish members among themselves and in union with the diocese and the entire Body of Christ throughout the world is at the service of the family as it seeks to learn and witness the faith. And learning and witnessing our Catholic religion is needed now more than ever.

(3) *The Catechism of the Catholic Church is an essential means to a learning and witnessing faith.* From the days of the Apostles, the Church has been engaged in preaching, teaching, and witnessing the Gospel of Christ. This is called the Ministry of the Word. As the Church expanded throughout the centuries, many ways were invented to fulfill this call. A unique form of this ministry was created by the Church at the Council of Trent in the face of the challenges of the Reformation — the *Roman Catechism*. Its adaptations in small catechisms and textbooks over the next four hundred years proved to be a remarkable tool for producing an enlightened and active faith for the universal Church.

Today we have the successor to that book in the new *Catechism of the Catholic Church*. It is at the service of the liturgy and Scripture and the universal teaching and evangelizing mission of the Church. Every Catholic family should have a copy of this *Catechism* along with the Bible. Just as adaptations were created to implement the *Roman Catechism*, so the same will be necessary for this new one. This is the purpose of the *Family Catechism*.

I hope that you will use this book to help you make a lifetime study of the full *Catechism of the Catholic Church*. My book is simply a means to an end, not just for study, but for living the faith of the Church.

Reverend Alfred McBride, O. Praem.

Chapter One

The Profession of Faith

The Crucifixion
— by Raphael

Lesson 1
My Soul Longs for You, O God

Resource: *CCC* paragraphs 26-49

Come, O Lord, and stir our hearts. Call us back to yourself. Kindle your fire in us and carry us away. Let us scent your fragrance and taste your sweetness. Let us love you and hasten to your side.

— St. Augustine, *Confessions*, 8, 4

Brother Luc Had No Regrets

On May 21, 1996, seven Trappist monks from the Atlas monastery in Algeria were martyred. The executioners belonged to the Group Islamic Army (GIA). They issued a communique which stated, "We have cut the throats of the seven monks, faithful to our promise to do so. . . . Praise be to God."

Three years before, the GIA had warned the monks of Atlas of this possibility. "The monks who live among the working classes can legitimately be killed." The monks resolved to stay. The Abbot General of the Order, Dom Bernardo Olivera, commented on their decision in these words: "The decision of our brothers of Atlas is not unique. All of us as monks and nuns of the Benedictine-Cistercian tradition take a vow of "stability" which binds us until death to our community and to the place where that community lives."

How can we understand the depth of this vow? The words of Father Christian, a monk of Atlas, to the head of the GIA explain it this way:

"Brother, allow me to address you as man to man, believer to believer. In the present conflict in which our country is living, it seems impossible to us to take sides. The fact we are foreigners forbids it. Our state as monks binds us to the choice of God for us which is prayer and the simple life, manual work, hospitality and the sharing with everyone, especially the poor. These reasons for our life are a free choice for each one of us. They bind us until death."

Abbot Olivera saw an essential link between their quest for God in the monastery and their martyrdom. "From the martyrdom of spiritual combat to the martyrdom of blood poured out, it is the same cry which calls to love and forgiveness and love of one's enemies. Life is stronger than death. Love has the last word." Their faith overcame any natural instinct for revenge. They took the words of Jesus literally and forgave their enemies. Their longing for God ended in absolute love.

15

Brother Luc, eighty-years-old, left behind a most touching memento of the whole affair. It was a cassette of a song that he hoped someone would play on the day of his funeral. It was Edith Piaf singing, "No, I have no regrets."

We Were Born With a Desire for God

Pope John Paul II's Apostolic Letter, "On The Coming of the Third Millennium," concerning the preparation for the Jubilee of the Year 2000, recalls that the Church of the first millennium was born from the blood of martyrs. The greatest witness to anyone's longing for God is the willingness to shed one's blood on behalf of this belief. That is what the monks of Atlas did. Their shining heroism illumines what is true of each one of us and all of our families. Every single human being possesses the inner drive to an absolute, an ultimate, an infinite, which is nothing less than God.

Man and woman are in search of God.

The *Catechism of the Catholic Church* opens with this profound truth about each of us. The opening chapter is entitled, "Man's Capacity For God." God created us in such a way that only in him will we find real personal fulfillment, truth, and happiness. Our human dignity rests on the fact that we are called to communion with God. The invitation to be friends with God begins the moment we come into being. God created us in an act of love and by that love holds us in being.

Modern culture tries to teach us that we are purely secular people. But God made us essentially religious. Even though America is thought to be a thoroughly secular country, it has more houses of worship per capita than any other industrialized nation. History shows that people have expressed their urge toward God in prayers, sacrifices, rituals, churches, temples, synagogues, and mosques right into the present age.

St. Paul was right when he told the Athenians, "He [God] made from one the whole human race to dwell on the entire surface of the earth, and he fixed the ordered seasons and boundaries of their regions, so *that people might seek God, even perhaps grope for him and find him* [emphasis added], though indeed he is not far from any one of us. For 'In him we live and move and have our being . . .' " (Acts 17:26-28).

If this be true, why have so many failed to find God?

Many reasons account for this. The presence of so many evils in the world overwhelm some and cause them to revolt against the very idea of a God who lets this happen. Religious illiteracy and indifference, which deprive people of even the basic knowledge about God, are other causes. Often wealth so distracts the rich that they never think of God. The scandalous behavior of some believers drives honest searchers away from religion. Last, personal sinfulness inclines the sinner to deny the sin, refuse to take responsibility for it, and hide from God. ". . . the man and his wife hid themselves from the LORD God among the trees of the garden" (Gen 3:8).

16

How then are we to find the God for whom we long?

God reveals himself in three ways:

(1) *Through Creation*: St. Paul tells us that the Creator can be known through the works of creation. St. Augustine puts this truth more dramatically. "Question the beauty of the earth. Question the beauty of the sea . . . question the beauty of the sky. . . . All respond: 'See, we are beautiful.' Their beauty is a profession. These beauties are subject to change. Who made them if not the Beautiful One who is not subject to change?" (*Sermon* 241, 2).

(2) *Through the Human Person:* If we think about what we are like, we notice that we want to know the truth and experience perfect beauty. We are attracted to moral goodness. We appreciate our freedom and struggle to maintain it. We are aware of the voice of conscience and try to live by it. We thirst for nothing less than the infinite and absolute happiness. These experiences make us aware of our souls and our spiritual nature. The more we realize these facts about ourselves, the more we are drawn to the reality of God.

(3) *Through Direct Revelation:* Wonderful as the world and the human person are as sources for knowing God, the ambiguity of the signs, caused by human sinfulness, required an explicit and assuring direct Revelation from God about his love for us, his plan for our salvation, and his inner life. In Sacred Scripture, as understood within the faith of the Church, we have a sure and certain guide to the extraordinary riches of God. Most of what we will be studying in the *Catechism* is derived from Scripture as prayed in the liturgy and transmitted to us by the Church, her Apostolic Tradition, and her teaching office (Magisterium).

In each of our lessons we will have a reflection section with some questions, the answers to which are taken from the *Catechism*. In addition, we will offer you some questions for personal application of the materials, followed by an invitation to prayer, and a concluding glossary.

Catechism Reflection

1. How do we know we are essentially religious beings?

"In many ways, throughout history down to the present, men have given expression to their quest for God in their religious beliefs and behavior: in their prayers, sacrifices, rituals, meditations, and so forth. These forms of religious expression, despite the ambiguities they often bring with them, are so universal that one may well call man a *religious being* . . ." (cf. Acts 17:26-28) (*CCC* 28).

2. Why do we lose our sense of being basically religious?

"But this 'intimate and vital bond of man to God' (*GS* 19, 1) can be forgotten, overlooked or even explicitly rejected by man. Such attitudes can have different causes: revolt against evil in the world; religious ignorance or indifference; the cares and riches of the world; the scandal of bad example on the part of believers; currents of thought hostile to religion; finally, the attitude of sinful man that makes him hide from God out of fear and flee his call [Cf. *GS* 19-21, *Mt* 13:22, *Gen* 3:8-10, *Jon* 1:3]" (*CCC* 29).

3. What natural help do we have for knowing God?

"When he listens to the message of creation and to the voice of conscience, man can arrive at certainty about the existence of God, the cause and end of everything" (*CCC* 46).

Connecting to Our Families

It is no secret that the culture treats us as though we were merely secular people with no religious nature. Popular music, films, and TV shows bombard us and our children with thousands of stimulants that appeal to our selfish wants. Secular newspapers and magazines belittle religious authority and stress the weaknesses and scandals of believers. We need to keep reminding ourselves that God has made us for himself and that our hearts will find true happiness only in him. We should look at the beauty of the world and think of the Creator. We must value silence, prayer, and faith. Mother Teresa puts it this way:

> Silence leads to prayer.
> Prayer leads to faith.
> Faith leads to love.
> Love leads to service.
> Service leads to peace.

1. How could this teaching about our basic religious nature help our young people maintain their link with God?

2. Paragraph twenty-nine of the *Catechism* lists six attitudes which make people forget their religious identity. Which of them, if any, do you see in your family life? What should be done to correct the situation?

3. How would the development of a sound "moral sense" help you open your heart to God more effectively?

Family Prayer

Jesus, Mary, and Joseph, your holy family was bound by prayer, faith, and love. We hope that our family life will be built on the same firm spiritual foundation. As we journey together through life on the path of faith, we ask your help and love to stay with us. We hope to remain faithful to our calling until the day when, joyfully, we shall be with you in the eternal joys of heaven.

Glossary

Religious Man: The *Catechism* teaches that every man and woman is born with a religious impulse and drive toward God.

Creation and Conscience: Two paths by which reason can know God.

Lesson 2

The Love That Never Ends

Resource: *CCC* paragraphs 50-141

Cry out at the top of your voice,
Jerusalem, herald of good news!
Fear not to cry out
and say to the cities of Judah:
Here is your God!

— Isaiah 40:9

A Reluctant Moses Meets God

I enjoy the shepherd's life. I like the long stretches of quiet especially when my flock is content. This serene life came to a halt the day I took the sheep to Mount Horeb. I was startled by a bush that caught fire. Brush fires, if blown by the wind, are always a clear and present danger. Instead, I saw a solitary bush aflame, yet its leaves and branches remained intact.

A feeling of mystery enveloped me. Fascinated, I approached the flaming sight. Then from the fire I heard a voice that ordered me, "Moses! Take off your sandals, for this is holy ground." Struck with awe and fear, I removed my sandals and fell to the ground, closed my eyes, not daring to look up. I wondered who was speaking to me. It seemed as though I was meeting God.

I soon found out. The voice said, "I am the God whom your fathers Abraham, Isaac, and Jacob worshiped. The wailing cries of the Israelite slaves in Egypt have pierced the very heavens. I have felt their sorrow and heard their grief. I want to liberate them. Moses, I want you to lead them to freedom."

I protested, "How can I, a shepherd with no military training or diplomatic skills, do such a thing?"

"You need to learn that my divine power works best in a humble heart. I achieve my goals on earth in those who depend on my strength rather than their own. My divine power is made perfect in human weakness."

"You are not worried about my fears that I can't do this?"

"I will be with you. I will give you the inner power and imagination you need to accomplish this."

I argued further, "Who are you? What is your name? The people will want to know . . . I want to know."

"Tell them that I am the same God who called Abraham to start a new nation, a people who would be my very own."

"And your name?"

"My name is I AM. Let your people know that their God is not a mere

19

nature god. Not the moon god of Babylon. Not the sun god of Egypt. Not the rain and earth god of the Philistines. I am a real God, a personal God, someone who knows you and loves you with a love that never ends."

"This mission frightens me. I am a poor speaker. I have no eloquence. They won't believe me."

"I will give you the words you need and teach you what to say."

"Forgive me, Lord, I just can't do it. I trip over my words. Please send someone else."

"Moses, you are trying my patience. All right, I will give you some human support. Your brother Aaron is a persuasive speaker. I will give you the words to share with him. He will serve as your spokesman. I will walk with both of you. Do you accept my call?"

"Yes, Lord, I believe in you. I will do as you say."

No longer would I be a simple shepherd of a little flock of sheep. God had revealed himself to me and given me the call to be the shepherd of my people Israel. I had received a fiery vision of the living God. With that vision came a responsibility that would consume me for the rest of my life.

Our Religion Begins with Revelation

The Moses story (Gen 3-4) is one of numerous narratives in Scripture which emphasize a major teaching of the *Catechism* that it is God who reveals to us his loving plan to save us from our sins. We do search for God and can know him through the visible things of creation. But we need a formal Revelation to know God's inner life and how he has for us a love that never ends. There is a kind of knowledge of God that we cannot achieve by our own powers. Only God can teach us this in Revelation.

God did this gradually in deeds and words over many centuries. In forming the Israelite people as a faith community, God planted in them the hope of salvation and the hope of a new and everlasting covenant that would be written on the human heart. God spoke to the patriarchs and then to the prophets and finally through his Son, Jesus Christ, the Son of God made man is the Father's perfect, revealed Word. St. John of the Cross described this truth in the following magnificent passage: "In giving us his Son, his only Word (for he possesses no other), he spoke everything to us at once in his sole Word — and he had no more to say . . . because what he spoke before to the prophets in parts, he has now spoken all at once by giving us the All Who is His Son" (*Ascent of Mount Carmel*, 2, 22).

Hence there will be no new public revelation. Catholic Church history also has examples of so-called "private revelations." In reflecting on these text we should note whether they are consistent with the public revelation of Sacred Scripture and the official interpretation of that revelation by the Church. We should also consider how private revelation is building up the Body of Christ and whether its bearers are examples of Christian holiness.

How Is Revelation Communicated to Us?

Revelation is communicated to us in the *Apostolic Tradition*. What does this mean? Christ the Lord embodied in his saving words and deeds the fullness of Revelation. He commissioned his Apostles to preach the Gospel of salvation and the kingdom, promised by the prophets and fulfilled in his paschal mystery.

The Apostles handed on the Gospel in two ways. (1) *Orally.* They proclaimed the revealed message of salvation in their preaching, their witness, and the institutions they established. They preached what Jesus taught them and what they learned from the prompting of the Holy Spirit. (2) *In Writing.* The message of salvation was written down by the Apostles and other men associated with them, under the inspiration of the Holy Spirit. This Apostolic Tradition was continued in what we call "Apostolic Succession." To make sure the Gospel would be saved in the Church, the Apostles created bishops as their successors and gave them their own teaching authority. This living transmission is called Tradition, which is distinct from Sacred Scripture but closely connected to it.

Sacred Tradition and Sacred Scripture are bound tightly together. They flow from the same divine wellspring of Revelation. Sacred Scripture is God's Word as put down in writing under the breathing of the Spirit. Sacred Tradition passes on the Word of God which was entrusted to the Apostles by Jesus and the Spirit. The first generation of Christians did not yet have a written New Testament. It is the New Testament which demonstrates vividly the process of a living Tradition.

How is the Word of God to be interpreted, whether in its written form or in Church Tradition? That responsibility has been given to the bishops, the successors of the Apostles in communion with the pope, the successor of St. Peter, chief of the Apostles. We call this teaching office the "Magisterium." The Magisterium is not superior to the Word of God, but its servant.

This is supported by the supernatural sense of faith which is welcomed by the People of God. In faith and prayer they penetrate ever more deeply and live more courageously the gift received in Divine Revelation. While there is no new Revelation, there is an ever fresh understanding and appreciation of it due to centuries of faith, witness, and deep contemplation under the guidance of the Holy Spirit.

Catechism Reflection

1. Why did God reveal himself?

"By love, God has revealed himself and given himself to man. He has thus provided the definitive, superabundant answer to the questions that man asks himself about the meaning and purpose of life" (*CCC* 68). "God has revealed himself fully by sending his own Son. . . . The Son is his Father's definitive Word, so there will be no further Revelation after him" (*CCC* 73).

2. What is the Apostolic Tradition?

"What Christ entrusted to the apostles, they in turn handed on by their preaching and writing, under the inspiration of the Holy Spirit, to all generations, until Christ returns in glory" (*CCC* 96). "The Church in her doctrine, life, and worship perpetuates and transmits to every generation . . . all that she believes (*DV* 8 §1)" (*CCC* 98).

3. How are Scripture and Tradition related?

" 'Sacred Tradition and Sacred Scripture make up a single sacred deposit of the Word of God,' (*DV* 10), in which, as in a mirror, the pilgrim Church contemplates God, the source of all her riches" (*CCC* 97).

Connecting to Our Family

Revelation tells you about God's love which never ends, a love which expresses forgiveness and salvation for all of us. God's covenant of love with us through Jesus finds an echo in the marriage covenant between husband and wife. Your Christian marriage symbolizes the love Jesus has for his Church. Jesus revealed the original meaning of marriage in which the spouses express a binding love for each other until the end of time. For this reason, Jesus established marriage as a sacrament of the Church, an effective sign that husband and wife are united in a communion with God and one another. The bond is sacred.

Revelation also teaches that the gift of love in marriage does not end there. Husband and wife become cooperators with God in the begetting of new life. The spouses not only surrender to each other in love but also to their children who reflect their love and symbolize their permanent unity. Parental love for children is a sign of God's love for everyone. Where having children is not possible, marital love still has its value. The couple can serve others by adoption, through educational services, by helping other families, and by aiding poor and disabled children.

The Christian family can find continual support in Revelation which is experienced today in the life of the Church Tradition — with its teachings, liturgy, prayer, and witness — as well as in Sacred Scripture. In a particular way, Scripture is the Word of God designed to pour spiritual strength into family life. The family Bible should not be a mere ornament in the home, but rather a "burning bush," a fiery Revelation of divine love bringing the power of the Holy Spirit into the family circle.

Read, study, and pray the Bible together. Prepare the Sunday Scripture readings together. Underline passages that speak to your hearts. Sing the Psalms to help the texts touch your hearts. God's "ear" is right next to all of your faith outpourings of the holy words. Look for guidance in Scripture for your family needs. A Scripture-centered home will connect you more intimately with the parish community at worship. The family is the domestic church that prepares the members for active participation in the parish and universal Church.

l. How have you experienced God as the one who takes the initiative in your lives? When it is said that religion begins with God, what does that mean to you? God completed all Revelation in Jesus Christ by speaking his total word in the Word made flesh. What should you do to meet Jesus as God's fullest Revelation?

2. What would help you make your home a "domestic church"? What symbols and deeds would make this possible? How do you see the domestic church leading family members to the parish and universal Church?

3. How do you honor the presence of Sacred Scripture in your home? What methods have you used to study and pray over the texts of Scripture? What have you learned from a faith involvement in Scripture?

Family Prayer

Loving Father, you loved us so much that you decided to share your inner life with us in the act of Revelation. You completed your revealing actions in your Son, Jesus Christ — the Word who is your total word. As a family, we praise and thank you for your splendid love by making the Revelation of Christ available to us in Sacred Tradition and Sacred Scripture, and in the Communion of the Church. Our family's love for one another needs the power of your Revelation so that it may be a love that never ends — just like your love for us. Thank you for this gift, and walk with us every moment of every day.

Glossary

Revelation: The name given to the various ways God has made known his reality, life, and love through created things; through the workings of human reason and conscience; through disclosures of his inner life in covenants with Noah, Abraham, Moses, and the prophets; and above all, perfectly, in his Son, Jesus Christ.

Apostolic Tradition: Christ entrusted his Revelation to the Apostles. They passed this on in their preaching and writing — guided by the Spirit — to their successors, the bishops in communion with the popes, successors of Peter.

Sacred Deposit of God's Word: Revelation is expressed in Sacred Tradition and Sacred Scripture which make up a single sacred deposit of God's Word.

Magisterium: The Magisterium is the pope and the bishops. It the name given to their teaching office, which has been entrusted to them by Christ for the purpose of giving an authentic interpretation of God's Word.

Lesson 3
The Blessed Assurance of Faith

Resource: *CCC* paragraphs 142-147

Faith is the realization of what is hoped for and evidence of things not seen.

— Hebrews 11:1

We Walk by Faith and Not by Sight

Picture a wire stretched between the bank building and the courthouse in your town. A woman stands on top of the bank building and announces her intention to walk across the wire to the courthouse. A crowd has gathered to witness this daring act. There is no net below to catch the woman should she fall. She asks the crowd if they believe she can make it across. Many say yes and encourage her to go ahead. Carefully and slowly she makes her way across, sometimes swaying and almost losing her balance. Reaching the other side, she hears the cheers from below. "Well done!" they cry. Then she holds up a wheelbarrow and asks the audience if they think she can make the trip back the other way pushing the wheelbarrow before her. Some nod in assent. Others shake their heads, unsure. She then singles out a man and yells, "Do you think I can make it?" He agrees that she can and smiles at her. Then she challenges him, "Then prove your faith in me by riding in the wheelbarrow!"

Rushing across the battlefields in World War II, the allies found many strange yet often inspiring things. Soldiers searched farms and houses looking for snipers. At one abandoned house they turned on their flashlights and went to the basement. There on the crumbling wall they saw a Cross. Beneath it was the lettering:

I believe in the sun — even when it does not shine.
I believe in love — even when it is not shown.
I believe in Jesus — even when he does not speak.

Two tadpoles were discussing the possibility of any world besides their own. One little tadpole said to the other, "I think I will stick my head above the water to see what the rest of the world looks like." The other tadpole said, "Don't be silly. Don't try to tell me there is anything in the world besides water."

So it is with us. Some tadpoles never think they can be frogs, even when they rise from their pond world. Some people believe there is nothing but what common sense tells them, but they could have so much more if they had faith.

Faith of Our Fathers and Mothers Living Still

In Revelation God reaches out to us and invites us to intimacy with him and his grace which offers us salvation from sin and guilt.

The response to Revelation's invitation is faith.

By faith we give our minds and hearts to God. St. Paul speaks of this as the "obedience of faith" (Rom 1:5, 16:26). The word *obedience* comes from the Latin word *ob-audire*, meaning to hear. Faith opens us to hearing God's loving words that tell us of our human dignity and our eternal destiny. We are meant to be both hearers of the Word and doers of the Word.

Scripture tells us that Abraham is our father in faith because he obeyed God's call to leave his homeland and become the father of a new people in another place which God would show him (Gen 12: 1-4). Read the eleventh chapter of Hebrews, which celebrates a number of Old Testament holy people who were models of faith.

The Virgin Mary most perfectly embodies the obedience of faith. When she visited her cousin Elizabeth, she heard Elizabeth say, "Blessed are you who believed that what was spoken to you by the Lord would be fulfilled" (Lk 1:45). From her "yes" to God at the Annunciation to her silent assent at the Cross, Mary's faith never wavered. Mary marvelously witnessed God's will. This is why the Church venerates Mary as the purest example of faith.

What Are the Characteristics of Christian Faith?

• Faith is personal. Faith says to God, "I believe in you. I entrust myself wholly to you and place my mind, heart, soul, and body in your hands." This faith includes belief in Jesus Christ and the Holy Spirit.

• Faith is communal. I do not believe all by myself. I am part of the Church, a community of believers. I join them in saying, "We believe in Father, Son, and Spirit." In a sense the Church is my faith support group. Our faith is, therefore, ecclesial. It would be hard, though not impossible, to have Christian faith if there were no one around me who believed. The family, the parish, the diocese, and the universal Church strengthen me by their communal faith.

• Faith is a gift. When St. Peter confessed that Jesus was the Son of the living God, Jesus praised God for this gift of faith to Peter. Peter did not know this about Jesus from his reason, from "flesh and blood," but by a grand gift of grace from the Father. Our faith is also just such a gift and a grace.

• Faith is a human act. The Holy Spirit makes faith possible, but we also use our intelligence and our capacity to trust. Grace builds on our natural human ability to know and trust in freedom and lifts these capacities to a supernatural level.

• Faith seeks understanding. While our intelligence by itself could never know the truths of such Revelation as the Trinity, the plan of salvation, or the divinity of Christ, our minds can be disposed to believe by the miracles of Christ and the saints, the teachings of the prophets, and the Church's growth and holiness. Moreover, our minds can probe the truths of Revelation to understand them more deeply and apply them more effectively in our lives. St. Augustine said, "I believe that I may understand and I understand that I may believe" (*Sermo* 43, 7, 9).

• Faith is certain. What we know by faith is more certain that what we know from reason, because we have the authority of God to guarantee it. Faith can indeed seem obscure to our minds at times, but the certainty of the divine light is greater than that of our intelligence. St. Anselm says that a "thousand difficulties do not make one doubt."

• Faith is a friend of reason. There can be no contradiction between faith and reason when they both deal with truth. Divine Truth does not contradict human truth since God is the author of truth wherever it appears. Methodical research in all branches of knowledge, so long as it is honest and does not break moral laws, is not in conflict with faith.

• Faith is free. No one should be forced against his will to have faith because the act of faith is by its nature a free act. We propose faith to others; we should not try to impose it on them. We offer people the option for Jesus Christ, the option for love. We try to make the case for Christ with all the love, energy, and persuasiveness that we can, but we do not force Jesus on others.

• Faith is belief in a message. Much of what is said above refers to faith in its personal, communal, and trusting terms. Our faith establishes a relationship with the Holy Trinity — with Jesus. Now Christ did say we should believe in him, but he also said we should believe in what he taught. He said, "I am the truth," but he also taught, "I have the truth." Our Apostles' Creed is an example of a summary of the Christian message. It is a creed that dates from the second century and was used at Baptisms. Our Nicene Creed dates from the fourth century and resulted from the first two ecumenical Councils (Nicaea and Constantinople) which clarified the Church's teachings on the humanity and divinity of Jesus, the divinity of the Holy Spirit, and the relationships of Father, Son, and Spirit in the Holy Trinity. The *Catechism of the Catholic Church* is an excellent example of the rich and satisfying message in which our faith believes.

• Faith tastes eternal life. St. Basil teaches that we see the blessings of faith now as experiencing the first taste of eternal life. It is true that the problems of our present lives make it difficult to appreciate the glory of the future life. Because of this, we should be inspired by such witnesses of faith as Abraham, who walked in God's path with irrepressible hope, and Mary, who journeyed in the night of faith. The saints are a cloud of witnesses who assure us that our commitment is not in vain but a blessed assurance of what we hope for and a conviction of the reality of things we do not see.

Catechism Reflection

1. What is Christian faith?

"Faith is a personal adherence of the whole man to God who reveals himself. It involves an assent of the intellect and will to the self-revelation God has made through his deeds and words" (*CCC* 176). "[This] faith is a supernatural gift from God. In order to believe, man needs the interior helps of the Holy Spirit" (*CCC* 179).

2. How is faith a human and ecclesial act?

" 'Believing' is a human act, conscious and free, corresponding to the dignity of the human person. 'Believing' is an ecclesial act. The Church's faith precedes, engenders, supports, and nourishes our faith" (*CCC* 180-181). "Faith is necessary for salvation" (*CCC* 183).

3. How can we persevere in faith?

"To live, grow, and persevere in the faith until the end we must nourish it with the word of God; we must beg the Lord to increase our faith [Cf. *Mk* 9:24; *Lk* 17:5; 22:32]; it must be 'working through charity,' abounding in hope, and rooted in the faith of the Church [*Gal* 5:6; *Rom* 15:13; cf; *Jas* 2:14-26]" (*CCC* 162).

Connecting to Our Family

Family prayer, nourishing love, moral training, and witness are the chief components of the conditions for the growth of faith in the family circle. The adage that "the family that prays together stays together" is still true. Grace at meals; family Scripture study; the celebration of the anniversaries of the Baptisms, Confirmations, and weddings of the family members; regular prayers for the deceased relatives; incorporating the great seasons of Advent, Christmas, Lent, Easter, and Pentecost within the family customs — these are some ways in which the life of faith comes alive in the home.

Prayer and faith must be lived out by parents and children through love and mutual respect for each other as persons with human dignity and images of God. Connected to this is the moral training of the young by parents or guardians, a discipline modeled by the adults. Example remains the most powerful form of religious training. This training should be conducted in a spirit of joy and freedom — a freedom to do what we should, not just what we want. All of it is meant to bring each human being in the family to his or her full potential as meant and designed by God.

Take the ten qualities of faith listed above and work on them in a cooperative manner. The *Catechism* in its wisdom has given us a comprehensive and inspiring vision of faith. Link all of this to your active participation in the life of your parish, its worship, communal gatherings, and social outreach to the needy. Faith is lived not only by generosity to one another at home, but also to the poor, sick, lonely, and others in need outside the home.

1. What have you been doing to deepen your personal faith in Jesus Christ? How do you maintain the freedom of your faith with the obligations that faith entails. How often do you pray, "I believe in you Lord; help my unbelief"?

2. Faith is an act that seeks understanding. How do you study your Catholic faith? In what way is your adult faith deeper than it was when you were a child? What do you do to help your young ones grow in their understanding of their faith?

3. Who are models of faith in your family and among your acquaintances? Who are your faith heroes and heroines, the ones who inspire you when the going gets tough? What models do you think are needed to help your children grown in their faith?

Family Prayer

Jesus, Mary, and Joseph, you modeled what a holy family should be and you showed us faith in action. Help us to see that we walk by faith and not by sight. We have not touched Christ's side nor seen his face nor heard his voice. Yet we believe that he is here. Help then, O Jesus, our unbelief and make our faith abound to come to you when you are near and seek where you are found.

Glossary

Faith: Faith is a surrender of our minds and wills to God who has revealed himself to us. This "obedience of faith" is personal, ecclesial, free, a gift, seeks understanding, works with our reason, is a source of certitude, and a foretaste of eternal life.

Apostles' Creed: The Apostles' Creed is a creed developed in the second century by the church at Rome for the sacrament of Baptism and accurately reflects the faith of the Apostles.

Nicene Creed: This creed was the result of the Councils of Nicaea (325) and First Constantinople (381) which addressed questions concerning the humanity and divinity of Christ and the divinity of the Holy Spirit. Normally, this is the creed used at Sunday liturgies.

Lesson 4

O Most Holy Trinity — Undivided Unity

Resource: *CCC* paragraphs 198-267

I Believe in God . . . I Believe in the Trinity
Most ancient of all mysteries,
Before your throne we lie.
Have mercy now and evermore,
Most holy Trinity.

— Frederick William Faber

On Easter Sunday 1966, *Time* magazine published a cover with a black field, upon which, in bold red letters, was printed the provocative question "Is God Dead?" The editors deliberately chose the day that celebrated Christ's Resurrection to new life to confront faithful Christians with a question based on a suddenly fashionable and radical theological discussion about the so-called death of God.

The idea was borrowed from the eccentric nineteenth-century German philosopher Friedrich Nietzsche. Designed to outrage believers and possibly stir up discussions about the secularization of the culture and even religion itself, the movement did have its lighter moments as the following humorous, imaginary sketch illustrates.

Imagine a conversation in heaven between the angel Gabriel and God.

Gabriel: Have you heard what they are saying about you down on earth?

God: No . . . what?

Gabriel: They are claiming you are dead and that Jesus is the man for others.

God: Who started this?

Gabriel: Nietzsche and some of his modern disciples.

God: What else do they teach?

Gabriel: They propose that your primordial transcendence has been changed into radical immanence.

God: What does that mean?

Gabriel: I don't know, but I have Augustine working on it.

God: What is Nietzsche doing now?

Gabriel: He is writing, "I was wrong," three million times on a huge blackboard.

Ten years later, *Time* featured a cover story about the "Jesus Movement," noting the revival of evangelical religion and faith in Jesus Christ as Lord.

Preachers and missionaries have always grappled with ways to communicate the mystery of God, especially the mystery of the Trinity. St. Patrick told the Irish that the Trinity was like a shamrock. The three leaves on the one stem are like the three divine persons in the one God. Others have used the colors in the flame of a candle. The red, white, and blue colors of the one flame stand for the three divine persons in the one divine nature. Some took the illustration of a tree. Its roots, trunk, and fruit differ in parts but belong to the one tree. So also the divine persons differ from each other but are united in the one divine nature. ". . . for I am God and not man, / the Holy One present among you. . ." (Hos 11:9).

After the *Catechism* has established the dynamic of a God revealing and ourselves responding in faith, it goes on to present the teachings of the Apostles' Creed. Hence it turns immediately to the meaning of the words, "I believe in one God." We think then first of God the Father and then of God as Trinity.

God has revealed himself as the one God, the only God. ". . . for I am God; there is no other!" (Is 45:22). In early biblical times there were many gods worshiped by various peoples. Through Revelation to Moses and the prophets, God made clear that the gods made of wood and stone and those identified with parts of creation (sun, moon, stars, trees, mountains) were not divine. There is only one God. "Hear, O Israel: the LORD our God is one LORD" (*RSV* Dt 6:4). What are we to say of this one and only God?

• God is Mystery. At the burning bush God told Moses his name, "I AM WHO I AM." This mysterious name discloses several truths about God: (a) God is living and personal; (b) God is near us and yet infinitely beyond us; (c) God communicates himself to us through our experience of created things, or particular persons, or through particular events such as Moses' experience of God at the burning bush; and (d) The hidden God imbues a visible reality. The revelation of God is mysterious or sacramental in character, as St. Augustine would say, "a visible sign of an invisible reality."

• God is Truth. This means that God tells us absolute truth and never deceives us. Such truth is more than an abstract idea. God's truth implies faithful action and loyalty to what he teaches. God is always trustworthy and constant. In other words, God is sheer fidelity. God will never let us down or go back on his promises to us.

• God is Love. As the biblical story of salvation unfolds, it becomes clear that God's motive for saving us was his love for us and his mercy toward our sins. The Bible compares God's love to a father for his son, to a mother's love of her children, to a bridegroom's affection for his beloved. God's love is stronger than any of our infidelities. St. John summarizes all this with his eloquent praise: ". . . God is love" (1 Jn 4:8). God is an eternal exchange of love among Father, Son, and Spirit and destines us to join in that exchange.

Holy, Holy, Holy, Lord God Almighty

We are all baptized "in the name of the Father, and of the Son, and of the Holy Spirit." The faith of all Christians rests on the Trinity. This is the most ancient and deepest of all mysteries of faith.

How was the mystery of the Trinity revealed?

The Old Testament often calls God "Father." This language of faith speaks of God as the origin of everything and the Divine Authority, but also it implies tenderness for his children. Moreover, God's parental tenderness can be expressed in terms of motherhood (Is 66:13). This emphasizes the intimacy between Creator and creature. The use of parental images for God is helpful but limited because parents can betray their roles. God transcends the distinction between the sexes. God is not a man nor a woman. God is simply God.

Jesus revealed God as Father in a new sense, not just as Creator. God is Father in relationship to his only Son. The Son is only Son in relation to his Father. The Council of Nicaea (325) declared the "Son is consubstantial with the Father," meaning the Son has the same divine nature as the Father.

The Spirit reveals the Father and the Son. Before the Passion Jesus announced the sending of the Holy Spirit. This Spirit had been at work in the preaching of the prophets. Now the Spirit would teach and guide the Apostles and disciples into all truth. The Father sent the Spirit in the name of the Son and the Son would send the Spirit once he had returned to the Father. The Spirit is another divine person with Jesus and the Father. The Spirit's appearance reveals the reality and work of the father and the Son. "We believe in the Holy Spirit, the Lord and giver of life" (Nicene Creed).

How do we speak of the doctrine of the Trinity?

Baptismal faith from apostolic times drew attention to the mystery of the Trinity. As time went on, the Church tried to clarify her understanding of the mystery, especially when there was need to defend the truth against those who denied it or deformed it. The Church borrowed three terms from philosophy to help her with this task. We use the term *substance or nature* to speak of the unity of God. We employ the term *person* or *hypostasis* to apply to the Father, Son, and Spirit to show the real distinction between them. We use the word *relation* to teach that their distinctiveness lies in the relationship of each to the others.

The dogma of the Trinity thus includes three truths of faith:

(1) The Trinity is One. We do not speak of three gods, but one God. Each person is fully God;

(2) The divine persons are truly distinct from each other. Father, Son, and Spirit are not just three shapes or modes of God, but three real identifiable persons. The Father is not the Son. The Son is not the Father. The Holy Spirit is neither Father nor Son;

(3) The divine persons relate to each other. Because of the manner in which they relate to one another, we can identify each person by that relationship.

What are the missions of the Persons of the Trinity?

The divine plan of salvation is the common work of the three divine persons of the Trinity. Still, each divine person performs this common mission according to a unique property. This is why we speak of the Father as Creator, the Son as Redeemer, and the Spirit as Sanctifier, even though all three in fact work together in these missions. When we glorify and praise one person we automatically praise all three.

Catechism Reflection

1. What does faith ask of us regarding the One God?

Our faith is monotheistic. " 'Hear O Israel: the LORD our God is one LORD. . .' (Dt 6:4; Mk 12:29). . . . Faith in God leads us to turn to him alone as our first origin and our ultimate goal, and neither to prefer anything to him nor to substitute anything for him. Even when he reveals himself, God remains a mystery beyond words. . . . The God of our faith has revealed himself as He who is; . . . God's very being is Truth and Love" (*CCC* 228-231).

2. How should we speak of the Holy Trinity?

"The mystery of the Most Holy Trinity is the central mystery of the Christian faith and of Christian life. God alone can make it known to us by revealing himself as Father, Son, and Holy Spirit" (*CCC* 261).

3. What are the relations and missions of the three divine persons?

The divine persons are inseparable in what they are and inseparable in what they do. "But within the single divine operation each shows forth what is proper to him in the Trinity, especially in the divine missions of the Son's Incarnation and the gift of the Holy Spirit" (*CCC* 267).

Connecting to Our Family

Every Christian family realizes that the glue that holds the family together is faith in the living God. Hence, there should be a conscious effort to live that faith. Parents and children and all relatives will be bound more intimately to one another when faith in God is expressed in the following manner:

• Make a conscious effort to become aware of God's greatness and magnificence. The wonderful discovery ahead of us is this: we are not made smaller by recognizing the grandeur of God. The more we admit, it the more our own greatness becomes evident because this glorious God made us and wants us to share in his divine life.

• Raise up songs of praise and thanksgiving within the family circle. Fund-raisers say, "You can never thank your donors enough." In other words, thankful appreciation increases the donations. Now God is the greatest of all donors. We thank and praise God for our gift of life and the talents we received. The more we do so, the more abundant is the quality of the gifts we have.

• Recognize the human dignity and unity of all people, affirming that such beauty is due to the fact that each person is made in the image and likeness of God. When we see that everyone is a "God reflector," we are

32

drawn into a world of beauty, reverence, and respect for one another that causes us awe before God and responsibility for one another.

• Deal with created things in such a manner that they never draw us away from God, but always are stepping stones to the divine. The gifts of creation are meant to support our needs, but also to attract us to the Creator. Accumulation of things for their own sake is a foolish goal. Greed is "fools' gold."

• Trust God with all your heart. When things are going well, this is easy. When suffering and trials come, then trust in God is tested. St. Teresa of Ávila says, "Let nothing trouble you. Let nothing scare you. Everything passes. God never changes. Patience obtains all. Whoever has God wants for nothing. God alone is enough."

1. What does your family need in order to become more aware of God's greatness and goodness? How is the constant praise of God and thanks for his gifts present in your home? What are some examples of the value of these attitudes which cause you joy?

2. What are some means you use to awaken a sense of each person's human dignity in your family? Why is it important to recognize each family member as an image of God?

3. What is your family's attitude toward money and possessions? How does such an attitude seem compatible with your faith in God the Creator? When serious troubles affect your family, what examples of trust in God have brought you through the test?

Family Prayer

O my God, Trinity whom I adore, help me to act as though I were already in eternity. I beg you to keep me in peace and let nothing disturb it. Bring me each minute, dear Lord, into your unchanging mystery. Make my soul your beloved dwelling place. May I never leave you alone in my heart but always be present to you completely and without reserve. Increase the watchfulness of my faith that I may adore your with all my heart, O Blessed Trinity, till my last breath.

Glossary

Person in the Trinity: The Church uses this term to designate the Father, Son, and Spirit in the real distinction among them. The Church takes philosophical terms and gives them unprecedented meaning to signify an ineffable mystery.

Substance or Nature in Trinity: The Church uses this term to speak of the divine "being" in its unity. Hence we speak of three divine persons in one divine nature or substance.

Relation in the Trinity: The Church uses this term to say that the persons of the Trinity are distinct and identifiable in their relations to one another.

Lesson 5

The Creation of the World

Resource: *CCC* paragraphs 279-354

God Creates an Ordered and Good World
All good gifts around us
Are sent from heaven above.
Then thank the Lord,
O thank the Lord for all his love.
— M. Claudius

In his book *Infinite in all Directions,* Freeman Dyson tells this story: "My youngest daughter came back from a music camp in Massachusetts carrying some monarch caterpillars in a jar. She found them feeding on milkweed near the camp. We also have milkweed growing in Princeton and so she was able to keep the caterpillars alive. After a few days they stopped feeding, hung themselves up by their tails and began to pupate.

"The process of pupation is delightful to watch. They squeeze themselves up into the skin of the pupa, like a fat boy wriggling into a sleeping bag that is three sizes too small for him. At the beginning you cannot believe that the caterpillar will ever fit inside, and at the end it turns out that the sleeping bag was exactly the right size.

"Two or three weeks later the butterflies emerge. The emergence is even more spectacular than the pupation. Out of the sleeping bag crawls the bedraggled remnant of the caterpillar, much reduced in size and with wet black stubs for wings. Then, in a few minutes, the body dries, the legs and antennae stiffen, and the wings unfurl. The bedraggled little creature springs to life as a shimmering beauty of orange, white, and black.

"We set her free in a nearby field and she flies high over the trees, disappearing into the sky. We hope that the move from Massachusetts to Princeton will not have disrupted the pattern of her autumn migration. With luck she will find companions to share with her the long journey to the southwest. She has a long way to go, most of it against the prevailing winds.

"The world of biology is full of miracles, but nothing I have seen is as miraculous as this metamorphosis of the monarch caterpillar. Her brain is a speck of neural tissue a few millimeters long, about a million times smaller than the human brain. With this almost microscopic clump of nerve cells, she knows how to manage her new legs and wings, to walk and to fly, to find her way by some unknown means of navigation over thousands of miles from Massachusetts to Mexico" (Harper and Row 1988, p. 33).

The Mystery of Creation

The marvel of the monarch butterfly is but one of millions of wonders that point us back to the Creator and the work of creation. The Bible begins the story of creation with these stately words: "In the beginning God created the heavens and the earth" (*RSV* Gen 1:1). God's creation is the beginning of his saving plans, the very start of the history of salvation that is realized in Christ. St. John teaches that Christ's salvation is the beginning of a new creation. The first words of his Gospel are the same as that of Genesis: "In the beginning. . ." (Jn 1:1).

The most tantalizing questions that all of us ask at one time or another are: Where did I come from? Where am I going? How did this world happen? Natural sciences have extensively investigated human origins, the development of the earth, and the cosmos itself. Pope John Paul II has stated that the Church acknowledges the value of some theories of evolution, while he also insists on our faith that God is Creator of the world and its developmental process and the Creator of the human soul. We recommend that you read and study the *Catechism* (283-285) with its analysis of the differences between the ways natural science, philosophy, and religion treat the question of origins and the meaning of what happened.

The most important texts in Scripture that deal with creation are found in the first three chapters of Genesis. Here are found the grand themes which command our attention about creation: ". . . its origin and its end in God, its order and goodness, the vocation of man, and finally, the drama of sin and the hope of salvation" (*CCC* 289). We should read these chapters with Jesus in mind and consider them in the light of all of Scripture and the living Tradition of the Church.

In our next lesson we will look at the creation of man in the image of God and the story of the Fall of Man. But here we should outline five teachings related to God's creation.

(1) Love and wisdom motivated God's creativity. To those who would say that the world is simply the result of chance or blind fate, we reply that our faith tells us that God made all this happen because he loved us. Creation is not a mere mechanical event, but the result of a wise Creator. Who can observe the splendor of the monarch butterfly and the complexity of its origin and behavior and not break out into song? "How manifold are your works O LORD! / In wisdom you made them all — " (Ps 104:24). Though we attribute the creation to the Father, we affirm that Father, Son, and Spirit together are the one principle of creation.

(2) God created the world out of nothing and said, "That's Good!" If you want to create a bread pudding you must use existing materials: eggs, cream, sugar, bread, cinnamon, ground lemon, and orange rinds. God had no preexisting materials. God created out of nothing. This teaching applies today when the Holy Spirit gives spiritual life to sinners by creating a pure heart in them. The Spirit's creativity will occur when bodily life is

given in the resurrection of the dead. We see this every day when the Spirit creates the light of faith in those who do not yet know God. Also, because creation originates from God's goodness, it shares in the divine goodness. How often we hear in Genesis, "And God saw that it was good" (*RSV* Gen 1:4).

(3) God's divine plan included his providence. Creation did not occur in its perfection. It is in process toward its proper fulfillment. God remains present to creation and its journey to its destiny. God cares for the whole world and everything and everyone in it. God is present to the process. *Divine providence is the name we give to the dispositions by which God guides his creation toward what it is meant to be.* Jesus taught this truth in his sermon about the lilies of the field that owe their beauty to God's attention (Mt 6:29-30). If God takes care of flowers that are here today and gone tomorrow, how much more will God care for us whom he calls to divine life? We can share in God's providential work by uniting ourselves to it in our acts, prayers, and energies and asking for the graces to do so.

(4) God's providence and the problem of evil. Why is there evil if God has created a good and ordered world and cares for us? There is no quick and easy answer to this. Our life of faith gives a partial answer to the problem of evil. People in their human freedom have sinned and caused evil, monstrous evil at times. God is never the cause of moral evil, but does permit it. God can bring good out of evil. The Joseph story in the book of Genesis teaches this lesson (Gen 45:8, 50:20). Note the eight elements of faith life which the *Catechism* lists in paragraph 309. Keep all these elements in mind when pondering the problem of evil. Faith calls us to firmly believe that God is the master of the world and its history. Even with our faith we must realize that on earth our knowledge is always partial. Only when we see God face-to-face will we finally understand the ways of providence that ordered creation to its Sabbath rest.

(5) God created the angels. That God created the angels is a truth of faith. They are spiritual beings who are servants and messengers of God. Accounts of the angels' activity may be found throughout the Bible, from Genesis to Apocalypse. An angel announced the Incarnation to Mary. Angels comforted Jesus after the temptation in the desert and also after the agony in the garden. Angels sang at Christ's birth and angels made the first announcement of his Resurrection to the women who came to the tomb on Easter morning. At every Eucharist we ask the angels to join us in praising the thrice-holy God. Our liturgy celebrates the existence and protection each of us receives from a personal guardian angel. The last book of the Bible says that angels will announce Christ's return and serve at the judgment.

Catechism Reflection

1. What does God witness in his act of creation?

"In the creation of the world and of man, God gave the first and universal witness to his almighty love and his wisdom, the first proclamation of the 'plan of his loving goodness,' which finds its goal in the new creation in Christ" (*CCC* 315). "God alone created the universe freely, directly, and without any help" (*CCC* 317).

2. What is the link between creation and God's glory?

"God created the world to show forth and communicate his glory. That his creatures should share in his truth, goodness, and beauty — this is the glory for which God created them" (*CCC* 319). This includes the angels as "spiritual creatures who glorify God without ceasing and who serve his saving plans for other creatures . . ." (*CCC* 350).

3. What do we mean by God's "providence"?

"God created the universe and keeps it in existence by his Word, the Son, 'upholding the universe by his word of power' (*Heb* 1:3) and by his Creator Spirit, the giver of life" (*CCC* 320).

Connecting to Our Family

There is a legend about a conversation between the Roman emperor Trajan and a wise old Jewish Rabbi. Trajan wanted to know how God could be present everywhere. "If your God is present everywhere, why don't mortal eyes see him?" The Rabbi replied, "God is everywhere, but mortal eyes cannot look directly into his face." Trajan found the answer unsatisfying. There must be a better way of explaining God's universal presence.

So the Rabbi took Trajan outside into the noonday sun. "Now look straight at the sun." "I can't,' replied Trajan, "the light would blind me." Smiling, the Rabbi said, "You see? You can't bear the light of one of God's creatures. How do you think you could stand looking directly into the stunning glory of the Creator? If the sun blinds your eyes, would not the light of God annihilate all of you? That is why we say that we cannot look at the face of God and live."

When there is an eclipse of the sun, we tell our children not to look at it directly. We show them how to use a kind of shadow box so they can see it without having their eyes harmed by radiation. The best way to see the presence of God in creation is to look at beautiful manifestations of God's artistry. Fresh snow on a mountain peak. A new rose at dawn with the drops of dew sparkling on its petals. The red glow of a sunset. The mystery of a full autumn moon, cool and enchanting to the view. Mother nature reveals the majesty of the Creator and warms us with his presence.

St. Thomas Aquinas teaches that the act of consecration at Mass is more like God's act of creation than that of a miracle, because the transformation of bread and wine into Christ's Body and Blood is the most profound kind of change our faith can know. Teach yourselves and your children to increase your faith in the mystery of God as Creator by becoming alert to the signs of God's presence in the world.

The scientist Linnaeus wrote over his door, "Live innocently. God is here." Is this not true of a good home as well? The miracle of the family calls for innocent living because the more innocence there is the greater will be the experience of the divine presence.

1. The best way to appreciate the truth of God as Creator is to become attentive to the beauty of creation. What are some encounters with the loveliness of the world that you remember and would share with your family? How can you draw your family to be attentive to the beauty of creation? In what ways can you fill your home and its environs with the living beauty of God?

2. Another way to think of the Creator is to practice the presence of God. What are some symbols you have in your home that would remind everyone of God's presence? What are some daily practices which could awaken your household to God's presence? Why does the smile of a child give you a hint of eternity?

3. A third way to be aware of the Creator is to use the Christian Sunday wisely. What are ways to slow down your family life on Sunday so you can appreciate your Creator and the gifts of creation? Read the *Catechism*, paragraph 344, which details the *Canticle of the Creatures* by St. Francis of Assisi. How can his song help your family to reach God through the charm of the creation?

Family Prayer

Father Creator of the sun, moon, and stars, of the hills and valleys, of the trees and flowers, and of each human person shining with your presence, we praise you and adore you. We thank you for the gift of beauty in creation and the gift of life which we enjoy. Remind us to look for you in the majesty of your earth, sea, and sky. Help us to sense your presence in our own created bodies and souls. Make our lives songs of praise and thanks for such magnificent gifts.

Glossary

Creation: God — Father, Son, and Spirit — created the world out of nothing. Done for love, creation becomes a "new creation" in Jesus Christ and his work of salvation.

Providence: God does not abandon the world after creation, but remains present to it and guides all creatures, including humans, with his wisdom and love to their ultimate destiny.

Lesson 6

Made in God's Image

Resource: *CCC* paragraphs 355-421

Christ the Lord . . . fully reveals man to man himself and makes his supreme calling clear.

— *Church in the Modern World,* [*GS*], 22

Behold — The Only One Greater Than Yourself

Never surpassed, the most absorbing television mini-series was the one based on Alex Haley's riveting autobiography, *Roots.* Haley's research uncovered the inspiring ritual surrounding the naming of his African ancestor who had been brought to America as a slave. The story touched Haley in the hidden depths of his personality and bonded him to his past in Juffure, Africa.

When Haley's ancestor, Kunta Kinte, was born, the first sounds the infant boy heard were the women pounding grain for the morning cereal and the *alimano* (holy man) chanting, "*Allah Akbar* — God is great!" Omoro, the father of the new child, spent the next seven days thinking about a new name for his son.

On the eighth day the villagers gathered for the ceremony of the naming of the new boy. The scene reminds us of Luke's gospel which tells the story of Zachary and Elizabeth gathering with their family and friends for the naming of their new child, whom they would call John — the future baptizer. In Juffure, two centuries ago, the *alimano* blessed the table piled with food for the naming banquet. Then he blessed the boy, asking God to give him a long life, success in bringing credit to his family and honor to the name he was about to receive.

Omoro took his son in his arms and three times whispered into his ear his new name — for he should be the first one to hear it. Then Omoro quietly revealed the name to the boy's mother. Last, he announced it to the whole assembly. "The first child of Omoro and Binta Kinte is Kunta." That night under the stars, Omoro lifted his son to the heavens and said, "Behold — the only One greater than yourself."

That naming ritual bonded the boy to his family, to his traditions, and to a descendant whose own identity was enriched by the memory. That remembered experience resonates with the biblical narratives of Abraham and Sarah, of Isaac and Rebecca, and of Jacob and Rachel. It speaks of family, created life, human dignity, and the profound relationship we all have with God.

O Wondrous Vision — Human Dignity

As we visualize the father of our opening story lifting up his child to the skies and acknowledging the supremacy of God, but also affirming the human dignity of the baby, we have an image to introduce us to God's creation of man and woman. "God created man in his own image, in the image of God he created him; male and female he created them" (Gen 1:27).

Images of God

God created us in his image. What does this mean? We are the only creatures who image God so richly. We image God in five ways:

(1) We can know truth and know God;

(2) We can love people, ourselves, and God;

(3) Each of us is a person and not a thing. Our self-worth and dignity come from God;

(4) We can know ourselves, control our lives, and enter into community with others — and should do so. This arises from our solidarity and unity with the whole human race; and

(5) We are called by grace to communion/covenant with God. By a faith surrender to God we share in the divine life as a result of the Gift Jesus obtained for us in his Incarnation and paschal mystery.

These five traits of being an image of God form the basis of how we should respect ourselves and others. They show us how much God has honored us and how precious each of us is in his sight. None of this is a passive matter. Images of God disclose the divine to one another through the acts of knowing, loving, covenant behavior, peace seeking, and faith. As a noun, we *are* images of God. As a verb, we *act* as images of God, especially when we identify with Jesus Christ, the truest image of God.

The Unity of Our Bodies and Souls

The human person is both physical and spiritual. Genesis says God took physical dust, formed a body, and breathed life into it. God has willed that we be a unity of soul and body. The word "soul" has multiple meanings: human life, the person, the innermost self, being God's image, that which is spiritual about us. The body is also an image of God because of its intimate relationship to the soul. Body and soul are distinct but form a unity which we call human nature.

Every human soul is created immediately by God. The soul is not produced by the parents. The soul is immortal, will not perish at death, and will be reunited with the body at the final resurrection. St. Paul often speaks of soul and spirit. This does not mean that spirit is another invisible reality apart from our souls, rather this is Paul's way of teaching us about our supernatural destiny. Moreover, the Bible frequently talks about the heart — at least one thousand times. The heart refers to the inmost depth of the soul where we make our most important commitments and decisions.

Ideally, soul and body work harmoniously together, and those aspects of the soul — spirit and heart — are unifying spiritual acts.

Male and Female

God deliberately willed and created man and woman. As human persons, men and women are equal, possess the same dignity, and are images of God — gifts directly given by God. But God is not the image of man and woman. God has no gender. Man and woman reflect the perfections of God. Hence, Scripture refers to God's love as fatherly, maternal, spousal. God created man and woman to be for one another. The man and the woman are each complete human persons but meant to complement their masculine and feminine natures. In marriage God unites man and woman into one flesh. They have spousal, unitive love and are open to the transmission of human life. As spouses and parents, they uniquely image God's creative work. God has called all humanity to be stewards of the goods of the earth, to make the gifts of creation available to everyone for their sustenance and well-being.

The Church interprets the symbolism of the Genesis narrative in the light of the New Testament and Tradition to teach us that our first parents received in paradise a life of original holiness and justice. So long as they remained faithful to God's will they would not have to suffer or die. Before the Fall, there was inner harmony within Adam and Eve and harmony between them, creation, and God. Their mastery of creation depended on their mastery of self.

The Fall — Original Sin

Everyone experiences evil. Sin is present everywhere and throughout all of history. It is foolish to ignore or deny it. The only way to understand sin is to be aware of our relationship to God. Sin is a human rejection of God and the breaking of our relationship with him. Only Divine Revelation can clarify the meaning of sin and its appearance at human origins. Without Revelation we will identify sin as "a developmental flaw, a psychological weakness, a mistake, or the necessary consequence of an inadequate social structure, etc." (*CCC* 387).

With the development of Revelation, the truth about sin becomes progressively clear. God's people in the Old Testament probed the story of the Fall in Genesis but they did not grasp its ultimate meaning. The meaning of the Fall only became evident in the death and Resurrection of Jesus and the work of the Holy Spirit, who convicts us of sin and reveals the Redeemer. The doctrine of original sin is the reverse side of the Good News of Jesus, who saves us from both original and actual sins. It has been noted that the "missing doctrine" in many of our homilies, religion books, and theological treatises is original sin. Because of this, Christ's saving act in the paschal mystery loses its meaning.

How should we read the account of the Fall? Genesis chapter three is written in figurative language that describes something that really happened to original man. Revelation teaches us that all of history is touched by the original sin committed by our first parents.

God created us to be his friends. This involved our free submission to him. God told our first parents not to eat of the tree of knowledge of good and evil. There were limits beyond which we should not go. Tempted by the devil, a fallen angel, man abused his freedom and disobeyed God. By this sin, Adam lost original holiness and justice for himself and for all human beings. St. Augustine gave the name "original sin" to this act. *We do not commit this sin, but inherit it at our birth.* Original sin is a deprivation of original holiness and justice — all the gifts and harmonies of paradise. In Christ's death and Resurrection there is a victory over all sin and the creation of a new life for us all. In Baptism, faith, and life in the Church, we are freed from sin's power (original and active) and filled with divine grace.

Catechism Reflection

1. Situate man and woman in God's intention for creation.

"[God] has destined all material creatures for the good of the human race. Man, and through him all creation, is destined for the glory of God" (*CCC* 353). "Man is predestined to reproduce the image of God's Son made man, the 'image of the invisible God' " (*CCC* 381).

2. How do our souls and body relate? Are we meant to be solitary?

" 'Man, though made of body and soul, is a unity' (*GS* 14 §1). The doctrine of faith affirms that the spiritual and immortal soul is created immediately by God. 'God did not create man a solitary being. From the beginning, "male and female he created them" (Gen 1:27). This partnership of man and woman constitutes the first form of communion between persons'(*GS* 12 § 4)" (*CCC* 382-383).

3. How do we know about Paradise and the Fall?

"Revelation makes known to us the state of original holiness and justice of man and woman before sin: from their friendship with God flowed the happiness of their existence in paradise" (*CCC* 384). " 'Although set by God in a state of rectitude, man, enticed by the evil one, abused his freedom at the very start of history. He lifted himself up against God and sought to attain his goal apart from him' (*GS* 13 §1)" (*CCC* 415).

4. What did Adam lose and how did that affect us?

"By his sin Adam, as the first man, lost the original holiness and justice he had received from God, not only for himself but for all human beings. Adam and Eve transmitted to their descendants human nature wounded by their own first sin and hence deprived of original holiness and justice; this deprivation is called 'original sin' " (*CCC* 416-417).

Connecting to our Family

Sandy said she loved Christmas Eve more than Christmas Day. She recalled that as a child there was one Christmas Eve that unsettled her. She had watched Dickens' *A Christmas Carol* and felt scared when the lights in her room were turned out. She imagined she saw Marley's ghost clanking toward her room and cried out for her father. He rushed in and knelt beside her bed, asked her what was the matter and calmed her fears. "Go to sleep now."

A little while later she cried out again and once more her father came. She couldn't get over her feeling that the ghost was coming. Her father said, "There is no ghost. God is with you in your heart to protect you. And your mother and I are just across the hall to make sure nothing happens to you. God is here." Sandy said, "I know he's here, but I wish he had some skin."

In fact God did acquire some skin. The first chapter of John's Gospel says that the Word of God became flesh and pitched his tent among us. St. Paul added that Jesus is the true image of the invisible God. Because of what Jesus did we can be like him, we can share in his life and become in action the image of God which we have been created to be.

All the members of your household have been made in the image of God with priceless human dignity and the capacity to know and love God, self, and others. Even though we are earthen vessels we are also glowing with the divine. Pray to the Holy Spirit:

> Breathe on me, breath of God,
> My soul with grace refine,
> Until this earthly part of me
> Glows with your fire divine.

1. Read again the five ways to be an image of God mentioned just after our opening story. How could your family act out being images of God more effectively? Why does this help your young ones get a better a self-image?

2. If someone asks you why there is evil in the world, what should you say? Why does the *Catechism* teach that we need Revelation to help us understand the existence of evil?

3. What is the connection between the sin of the first Adam and the death and Resurrection of Jesus, the second Adam? What can you learn from St. Paul's teaching that where sin flourished, grace was more powerful because of Jesus?

Family Prayer

O God, Father and Creator of the human race, awaken in us a reverence for our human dignity. Help us to see within ourselves your divine image which in your love you endowed us. Show us how to live out our creative calling, to help this world be a genuine reflection of your glory. Enable us to honor everyone we meet and to be responsible stewards of the creation you have entrusted to us. We praise, love, and adore you and celebrate your presence.

Glossary

Original Holiness and Justice: Revelation teaches that before sin, man and woman lived in a state of original holiness and justice. There was no death and they lived in harmony with themselves, creation, and God.

Original Sin: By their disobedience, Adam and Eve were deprived of original holiness and justice. We inherit from them this deprivation which is called original sin.

Effects of Original Sin: Because of original sin, human nature is weakened. We are affected by ignorance, suffering, death, and the inclination to sin, which is called concupiscence.

Devils: Satan (the devil) and other demons are fallen angels who defied God. They tempt us to revolt against God.

Protoevangelium, "First Gospel": God did not abandon us after the Fall, but announced that a Messiah would come, that there would be a "battle between the serpent and the Woman, and of the final victory of a descendant of hers" [cf. Gen 3:9, 15] (*CCC* 410).

Lesson 7

Son of God and Son of Mary

Resource: *CCC* paragraphs 422-570

He came down from heaven to earth,
who is Lord and God of all,
and his shelter was a stable,
and his cradle was a stall;
with the poor, the scorned, the lowly,
lived on earth our Savior holy.
— Cecil F. Alexander

Behold the Savior of the World

In the last year of his life, St. Francis of Assisi told his friends, "This will be my final Christmas. I want to celebrate it in a new way." At the beginning of Advent, Francis and a few of his disciples had moved to a hillside overlooking the mountain town of Greccio. Several grotto-like caves lined the hilly property. A friend of Francis gave him and his brothers the land to use as a hermitage.

Francis and his community transformed one of the caves into a Bethlehem scene. They spread straw on the floor, installed a manger filled with straw and brought in an ox and a donkey. An altar was built for Mass. On Christmas Eve, one hour before midnight, the villagers of Greccio came in procession to celebrate the feast with Francis. Their streams of lanterns and candles looked like stars coming across the valley. As they sang the timeless Christmas carols of Umbria, their voices seemed to echo the Gloria of the angels in Luke's Gospel.

When they arrived at the cave, they were charmed by the sight of the ox and donkey and manger. The Eucharistic celebration began. At homily time, Francis stood by the manger to talk about the birth of Jesus. A spell of religious awe overtook the listeners. A golden light filled their assembly. They saw Francis reach into the *empty* manger and lift out a baby and cradle him in his arms.

And then he held the baby out to them, saying: "My brothers and sisters, behold the Savior of the world." They experienced the mystery of the Incarnation.

After the Eucharist, Francis disappeared. Not until dawn, when the morning star hovered in the sky, did someone find him. He was absorbed in prayer, his face turned toward Bethlehem.

I Believe in Jesus Christ, the Only Son of God

It has been said that Francis of Assisi is the saint who has been most like Jesus. Grace worked in him so strongly that the face of Christ could be seen in his presence. The Christmas scene at Greccio is compelling evidence of this truth. For him, to live was Christ.

God the Father sent his Son to us in the fullness of time to redeem us from sin and give us divine life. God the Son, the Word of God, became flesh of the Virgin Mary. God the Holy Spirit, by his divine power, effected the conception of Jesus in the womb of Mary and moved the Apostle Peter to declare of Jesus, "You are the Messiah, the Son of the living God" (Mt 16:16). The Incarnation is the work of the Trinity.

All Christian preaching and teaching of religion should be centered on Jesus Christ. We proclaim Jesus to lead all people to faith in him and so receive his salvation from sin and the graces of divine life.

Jesus — Christ — Son of God — Lord

The name *Jesus* means, "God saves." St. Peter testified that "There is no other name under heaven given among men by which we must be saved" (*RSV* Acts 4:12). The word *Christ* means "Messiah" or "anointed one." The Father sent the Holy Spirit to anoint Jesus as Messiah who would act as priest, king, and prophet, giving the complete meaning to these roles already present in the Old Testament. This messianic consecration was revealed at the baptism of Jesus.

The Old Testament used the title "Son of God" for angels, the chosen people, and their kings. It implied a special intimacy between God and his creatures. But when Simon Peter called him "Son of the living God," and when St. Paul uses a similar title for Jesus, they are attributing to him a *divine* Sonship. At the baptism and transfiguration, the Father designated Jesus as his "beloved Son." After the Resurrection, Christ's divine Sonship became evident in the power of his glorified humanity.

The name of God which Moses heard at the burning bush is rendered *YHWH* in Hebrew and *Kyrios* in Greek and *Lord* in English. Lord refers to the divinity of Israel's God. In the New Testament the title "Lord" was applied to Jesus as well as the Father. Still, it is true that in the Gospels people often addressed Jesus as Lord simply as a title of respect. But in the Easter narratives the Holy Spirit enlightens the holy women and the disciples to recognize the divine mystery of Jesus. The title infers adoration. "My Lord and my God!" (Jn 20:28). "The title 'Lord' indicates divine sovereignty. To confess or invoke Jesus as Lord is to believe in his divinity" (*CCC* 455).

The Son of God Became Man

Why did the Word become flesh? For our salvation.
- The Word became flesh to reconcile us to God.
- The Word became flesh to help us know God loves us.

• The Word became flesh to show us how to be holy.

• The Word became flesh to give us divine life. "For the Son of God became man so that we might become God" (St. Athanasius, *De inc*, 54, 3).

• The term *Incarnation* means that the Son of God assumed a full human nature, like us in all things except sin (Jn 1:14; Phil 2:5-8; Heb 10:5-7; 1 Tim 3:16).

Jesus Christ is true God and true man. Jesus is not part God and part man, nor a confused mixture of humanity and divinity. He is fully human and fully divine. The first heresies (Gnosticism, Docetism) denied his humanity. Christian faith reasserted Christ true "coming in the flesh." The next major heresy, Arianism, claimed that Jesus was not truly divine, but was formally "adopted" by the Father after the Resurrection. The Council of Nicaea (325) reaffirmed that Jesus was truly God, "begotten, not made, of the same substance as the Father."

A third heresy, Nestorianism, said that Jesus had a human person that was joined to the divine person. The Council of Ephesus (431) proclaimed that the faith of the Church holds that Christ's humanity — body and soul — has no other subject than the divine person of the Son of God from the moment of his conception by Mary. She is therefore truly the mother of God.

The fourth heresy, Monophysitism, said that Christ's human nature disappeared when the divine person assumed it. The Council of Chalcedon (451) declared that Christ's human nature remained intact at the Incarnation. Christ's divine and human natures remained together without change, confusion, or division — united by the divine person of the Son of God.

How Is the Son of God Man?

Vatican II states, "The Son of God . . . worked with human hands, He thought with a human mind, acted by human choice, and loved with a human heart. Born of the Virgin Mary, He has truly been made one of us, like us in all things except sin" (*Church in the Modern World, [GS]*, 22, 2).

Jesus learned and grew humanly. He ". . . increased in wisdom and in stature, and favor with God and man" (Lk 2:52). Still the Son of God in his human knowledge displayed the divine penetration he had into the secrets of the human heart. "By its union to the divine wisdom in the person of the Word incarnate, Christ enjoyed in his human knowledge the fullness of understanding of the eternal plans he had come to reveal [Cf. *Mk* 8:31; 9:31; 10:33-34; 14:18-20, 26-30]. What he admitted to not knowing in this area, he elsewhere declared himself not sent to reveal [Cf. *Mk* 13:32; *Acts* 1:7]" (*CCC* 474).

Jesus possessed a human will as well as a divine one. The two wills cooperated in such a way that he willed humanly in obedience to the Father what he had decided divinely with the Father and the Spirit for our salvation.

Jesus had a real human body. In the Body of Jesus we see our God made visible to help us love the God we cannot see.

The Mysteries of Christ's Life

" 'The whole of Christ's life was a continual teaching: his silences, his miracles, his gestures, his prayer, his love for people, his special affection for the little and the poor, his acceptance of the total sacrifice on the Cross for the redemption of the world, and his Resurrection are the actualization of his word, and the fulfillment of Revelation (John Paul II, *CT* 9)' " (*CCC* 561).

We speak of the events in Christ's life as "mysteries" because they reveal God's saving plan for us and give us a way of entering into communion with God. Jesus makes it possible for us to live in him all that he lived here on earth.

"We must continue to accomplish in ourselves the stages of Jesus' life and his mysteries and often beg him to perfect and realize them in us and in his whole Church. . . . For it is the plan of the Son of God to make us and the whole Church partake in his mysteries and to extend them and to continue them in us and in his whole Church. This is his plan for fulfilling his mysteries in us" (St. John Eudes, *Liturgy of the Hours*, Week 33, Friday *Office of Readings*).

In this book we can only allude to the major mysteries of Christ's life to give you an overview. Your own meditations and studies will draw you into the inexhaustible riches of Jesus as found in Scripture and the Tradition of the Church. Here is a list of the principal mysteries of Christ's life. Come to them with faith, prayer, and an open heart:

• Preparing for Jesus. God prepared for the Messiah through the centuries of the First Covenant and the immediate work of John the Baptist. The Church's Advent liturgy celebrates this mystery each year.

• The Birth of the Messiah. The Christmas story and the events of Christ's infancy (circumcision, Epiphany, presentation in the temple, flight into Egypt, Holy Innocents, and the return from Egypt) introduce us to the mystery of the Incarnation. Linked to this is Christ's hidden life and its lessons, especially from the finding in the temple.

• The Mysteries of Christ's Public Life:

(1) *The Baptism.* Jesus begins his public life at his Baptism by John the Baptist. The Gospels portray Jesus as the servant who totally dedicates himself to redeeming us in the "Baptism" of his Passion and death.

(2) *The Temptation in the Desert.* In his encounter with Satan, Jesus appears as the humble Messiah who overcomes the devil by complete obedience to the Father's plan for our salvation.

(3) *The Proclamation of the Kingdom.* Jesus inaugurates the kingdom of heaven on earth through his preaching, parables, miracles, and the glorious witness of his personal life. He establishes the Church which is the seed and the beginning of this kingdom. Peter received the keys of the kingdom from Jesus.

(4) *The Transfiguration and Ascent to Jerusalem.* Jesus strengthens the

faith of the Apostles by his transfiguration. They needed this encouragement in the light of his coming Passion. Jesus radiated his divine glory in his Body on the mountain and does so in a more hidden manner now in the sacraments. Jesus then ascends to Jerusalem, freely and knowingly, to accept violent death to save us from our sins.

(5) *Palm Sunday*. Jesus enters Jerusalem as the Messiah-King and in so doing manifested the coming of his kingdom. This will be accomplished by his death and Resurrection.

Catechism Reflection

1. Why did the Son of God become man?

" 'The only-begotten Son of God, wanting to make us sharers in his divinity, asummed our nature, so that he, made man, might make men gods' [St. Thomas Aquinas, *Opusc.* 57:1-4]" (*CCC* 460).

2. Describe the doctrine of the Incarnation.

"At the time appointed by God, the only Son of the Father, the eternal Word, that is, the Word and substantial Image of the Father, became incarnate; without losing his divine nature he has assumed human nature" (*CCC* 479). "The Incarnation is therefore the mystery of the wonderful union of the divine and human natures in the one person of the Word" (*CCC* 483).

3. How are the divinity and humanity united in Jesus Christ?

"Jesus Christ is true God and true man, in the unity of this divine person; for this reason he is the one and only mediator between God and men" (*CCC* 480).

(The doctrines concerning the Blessed Virgin Mary, Mother of God — and her relationship to Christ and the Church — will be discussed in a separate chapter.)

Connecting to Our Family

A quote from a meditation of Paul VI about the Holy Family is relevant to our family life today. He draws three lessons from the reflection on the life of the Holy Family at Nazareth: The Lesson of Silence. The Lesson on Family Life. The Lesson on Work.

"The home at Nazareth is the school where we begin to understand the life of Jesus — the school of the Gospel. First then, a lesson of silence. May esteem for *silence*, that admirable and indispensable condition of mind, revive in us. . . . A lesson on *family life*. May Nazareth teach us what family life is, its communion of love, its austere and simple beauty, and its sacred and inviolable character. . . . A lesson of *work*. Nazareth, home of the 'Carpenter's Son,' in you I would choose to understand and proclaim the severe and redeeming law of human work. . . . To conclude, I want to greet all the workers of the world, holding up to them their great pattern, their brother who is God [Paul VI, At Nazareth, January 5, 1964, *Liturgy of the Hours*, Feast of the Holy Family, *Office of Readings*]" (*CCC* 533).

1. When is your home quiet and at peace? How could a zone of silence be introduced? Why is it needed? How present is Jesus to your family life? How could Jesus be closer to all of you?

2. How strong is your sense of family and mutual bonding? What helps your family sense its deep identity? What best brings out the beauty and simplicity of your family? What can you learn from Jesus, Mary, and Joseph?

3. How are the work responsibilities handled among you? While work is needed for family support, how does it hinder or help family development? How does work produce human fulfillment?

Family Prayer

Son of the living God, we adore you and stand in awe that you became the son of a human family. You are our teacher, and like your mother, we want to ponder in our hearts your every word and deed. Teach us the holiness of human love and all the family values we need for our human fulfillment and divine salvation. Help us to live as your holy family did, united in respect and love. Amen.

Glossary

Jesus: The name *Jesus* means, "God saves." There is no other name by which we are saved.

Christ: The word *Christ* means "Messiah" or "anointed one."

Son of God: Son of God may refer to angels, the chosen people, and their kings. It implied intimacy between God and his creatures. But when Peter and Paul call Jesus the "Son of God," they attribute to him divine Sonship. At the Baptism and Transfiguration the Father designates Jesus as his "beloved Son."

Lord: Moses heard God's name as *YHWH* which is *Kyrios* in Greek and *Lord* in English. The New Testament calls the Father and Jesus Lord. "To confess or invoke Jesus as Lord is to believe in his divinity" (*CCC* 455).

Lesson 8
The Death and Resurrection of Jesus

Resource: *CCC* paragraphs 571-682

Now the green blade rises from the buried grain,
Wheat that in the dark earth many days has lain;
Love lives again that with the dead has been:
Love is come again like the wheat that springeth green.
— John Macleod Crum

A Journey to Glory

In 1960, Adam Bujak, a young Polish photographer from Krakow, decided to take pictures of the traditional rural rituals of Catholic Poland. He believed that his work would be more authentic if he joined the people in their pilgrimages, many of which dated from the Middle Ages. He needed to earn the pilgrims' trust so they would be willing to share their stories and experiences with him. Only after his presence was accepted by the pilgrims did he venture to take the pictures. His photographs remind us of the mystical style used by the Swedish filmmaker Ingmar Bergman in his movies "The Virgin Spring" and "The Seventh Seal."

With American journalist Marjorie Young, Bujak published a book called *Journeys to Glory: A Celebration of the Human Spirit*. The third of his photo-essays is titled "The Celebration of the Sufferings of the Lord." It shows a place in a remote farming area of Poland where 150,000 people gathered during Holy Week to reenact the Passion of Christ at the Chapel of the Council of High Priests and Elders.

"They gather around a life-sized wooden statue of Jesus, whose hands are chained to a pole and on whose body wound marks can be seen," says the narrative accompanying the pictures. "The statue portrays Jesus, not as an elegant figure, but as a simple peasant. Pilgrims place candles around him and talk to him as a friend. They stroke his face lovingly and tell him their problems. Some ask for cures or to be able to see or hear better. Others kiss his hands and his face and prostrate before him."

This is a world of awesome drama, emotion, and meaning. Through the focus of Christ's Passion, universal experiences are lived anew. Celebrating the mysteries regenerates the participants. The new life of Easter is only three days hence.

Lift High the Cross — The Love of Christ Proclaim

The Apostles and the Church which follows them have made the paschal mystery of the death and Resurrection of Jesus the center of the Good News proclaimed to the world.

The opposition to Jesus by the religious leaders of his time, which led to the Cross, focused on their misunderstanding of his teaching and behavior toward the Law of Moses, the temple, and certain religious customs.

In reality Jesus upheld the Mosaic Law, explained its deepest meaning, and brought it to its intended fulfillment. "Do not think I have come to abolish the law or the prophets. I have come not to abolish but to fulfill" (Mt 5:17).

Jesus honored the temple, made pilgrimages to it, and fervently protected this dwelling of God among us. The temple foreshadowed his own life. His prediction of the destruction of the temple symbolized his own death as well as the arrival of a new age in which his Body would be the definitive temple.

When Jesus forgave sins he disclosed himself as the Savior God. Jesus invited the religious authorities to believe in him. They needed an act of faith that required a death to self and a rebirth influenced by grace. Tragically, the religious leaders misunderstood him, saw him as a threat, and accused him of blasphemy. They acted partly out of ignorance but also from the hardness of unbelief.

Not all the people opposed him. Nicodemus and Joseph of Arimathea were secret disciples. Many believed in him, though imperfectly (Jn 10:19-21, 12:42). Nonetheless, Caiphas and the Sanhedrin declared Jesus a blasphemer and handed him to the Romans, accusing him of political revolt.

Still, the Jewish people should not be held collectively responsible for the death of Jesus. ". . . what happened in His passion cannot be blamed upon all the Jews then living, without distinction, nor upon the Jews today . . . the Jews should not be presented as repudiated or cursed by God, as if such views followed from the holy Scripture" (*Non-Christian Religions, [NA]*, 4). The truth of the matter is that *". . . sinners were the authors and ministers of the sufferings the divine Redeemer endured"* [emphasis added] (*Roman Catechism*, I, 11).

". . . Christ died for our sins in accordance with the scriptures" (*1 Cor* 15:3). It was because God loved us that he sent his Son to expiate our sins, thus reconciling the world to himself. In pure freedom, Jesus offered himself for our salvation. At the Last Supper, through the institution of the Eucharist, Jesus made his sacrificial offering present and symbolized its forthcoming occurrence.

By his death on the Cross, Jesus ransomed us from our sinfulness. His loving obedience to the Father corrected the disobedience of Adam. He fulfilled the atoning mission of the suffering servant of Isaiah by bearing our sins and justifying many. We are called to identify with the Cross and redemptive suffering. "Apart from the Cross, there is no other ladder by which we may get to heaven" (St. Rose of Lima).

Jesus died and was buried in a tomb. The divine person continued to possess Christ's soul and body though they were separated in death. Hence his Body did not corrupt. In our Apostles' Creed we say that Jesus descended into hell. The scriptural name for the abode of the dead is *Sheol* in which place the dead were deprived of the vision of God — both the damned and the just who waited for the redeemer. Jesus did not deliver the damned, but rather the just who yearned for him. On Holy Saturday we read with the Church:

> "Today a great silence reigns on earth, a great silence and a great stillness. A great silence because the King is asleep . . . he has gone to free from sorrow Adam in his bonds and Eve, captive with him. 'I am your God, who for your sake have become your son. . . . I order you, O sleeper, to awake. I did not create you to be a prisoner in hell. Rise from the dead, for I am the life of the dead' " (*Liturgy of the Hours*, Holy Saturday, *Office of Readings*).

The Day of Resurrection! Earth, Tell It Out Abroad!

On the third day Jesus rose from the dead. The Resurrection of Jesus is the central truth of our faith. It was believed and lived by the first Christian community, passed on by Apostolic Tradition, confirmed in the New Testament, and preached as an essential part of the paschal mystery along with the Cross.

Easter really happened historically as evidenced by the appearances of the risen Christ and the testimony of numerous witnesses (1 Cor 15:3-4). The empty tomb prepared the holy women and the Apostles to encounter the risen Lord. St. John looked at the empty grave and the linen cloth. ". . . He saw and believed" (Jn 20:8).

Mary Magdalene and the holy women came at dawn to anoint Christ's body. They were the first to encounter the risen Jesus. These women who were the first messengers of Easter to the Apostles themselves. Magdalene is called *Apostola Apostolorum,* the Apostle to the Apostles. Then it was Peter and the Apostles, the foundation stones of the Church, who saw Jesus and became his witnesses. St. Paul, St. James, and five hundred others also testified that they met the risen Lord.

What was Christ's Body like? He could be touched, seen, and was able to eat a meal. He was not a ghost. He even bore the marks of his Passion on his hands, feet, and side. But he also carried the qualities of a glorified body, not limited by space or time but able to be present how and where he willed. In this he was different from Lazarus and the daughter of Jairus who simply returned to ordinary earthly life and would die again. Christ rose from death to another life beyond time and space. His Body is permeated with the power of the Spirit. He is now a man of heaven.

However, the Resurrection was a transcendent event, an experience beyond the realm of history. No one saw the Resurrection. No evangelist describes it. No one can tell us how it happened physically. Nor can eye or ear or hand perceive how the essence of Christ's life passed over into another form. Though he could be seen, heard, and touched, his Resurrection is essentially a religious mystery which requires our faith to accept. The New Testament texts always speak of faith in the risen Jesus even by those who actually encountered him.

Easter was a work of the Holy Trinity. The Father's power raised up Jesus. The Son used his divine power to rise from the dead. The Holy Spirit gave life to Christ's dead humanity. Working together in inexpressible love, the Trinity gave us the gift of Christ's Resurrection which is the pledge of our own resurrection when Christ shall come again.

What is the meaning of the Resurrection for us?

• Without it, our faith in Christ would be in vain. Easter confirms that all Jesus said and did is truthful and saving.

• It fulfilled all the promises of the Old Testament and of Jesus himself.

• The Resurrection demonstrates the divinity of Jesus. ". . . When you lift up the Son of Man, then you will realize that I AM. . ." (Jn 8:28). The "I AM" statements of Jesus in John's Gospel link Christ to the name of God at the burning bush.

• Easter provides the second half of the two parts of the paschal mystery. At Calvary Jesus freed us from sin. At Easter he offers us the way to divine life.

• The Resurrection is the principle and source of our own resurrection, first by the justification of our souls and then new life for our bodies at the general resurrection of the dead.

The Ascension of Jesus tells us of Christ's humanity definitively entering heaven. He is seated at the right hand of the Father where he fulfills the prophecy of Daniel that he would be "given dominion, glory, and kingdom" (*RSV* Dan 7:14). There Jesus intercedes for us before the Father so that we have a continuous outpouring of the Spirit as we go forth to evangelize and witness his Kingdom of love, justice, mercy, and salvation.

Jesus will come again in glory to judge the living and the dead. This will happen on Judgment Day when the final victory over evil will become evident. Everyone will be judged according to whether they accepted or refused his grace.

Catechism Reflection

l. Did Jesus really die?

" 'By the grace of God,' Jesus tasted death 'for everyone' [*Heb* 2:9]. In his plan of salvation, God ordained that his Son should not only 'die for our sins' [*1 Cor* 15:3] but should also 'taste death,' experience the condition of death, the separation of his soul from his body, between the time he expired on the cross and the time he was raised from the dead"(*CCC* 624)."In his human soul united to his divine person, the dead Christ went down to the realm of the dead. He opened heaven's gates for the just who had gone before him" (*CCC* 637).

2. What does faith in Christ's Resurrection tell us?

"Faith in the Resurrection has as its object an event which is historically attested to by the disciples, who really encountered the Risen One" (*CCC* 656). "Christ the 'first-born' from the dead (*Col* 1:18), is the principle of our own resurrection . . ." (*CCC* 658).

3. What happened at Christ's ascension?

"Christ's ascension marks the definitive entrance of Jesus' humanity into God's heavenly domain, whence he will come again [cf. *Acts* 1:11]" (*CCC* 665).

4. What will Jesus do on Judgment Day?

"When he comes at the end of time to judge the living and the dead, the glorious Christ will reveal the secret disposition of hearts and will render to each man according to his works and according to his acceptance or refusal of grace" (*CCC* 682).

Connecting to Our Family

How can the paschal mystery of Christ's death and Resurrection affect our family life today? The following story can shed some light on a response to the question.

At the end of World War II, a small French village began to rebuild the structures battered by shell fire. American soldiers helped them. Their last project was the restoration of their parish church and the statue of Christ that had stood in front of the church. Stone by stone they lovingly collected the pieces of the statue. They found every part except the hands.

They held a meeting to discuss what should be done. Ought they to hire a sculptor to carve new hands and attach them to the arms? They finally decided to leave the statue handless and put an inscription beneath it. Visitors, tourists, and pilgrims who see that statue today read a carved statement at its base. It says, "I have no hands . . . but yours."

Because of his Resurrection, Jesus can be present to each of us. But he needs our willing cooperation to be able to touch people with his love, forgiveness, and salvation. Our calling is to be Christ's healing and caring hands in our homes, neighborhoods, parishes, and the larger community. We become the hands of Christ when we bear the affection of Jesus to all whom we meet. Some say that every human being needs four hugs a day — four direct, obvious, and unabashed gestures of affection. Children need oceans of love so they can be vessels of Christ when it is their turn to sail the choppy waters of life. Husbands and wives need unending streams of love from each other, a love that never ends. When the Christian home is a domestic church, it will have all the members acting as the hands of Christ — healing, caring, and loving.

1. The Sign of the Cross leads to the dawn of Easter. How is the Cross honored in your home? How are crises, setbacks, sorrows — forms of living the Cross — handled with faith among you? How do you balance patient endurance with problem solving? Do you permit your family to share their anxieties, concerns, and pains with attentive, understanding ears and hearts?

2. The Gospel is good news, meant to fill us with joy. Christ's Resurrection should fill us with hope and joy. What brings joy to your family? What do you do to increase the sense of hope? Who are the best witnesses of Christ's risen presence of hope among you?

3. Are you willing to think about the next life and what it means for the present one? Why is the future resurrection of our bodies an important teaching for respect for our bodies today?

Family Prayer

We adore you, O Jesus, for by your holy Cross and Resurrection you have redeemed us from our sins and given us divine life. We ask you to walk with us when we have our own way of the Cross in the inevitable troubles of our family life. We also ask you to sit with us when we celebrate the explosions of joy we experience in one another's laughter and love, these moments when we touch your Easter presence in our midst. In these ways, may we live your paschal mystery from day to day. Amen.

Glossary

Paschal Mystery: Refers to the saving death and Resurrection of Jesus Christ. We experience this mystery and its effects in the celebration of the sacraments.

Lesson 9
The House of God and Gate of Heaven

Resource: *CCC* paragraphs 683-962

And this shall be our anthem:
One Church, One Faith, One Lord.
— Edward Plumpire

The Church With a Human Face

"See everything. Correct a little. Forget the rest." This was the wisdom of good Pope John XXIII. Soon after his election, a number of people asked him, "What titles will you bestow on your relatives?" For centuries many popes had made their relatives, even those from humble backgrounds, counts and countesses. Pope John smiled and said, "Call them my brothers, sisters, nephews, and nieces. I believe that should be enough nobility for them."

Pope John loved people and liked to have company. He discovered that popes were expected to dine alone. He did not like the custom so he began inviting his secretary, Monsignor Capovilla, to join him at meals, then the cardinals living in Rome and finally the world's bishops who came for visits to report on their dioceses. One day a prominent visitor commented on the solitary eating habits of Pius XII. "Yes, well I value tradition as did my esteemed predecessor. But I must confess I never found any place in the Bible which suggests the pope should eat alone."

Pope John enjoyed taking walks in the Vatican gardens. His predecessor also liked to stroll in the gardens, but always did it at the same hour every day. The caretakers of the Basilica would then close the doors to the outdoor balcony around the dome of St. Peter's so the people would not see the pope in the gardens. Pope John was unpredictable about the timing of his walks. The caretakers did not know what to do.

"Why must you do anything? Why must you close the balcony at all?"

"Because otherwise people would see you, Holiness! The people, all those tourists."

John paused a moment and then said, "Don't worry about it. I promise not to do anything that would scandalize them."

Custom then required the pope to wear red slippers everywhere. John said he could hardly be expected to take good walks in these. So he hired a shoemaker to make sturdy leather walking shoes for him — and dye them red! Soon he heard people calling him "Johnny Walker."

These humorous tales from the life of Pope John show us why he was loved so much. He put a "human face" on the Church, witnessing the warmth of Jesus and creating an inviting attitude. The more he did, the more the divine side of the Church and its religious mystery became attractive to millions.

Part One: The Spirit and the Church

Before we begin our meditation on the Church, we must first ponder the teaching about the Holy Spirit who manifested the Church and continues to sustain it.

The Holy Spirit is the last of the persons of the Trinity to be revealed. St. Gregory of Nazianzus gives us an excellent picture of God's teaching method, slowly unfolding the truth about the Trinity. "The Old Testament proclaimed the Father clearly, but the Son more obscurely. The New Testament revealed the Son and gave us a glimpse of the divinity of the Spirit. Now the Spirit dwells among us [in the Church] and grants us a clearer vision of himself" (*Theological Prayer*, 5, 26).

St. Gregory goes on to say that we needed first to grasp God as Father, then we could proceed in faith to accept the Revelation of the divinity of the Son. Finally we would be ready to receive the disclosure of the divinity of the Spirit. In this way we advanced from glory to glory until we beheld the whole mystery of the Trinity.

The Holy Spirit is involved in the divine plan of salvation just as much as the Father and the Son. The Holy Spirit is truly God. That is why the Church teaches that the Spirit is "consubstantial with the Father and the Son and is inseparable from them." The Spirit has the same "substance" or divine nature as they do. The Spirit has the same mission as the Son in the cause of our salvation. When the Father sends us the Son, he also sends the Spirit to save us from sin and give us divine life.

The word *Spirit* comes from the Hebrew *ruah* which means "breath, air, wind." The Spirit is God's breath filling us with divine life, making our souls pure, sustaining our immortality until we love what God loves, until we do what God wants of us, until this earthly part of us glows with fire divine.

Scripture calls the Spirit the *paraclete*, meaning our advocate and consoler. Jesus prayed to the Father to send us the Spirit to teach us truth, to remind us of what Jesus had taught.

Tradition uses many symbols to illustrate the Spirit's actions;
• Water, signifying the Spirit's saving action at Baptism;
• Oil and Seal, by which the Spirit anoints us at Confirmation;
• Fire, by which the Spirit transforms us into Christ;
• Cloud, the shining glory that led Israel in the desert, dwelt on the ark, overshadowed Mary at the Annunciation, and was present at Christ's baptism and transfiguration. This image emphasizes how the Spirit makes us *experience* God's effective presence.

The Spirit participates with the other persons of the Trinity in the unfolding plan of salvation: at creation, in the promise to Abraham, in the appearances of God at Sinai and elsewhere, in the giving of the Law, and, above all, in the preaching of the prophets and the expectation of the Messiah. Our creed says the Spirit "spoke through the prophets."

It is clear how powerfully the Spirit acted in the ministry of John the Baptist and the conception of Jesus in the womb of Mary. The whole ministry of Jesus is a joint mission of salvation with the Spirit. How often the Gospels say Jesus is led by the Spirit or that Jesus acted in the Spirit. Immediately after his death and Resurrection, Jesus on Easter night gave the Holy Spirit to his Apostles, breathing on them this divine gift of the third person of the Trinity. *From that moment on the mission of Jesus and the Spirit becomes the mission of the Church.*

Catechism Reflection

1. How close is the work of the Spirit to the Father and the Son?

"From the beginning to the end of time, whenever God sends his Son, he always sends his Spirit: their mission is conjoined and inseparable" (*CCC* 743). "The Holy Spirit, whom Christ the head pours out on his members, builds, animates, and sanctifies the Church" (*CCC* 747).

2. How do we come to know the Spirit in the Church?

"The Church, a communion living in the faith of the apostles which she transmits, is the place where we know the Holy Spirit:

— in the Scriptures he inspired;

— in the Tradition, to which the Church Fathers are always timely witnesses;

— in the Church's Magisterium, which he assists;

— in the sacramental liturgy, through its words and symbols, in which the Holy Spirit puts us into communion with Christ;

— in prayer, wherein he intercedes with us;

— in the charisms and ministries by which the Church is built up;

— in the signs of apostolic and missionary life;

— in the witness of saints through whom he manifests his holiness and continues the work of salvation" (*CCC* 688).

3. What did the Holy Spirit accomplish in Mary?

"In the fullness of time the Holy Spirit completes in Mary all the preparations for Christ's coming among the People of God. By the action of the Holy Spirit in her, the Father gives the world Emmanuel, 'God-with-us' (*Mt* 1:23)" (*CCC* 744).

Part Two: I Believe in the Catholic Church

The Church is the work of the Trinity. The Father called the Church into existence. The Son founded the Church. The Spirit manifested and sustains the Church.

The word *church* comes from the Hebrew *qahal*. It means a "called community." Hence, the Church is not created by the self-determination of the members. The Greek translation is *kyriake*, which became the German *kirche* and the English word *church*.

The word *church* refers to a parish, diocese, universal church, liturgical gathering, or witnessing community as well as the church building. What is the origin, founding, and mission of the Church?

We can only sketch here the highlights of the answer to this question which is better developed in the *Catechism*, paragraphs 758-768.

The Father planned the Church. There was a gradual creation of God's family through a series of covenant experiences with the Old Testament People of God. Jesus accomplished the Father's plan first by preaching and witnessing the Good News of the kingdom of salvation, love, justice, and mercy. Jesus initiated a visible structure for the Church through the twelve Apostles with Peter as its head.

The Church is *born* in Christ's self-giving sacrifice and Resurrection for our salvation. The Church is *anticipated* at the Last Supper through the institution of the Holy Eucharist and the consecration of the Apostles — as evidenced in Christ's priestly prayer in John chapter seventeen, especially verse seventeen. The Church is *fulfilled* at the Cross. Just as Eve was taken from the sleeping side of Adam, so now Church flows from the sleeping side of Christ through the water and blood, symbolizing Baptism and the Eucharist.

The Spirit manifested the Church at Pentecost, coming upon Mary, the Apostles, and disciples with transforming fire, making them into a visible Church. Immediately, Peter preaches the Gospel, baptizes converts, and forms the Great Community. This community grows by listening to the teaching of the Apostles, forming fellowship, celebrating Eucharist, and sharing goods in common. The missionary effort of the Church grows in all directions.

The Spirit bestowed charisms and gifts on them for the hierarchy and other ministries of the Church. The Church begins her earthly pilgrimage that will be perfected in glory.

The Church Is a Mystery of Faith, a Sacrament of Salvation

The Church has a visible and invisible aspect. The visible Church is a public institution, with a hierarchical government, laws, and customs. This is its earthly and human side. St. Robert Bellarmine said the Church is as visible "as the kingdom of Naples."

The invisible Church is the Body of Christ, the Temple of the Spirit — a divine reality held together by the gifts and graces of God. It is present on earth but transcends it. This visible and invisible truth about the Church is one complex reality ordered to the holiness of its members.

The Church is a mystery of faith. It is planned, founded, and sustained by God. It is the universal sacrament of salvation. A sacrament is a sign that does three things: (1) Points to a divine reality; (2) contains that reality; and (3) produces that reality in us. When we speak of the Church as the sacrament of salvation we mean that it *points* to salvation and the kingdom of heaven, *and contains* and *produces* that reality in us when we open our hearts to the Church and her sacraments in faith.

How does this happen? The Spirit communicates the grace of Jesus Christ to us through the Church and her seven sacraments. By the will of Christ the Savior, the Church is the divinely appointed instrument of salvation in the world. All salvation comes from Christ the head through the Church which is his Body.

The Church is such a rich reality that images are used to illumine this treasure of grace. Three images in particular: People of God, Body of Christ, and Temple of the Spirit.

The People of God possess seven characteristics.

(1) They are called by God's Word, not by self-choice.

(2) They require a spiritual birth in faith, conversion, and Baptism.

(3) They have for their head Jesus and the pope as his vicar.

(4) All members have dignity as sons and daughters of God in whom the Spirit dwells.

(5) Their [the Church's] Law: To love as Jesus did.

(6) Their Mission: To be the salt and light of unity, hope, and salvation for everyone on earth.

(7) Their Destiny: The kingdom of God, begun on earth, perfected in heaven."The Church is the Body of Christ. Through the Spirit and his action in the sacraments, above all the Eucharist, Christ, who once was dead and is now risen, establishes the community of believers as his own Body. In the unity of this Body, there is a diversity of members and functions. All members are linked to one another, especially to those who are suffering, to the poor and persecuted" (*CCC* 805-806). "The Church is the Temple of the Holy Spirit. The Spirit is the soul, as it were, of the Mystical Body, the source of its life, of its unity in diversity, and of the riches of its gifts and charisms" (*CCC* 809).

The Four Marks of the Church: One, Holy, Catholic, Apostolic

The four marks of the Church — one, holy, catholic, apostolic — are inseparably linked to each other. They are always found in the Church and are essential to the Church's mission. Only faith can see this. The Church's history of saints, holiness, durability, stability, and charitable endeavor testify to her believability and divine mission.

At the same time, because of the sinfulness of the membership, these marks are not always wholly realized. Hence the marks are both a reality and a challenge.

• The Church is one. This reflects the unity of the Trinity. The Spirit is at work to unify the Church and reconcile its members. This unity includes a diversity of gifts, talents, cultures, and rites. The bonds of unity include the one faith received from the Apostles, the sacraments and Christian community, and the apostolic succession with the bishops as signs of unity and the pope as vicar of Christ. This unity has been injured by heresy, apostasy, and schism. The ecumenical movement is designed to restore the unity of the Church (cf. *CCC* 818-819, principles for ecumenism).

• The Church is holy. The founder is holy. Jesus makes holiness available to us by his paschal mystery. The Holy Spirit gives us this holiness which is participation in God's life. Though the Church is holy, there is sinfulness in the members, sins which can be forgiven by the sacrament of Reconciliation. The Church confirms its holiness when she canonizes saints who are models of holiness.

• The Church is catholic. The word means universal. All the means of salvation are found in the Church. We have the fullness of the faith, the sacraments, and apostolic succession. We are sent by Jesus to all nations. We are commissioned to speak to the conscience of all peoples. The Church strives to relate to every nation, culture, and religion. The Church is the sacrament of salvation for all people. This mark of the Church involves his missionary call to bring Christ's Kingdom and salvation to everyone.

• The Church is apostolic. This means the Church is founded by the Apostles. It is built on the twelve Apostles who were called and trained by Jesus and on whom he made the foundation of the Church. The Church gives us the teaching of these Apostles. The Church continues to be taught by the successors of the Apostles: the college of bishops, assisted by the priests and united to the pope, the successor of Peter. The Church is also apostolic in the missionary meaning of the word, a calling already treated under the mark of being catholic. The reader is encouraged to read and study the *Catechism*'s treatment of the Church's Magisterium, *CCC* 888-892. (The relationship of Mary to the Church will be treated in the chapter on Mary.)

Catechism Reflection

1. How is the Church of Christ in the Catholic Church?

"The sole Church of Christ which in the Creed we profess to be one, holy, catholic, and apostolic, . . . subsists in the Catholic Church, which is governed by the successor of Peter and by the bishops in communion with him. Nevertheless, many elements of sanctification and of truth are found outside its visible confines (*LG* 8)" (*CCC* 870).

2. What is the relation of the pope, bishops, priests, and deacons?

"The bishop of the Church of Rome, successor to St. Peter, is 'head of the college of bishops, the Vicar of Christ and Pastor of the universal Church on earth' (CIC, Can. 331)" (*CCC* 936). "The Bishops, established by the Holy Spirit, succeed the Apostles. They are 'the visible source and foundation of unity in their own particular Churches' (*LG* 23). Helped by the priests, their co-workers, and by the deacons, the bishops have the duty of authentically teaching the faith, celebrating divine worship, above all the

Eucharist, and guiding their churches as true pastors . . . (*CCC* 938-939).

3. What is the role of the laity in the Church?

"Lay people share in Christ's priesthood: ever more united with him, they exhibit the grace of Baptism and Confirmation in all dimensions of their personal, family, social, and ecclesial lives, and so fulfill the call to holiness addressed to all the baptized. By virtue of their prophetic mission, lay people 'are called . . . to be witnesses to Christ in all circumstances and at the very heart of the community of mankind' (*GS* 43§4)" (*CCC* 941-942).

4. What is the "Consecrated Life?"

"The life consecrated to God is characterized by the public profession of the evangelical counsels of poverty, chastity, and obedience, in a stable state of life recognized by the Church" (*CCC* 944).

5. What is the Communion of Saints?

"The Church is a 'communion of saints': this expression refers first to the 'holy things' (*sancta*), above all the Eucharist, by which 'the unity of believers, who form one body in Christ, is both represented and brought about (*LG* 3). The term 'communion of saints' refers also to the communion of 'holy persons' (*sancti*) in Christ who 'died for all,' so that what each one does or suffers in and for Christ bears fruit for all. 'We believe in the communion of all the faithful of Christ, those who are pilgrims on earth, the dead who are being purified, and the blessed in heaven, all together forming one Church; and we believe that in this communion, the merciful love of God and his saints is always [attentive] to our prayers' (Paul VI, CPG §30)" (*CCC* 960-962).

Connecting to Our Family

Our families are domestic churches, where we intimately live our lives as God's holy people, as the Body of Christ and Temples of the Holy Spirit. Within the Christian family is the possibility of planting the seeds of the marks of the Church: unity among the family members, the quest for holiness on the part of all, a sense of identity with the universal Church and its missionary awareness, and a desire to be in communion with Apostolic Tradition as embodied in the service of the pope, bishops, priests, and deacons to the Catholic community.

1. How would you apply these images of Church to your family witness: People of God, Body of Christ, Bride of Christ, Temple of the Spirit?

2. What needs to be done to make reconciliation a reality in your family? How do you witness the missionary call of the Church? What helps you identify your calling in Baptism and Confirmation to bring Jesus to others?

3. How has the Holy Spirit been a vital presence in your home? Why is awareness of the Spirit's warm and consoling action so important in being a living witness to Christ for you?

Family Prayer

Come, Holy Spirit, and breathe into our family the warmth of your love. Pour into us your wisdom, knowledge, understanding, courage, counsel, piety, and fear of the Lord. With grace refine our souls until this earthly part of us glows with your fire divine. Show us how to love the Church and to be grateful for this precious gift from God. Fill us with the energy we need to share our faith with others so they too may know Jesus Christ and the gifts of salvation from sin and divine life. We praise you with all our hearts. Amen.

Glossary

People of God: An image of the Church highlighted by Vatican II. God calls people to community with the Trinity and one another within the Church to listen to his Word, celebrate the sacraments, and witness Christ to the world.

Ministerial Priesthood: By Holy Orders, bishops, priests, and deacons are called to minister to the sanctification, guidance, and instruction of the faithful.

Priesthood of All the Faithful: By Baptism all believers are initiated into the priesthood of the faithful to witness Christ for the sanctification of the world.

Canonization: The Church process that examines the lives of members who exhibited heroic virtue and concludes that they are now saints in heaven. They serve as models of Christian living and intercede for us before God.

Lesson 10
The Face That Most Resembles Christ

Resource: *CCC* paragraphs 466; 484-
511; 963-975; 2673-2679

Look now upon the face that is most like the face of Christ, for only
through its brightness can you prepare your vision to see him.
— Dante, *Divine Comedy*, Par. XXXII, 85-87

Why Are Two Billion Hail Marys Said Daily?

During his daily radio broadcast, Cardinal Cushing, Boston's archbishop in mid-century, liked to lead his flock in reciting the Rosary. The
popular cardinal loved to say, "I pray that the Virgin Mary will get me into
heaven fifteen minutes before the devil knows I'm there."

He would have been fond of the following story. Once upon a time, the
Lord went walking through the streets of heaven, and he saw a lot of people
who had no business being in heaven at all. So our Lord went to St. Peter
who guarded the gates of heaven.

And he said, "Simon Peter, I'm disappointed in you. There are people
here who shouldn't have been admitted, yet you let them in."

"Lord, it's not my fault. I had nothing to do with it."

"Well, who let them in?"

"I don't want to tell you, because I'm not sure how you will take it."

"You should tell me. I have a right to know."

"All right, if you must know. I tell those folks they can't get in. But
then they go around to the back door and your mother lets them in."

When the Holy Spirit touched the womb of Mary two thousand years
ago, the Virgin predicted, "All generations will call me blessed." She was
absolutely right. Of all the women who have ever lived, the mother of
Jesus Christ is the most celebrated, the most portrayed, the most honored
in the naming of girl babies and churches. Even the Moslems honor her,
strengthened by the fact she is mentioned thirty-four times in the Koran.

The late twentieth century has become the age of the Marian pilgrimage. Examples: Attendance at Lourdes has jumped ten percent to 5.5 million annually. Many of these are people twenty-five or younger. The young
ones dance, sing, and praise out loud exuberantly. At Fátima, 4.5 million
pilgrims a year visit. In Czestochowa, Poland, the stream of pilgrims has
increased to five million a year. In Emmitsburg, Maryland, the number
has suddenly doubled to 500,000 a year at their national shrine of Our
Lady of Lourdes.

Most astonishing of all, ten million flocked to Guadalupe last year to pray to Our Lady.

Pope John Paul II openly shares his devotion to Mary. His coat of arms contains a large "M" for Mary and his motto is "Totus Tuus" (All Yours). He believes Mary saved him from death when he was shot while in St. Peter's Square. One observer at that scene says that just as the assassin raised his gun to shoot him, the Pope suddenly bent down to look at a picture of Our Lady of Fátima being held up to him. In that instant his body was just enough out of line that the bullet did not accomplish its fatal intent.

John Paul noted that the assassination attempt occurred on May 13, the exact anniversary of the first apparition at Fátima. The Pope recovered and one year later he went to Fátima to thank Mary for his life. One million people joined him in that act of joyous gratitude. Today in the Vatican gardens there is a new statue of Our Lady of Fátima. The stone pedestal has a simple inscription: May 13, 1981.

The answer to the question "Why are two billion Hail Marys said daily?" is found in these stories of Mary's outreach to the world and her intercession for us with her Son Jesus. Our study of the *Catechism*'s teachings about Mary further reinforce the meaning of Mary's role in the Church and the history of salvation.

Conceived by the Spirit — Born of the Virgin Mary

The *Catechism* teaches about Mary principally in three places: the section about Jesus Christ; the section about the Church; and in the fourth part dealing with prayer.

When the angel Gabriel appeared to Mary at the Annunciation, the *fullness of time* had arrived. Scripture speaks of time in two ways: *chronos*, or clock time and *kairos*, or fulfillment time. The seconds and minutes of history flow inexorably, but there are moments full of grace in which God accomplishes his will in history. This is *kairos*, the sacred moment. All the promises about a Messiah are now about to be accomplished in Mary of Nazareth.

"How can this be since I do not know a man?"

"The Holy Spirit will come upon you."

The moment is Trinitarian. The Father will send the Holy Spirit, Lord and giver of life, to sanctify the womb of Mary and cause her to conceive the Son of God in the flesh.

What the Catholic Church believes about Mary is based on what it believes about Jesus Christ. What we teach about Mary increases our understanding of Jesus.

The Father willed that the Incarnation be preceded by a "yes" from the predestined mother. From all eternity God had chosen Mary to be the mother of his Son. But he also willed that her cooperation be a free assent.

The mission of many holy women prepared for Mary. Despite the disobedience of Eve, she received the promise of a descendant who would conquer the evil one. Throughout Old Testament history, God chose the powerless to give evidence of his promise: Sarah, Hannah, Deborah, Ruth, Judith, Esther, and many other women. Mary, a Daughter of Zion, stood out among all these poor and humble of the Lord who waited for the Messiah with confidence and hope (cf. *CCC* 490).

God enriched Mary with the graces she needed to be the mother of the Savior. Gabriel greets her as a woman, "full of grace" (*RSV* Lk 1:28). Her "yes" to God, freely given, was itself a testimony to grace.

Immaculate Conception

For centuries, the Church meditated on this singular gift of Mary as the woman, "full of grace." Under the guidance of the Spirit, the Church came to realize that Mary was immaculately conceived, meaning that she was conceived without inheriting original sin. Pope Pius IX proclaimed this teaching as a dogma of the Church in 1854. "The Blessed Virgin Mary was, from the first moment of her conception, by a singular grace and gift of almighty God and by virtue of the merits of Jesus Christ, Savior of the human race, preserved immune from all stain of original sin" (*Ineffabilis Deus*, 1854).

Mary needed to be redeemed by Jesus just like everyone else. She was saved from original sin at her conception by the anticipated merits of Jesus which he would achieve for us at the Cross and Easter. Grace continued to work in her so that she remained sinless throughout her life. We should note here that the immaculate conception does not refer to the virginal birth of Jesus, but rather to Mary's being conceived without inheriting original sin. The Fathers of the Eastern tradition call her the "All Holy" (*Panagia*) and celebrate her as free from any stain of sin.

Mary replied to Gabriel, "Be it done to me according to your word." Mary responded with the obedience of faith. Without a single sin to restrain her, she gave herself entirely to the work of her Son and served the mystery of salvation with him. We recommend that our readers study and pray over the encyclical *The Mother of the Redeemer* by Pope John Paul II. He has given us an inspiring meditation on the faith of Mary, first extolled and admired by Elizabeth at the visitation when she said to Mary, "Blessed are you for having believed."

Mother of God — Theotokos

In the year 431, St. Cyril of Alexandria led a delegation of bishops to the Council of Ephesus. Bishop John of Antioch led a contingent of bishops from Syria. Pope Celestine I sent three legates. St. Augustine had been invited, but died before the council opened. The best known decision of that council was to declare that Mary was the *Mother of God* (*Theotokos* or God-Bearer).

Why were they moved to this development of the ancient faith of the Church about Mary? Because the Patriarch of Constantinople, Nestorius, was teaching that the child born of Mary was only human. Mary was simply the Christ-bearer, not the God-bearer. Nestorius could not accept the idea that Mary was God's mother. He explained his position by saying that there were two persons in Jesus, a human and a divine one. After Jesus was born the divine person of the Word united himself to the human Jesus and so Jesus then became divine.

The Council Fathers rejected this teaching. They asserted that the Son of God was united to the humanity of Jesus at his conception. "He made the birth of his flesh into his own flesh. Thus we do not hesitate to call the Holy Virgin: "Mother of God." Mary was the mother of the whole Jesus Christ, divine and human. The Fathers were making a statement primarily about Jesus (cf. *CCC* 466).

Mary Always a Virgin

The Church believes that the Holy Spirit's power made possible the conception of Jesus in Mary's womb. There was no human Father. The Gospels present the virginal conception of Jesus as a divine work that surpasses all human understanding. The meaning of this event is accessible only to faith.

As the Church's faith in this mystery deepened, it came to confess that Mary remained a virgin while giving birth to Jesus and also afterwards. The liturgy of the Church speaks of Mary as "ever virgin." Some have objected that this could not be true since the Scriptures speak of the "brothers and sisters" of Jesus. St. Jerome, in his book *Against Helvidius*, defended Mary's perpetual virginity, claiming that the word for siblings could also mean cousins. The Eastern Church had an alternate tradition that these brothers and sisters were the children of Joseph by a previous marriage.

At the Council of Capua in 392, St. Ambrose upheld the Church's position about Mary's perpetual virginity. This was reconfirmed by Pope Siricius. In 1992, Pope John Paul went to Capua to celebrate the sixteen-hundredth anniversary of that Council. On that occasion he preached on the gift and mystery of Mary's total virginity. Jesus is Mary's only son, but her spiritual motherhood extends to all whom he came to save.

The *Catechism* gives five reasons for Mary's virginal motherhood:
• It emphasizes God's absolute initiative in the Incarnation. Jesus has only God as Father;
• It highlights that Jesus is the New Adam who begins the new creation. The Spirit dwells in him with divine fullness, from whom we receive a multitude of graces;
• We are made participants in divine life, not from flesh or human intentions but by God alone. This life is virginal for it comes only from God;
• This is a sign of Mary's faith not diluted by any doubt. She gave God the undivided surrender of her whole self.

• As both virgin and mother, Mary symbolizes the Church. In receiving God's Word, the Church preaches and baptizes and begets sons and daughters in Christ. The Church is virginal by her pure fidelity to Christ, her spouse.

Mother of the Church

It was Vatican II which developed the title "Mother of the Church" for Mary. From Christ's conception until his death, Mary was united to her Son in his work of salvation. Her pilgrimage of faith brought her to the Cross where she joined her son's sacrifice and lovingly consented to it. Jesus asked her to look at John, and by extension to all of us, and said, "Woman, behold, your son" (Jn 19:26-27).

Mary prayed with the Apostles and disciples after the Ascension and begged for the Spirit who came at Pentecost. She was present at the Incarnation of the physical Christ — and at the manifestation of the Mystical Body at Pentecost.

In the mystery of her Assumption, Mary was granted a unique participation in her Son's Resurrection and a forecast of our resurrection. "Finally, the Immaculate Virgin . . . when the course of her earthly life was finished, was taken up body and soul into heavenly glory, and exalted by the Lord as Queen over all things, so that she might be more fully conformed to her Son, the Lord of lords and conqueror of sin and death" (Pius XII, *Munificentissmus Deus*, 1950: *[DS]* 3903).

Pope Paul VI has written a wonderful book — *Marialis Cultus* — on devotion to Mary, based on the Scriptures, councils, liturgy, and popular piety. His warmhearted direction is inspiring and faith enriching, and deserves our prayerful meditation.

Finally, in Mary we behold what the Church is already like during the pilgrimage of faith — and what the Church will become at the end of the journey. Mary is an icon of the Church as well as sign of hope and comfort for all of us.

Catechism Reflection

1. What is the role of Mary's faith in the plan of salvation?

"The Virgin Mary 'cooperated through free faith and obedience in human salvation' (*LG* 56). She uttered her yes 'in the name of all human nature' (St. Thomas Aquinas, *STh* III, 30, 1). By her obedience she became the new Eve, the mother of all the living" (*CCC* 511).

2. What is the Church's teaching about Mary's virginity?

"Mary 'remained a virgin in conceiving her Son, a virgin in giving birth to him, a virgin in carrying him, a virgin in nursing him at her breast, always a virgin' (St. Augustine, *Serm* 186, 1: *PL* 38, 999): with her whole being she is the 'handmaid of the Lord' (*Lk* 1:38)" (*CCC* 510).

3. What are ways to have devotion to Mary?

"The Church rightly honors 'the Blessed Virgin with special devotion.

From the most ancient times the Blessed Virgin has been honored with the title "Mother of God," to whose protection the faithful fly in all their dangers and needs. . . . This very special devotion . . . differs essentially from the adoration which is given to the incarnate Word and equally to the Father and the Holy Spirit, and greatly fosters this adoration' [*LG* 66]. The liturgical feasts dedicated to the Mother of God and Marian prayer, such as the rosary, an 'epitome of the whole Gospel,' express this devotion to the Virgin Mary" [Cf. Paul VI, *MC* 42; *SC* 103] (*CCC* 971).

Connecting to Our Family

For many years, the late father Patrick Peyton preached the power of the Rosary under the motto "The Family That Prays Together Stays Together." His vibrant devotion to Mary inspired hundreds of thousands of families to turn to Mary to help them with family stability and the acquiring of family values.

The need for family devotion to Mary is greater today than ever. Each time we turn to Mary she brings us closer to Jesus. Two thousand years after the Nativity, the mother is Jesus is more beloved and powerful than ever.

In a *Life* magazine cover story on Mary, Robert Sullivan writes: "My habit as an adolescent was to pray to Jesus. I was a boy; he had been a boy. I figured he would understand me better. Later my pleas became more consequential. Life decisions — career changes, marriage — led to appeals for blessings and guidance; a family member developed a cancer, and lunchtime novenas at St. Pat's were squeezed into the day. I found myself praying to Mary.

"Something in my training? About motherhood?

"Something about intercession? Yes.

"Something about Mary? Indeed."

Look again upon the face that most resembles the face of Christ. Only through Mary's brightness can you most prepare to see the face of Jesus.

1. What forms of devotion to Mary occur in your family today? What images of Mary adorn your walls? Do your family members know how to say the Rosary? Do you ever pray together as a family?

2. How much are you aware of and involved in the liturgical feasts of Mary: Immaculate Conception, Assumption, Annunciation, Nativity of Mary, etc.? If you have made pilgrimages to one of Mary's shrines, how did the experience affect your faith life?

3. How have you learned to turn to Mary in times of trouble and ask her intercession with Jesus?

Family Prayer

Mary, Mother of Jesus, Mother of the Church and our Mother, we celebrate your undivided surrender of yourself to God. We admire you as the chief woman of faith in the Church and strive to imitate this virtue. We say with Elizabeth, "Blessed are you for having believed." When Jesus said, "Blessed are they who hear the Word of God and keep it," he thought of you who acted out this truth better than anyone else. May we also listen to God's Word and respond to it with the obedience of faith just as you did. We fly to your protection so that we may draw ever closer to Christ. Amen.

Glossary

Immaculate Conception: The Church's teach that Mary was conceived without original sin. She was redeemed by the anticipated merits of Jesus Christ and lived her full life without sin.

Ever Virgin: The Church's faith holds that Mary was a virgin in conceiving and bearing Jesus and remained so for the rest of her life.

Lesson 11
Last Things: Death, Judgment, Heaven, Hell

Resource: *CCC* paragraphs 988-1066

I have come to consider death as a friend.
— Joseph Cardinal Bernardin

Teaching Us How to Die

The late Cardinal Bernardin said he had three fears in life: the fear of being falsely accused, the fear of getting cancer like his father, and the fear of dying. All that he feared happened to him. He was falsely accused of sexually abusing a Mr. Cook who arrived at this idea through "recovered memory" while in therapy. Cook, dying of AIDS, subsequently retracted his accusation. The Cardinal met with him, forgave him, anointed him, and gave him back his dignity.

Bernardin then was afflicted with cancer and the prospect of a painful dying process. At one point his bones were so brittle from stenosis that he snapped a rib when bending over. He noticed that illness tended to pull him inside himself to focus on his pain. He felt sorry for himself and depressed. He wanted to withdraw from people.

He learned to turn outward to Jesus and his message and to open himself to God's grace. Christ helped him to begin to think of other people and their needs. He decided to walk with them in their trials. When referred to a cancer clinic, he refused the offered private entrance and went into the waiting room his fellow sufferers. He approached and comforted each one and followed up with phone calls and notes. In the last three months of his life, he acquired a "special parish" of six hundred people like himself, and he gave them hope and love. He loved to go to parishes and conduct services for the Anointing of the Sick. For him, death was not the end. It was the transition to life eternal.

In his last week on earth he wrote three letters. The first he sent to the Supreme Court of the United States. He begged the justices not to approve of physician-assisted suicide. "As one who is dying, I have come to appreciate in a special way the gift of life." He added that to approve of a new right to assisted suicide would endanger America and send the false signal that a less-than-"perfect" life was not worth living.

His second letter was a handwritten one to the United States bishops assembled for their autumn meeting in Washington, D.C. He asked them for their prayers that God would give him the grace to make it through each day. Last, he sent out his Christmas cards early to his priests and many friends.

He taught us all that approaching death meant learning new lessons of faith and new lessons to share with others. He was well prepared. "I know that just as God called me to serve him to the best of my ability throughout my life on earth, he is now calling me home."

I Believe in the Resurrection of the Body

"On no point does the Christian faith encounter more opposition than the resurrection of the body" (St. Augustine, *On the Psalms*, 88:5). God revealed the resurrection of the body gradually. Faith in God as Creator of body as well as soul led the believing community to confess the resurrection of the dead. The Maccabean martyrs were clear, ". . . the King of the universe will raise us up to an everlasting renewal of life, because we have died for his laws" (*RSV* 2 Mac 7:9).

The Pharisees looked for resurrection, but the Saducees did not.

Jesus raised the dead to life in his own ministry as a symbol of future resurrection. Strictly speaking, the raising of Lazarus and the daughter of Jairus were resuscitations, not resurrections, for they died again. Jesus associated resurrection of the body with himself. "I am the resurrection and the life" (Jn 11:25).

What is resurrection? At death the soul leaves the body to meet God. The soul waits for reunion with the body.

Who will rise? All dead people will rise. The good will rise to life with God. The evil will rise to the eternal death of hell.

How will this happen? Jesus received his own body back, even with the scars of the crucifixion. But his body was a glorified one with new supernatural qualities. The same will be true of ourselves. One of the best scriptural passage for this teaching is First Corinthians, chapter fifteen.

Though we make many attempts to explain resurrection, the "how it happens" exceeds our imagination and understanding. The seed/flower image can be useful because it establishes identity between the old and new body. It shows the glorious difference. It describes the change in dynamic terms.

When will the resurrection happen? At the last day at the end of the world, a date unknown to us.

Through our Baptism we know by faith that we have already begun the process of resurrection because we have been united to the risen Jesus. Therefore our bodies, as well as other peoples' bodies, deserve reverence, especially the suffering in hospitals, nursing homes, and hospices.

Dying in Christ

Death is the end of earthly life. The paths of glory lead but to the grave. Because death comes for us all, there is a sense of urgency that pushes us to fulfill what we dream about ourselves.

Two of the best-known philosophers of the twentieth century, Sartre and Heidegger, claimed that meditation on death inspired their lifelong quest to find meaning in life. Sartre said, "I am free to make meaning out of my life despite my mortality." His mental brush with death awoke in him the passion to make sense out of life.

Heidegger, too, contemplated the role of death in his life. He saw his life inevitably moving toward death. He noted that death would cancel out all the things he would still like to do. Instead of being depressed by this, he resolved to look at all of life's possibilities, thus to fulfill himself as much as he could.

What these men discovered at the human level about death's effect on life is even more true for the believer in Jesus. Christ resolutely looked at death and did not deny it. He taught us that this brings a divine meaning to our lives and that it called us to see the possibilities which life on earth holds for us. But far more, Jesus instructed us to see that death is not the cancellation of possibilities, but the prelude to an even greater life beyond the grave. The soul is immortal. And one day, in Jesus, our bodies will rise again.

Death is a result of sin. The Church's Magisterium interprets Scripture and Tradition to mean that sin caused death to enter the world. Had we not sinned, we would not die.

Death is transformed by Jesus. Accepting death by a free submission to the Father's will, Jesus transformed death into an act that both conquered sin and overcame death for us. Jesus took the experience of death which frightens so many people and removed its finality. It is not the end. It is the beginning of a new life. In death we are not obliterated. We pass into a new world where we can live with God in eternal rest and joy.

Listen to the saints:

"My earthly desire has been crucified . . . there is living water in me, water that murmurs and says within me: come to the Father" (St. Ignatius of Antioch, *To the Romans*, 6:1-2).

"I want to see God. In order to see him, I must die" (St. Teresa of Ávila, *Life*).

"I am not dying. I am entering into eternal life" (St. Thérèse of Lisieux, *The Last Conversations*).

We should prepare for death by avoiding sin and living a life of virtue. Since we will die as we have lived, it makes sense to spend each day full of love for others and always deepening our friendship with God. So when death comes, we will not have to rage against the dying of the light, for death shall have no dominion over us. We can go gently into that good night. As a ripe fruit falls quietly from the tree, so we will fall peacefully into the heart of God. Cardinal Bernardin said it best, "I learned to treat death as a friend."

Judgment, Heaven, Purgatory, Hell

The Church stands with the dying to absolve them from their sins, to anoint them with spiritual strength, and give them Jesus in the Eucharist (viaticum) as food for the final journey. At the funeral liturgy, the Church commends the person to God in these beauitful words:

> May holy Mary, the angels, and all the saints
> come to meet you as you go forth from this life . . .
> May you see your Redeemer face to face.

Immediately after death we face the *particular judgment*. Depending on the state of our souls, we enter heaven, purgatory, or hell. St. John of the Cross sums up the judgment in this touching sentence, "At the evening of life, we shall be judged by our love."

Heaven

If we die in the grace of God and have no need of further purification, we will go straight to heaven. In heaven we will find perfect and unending happiness at last. This will be caused by a perfect communion with the Holy Trinity, the Blessed Mother, the angels, and saints. Jesus Christ opened heaven to us by his death and Resurrection. We will enjoy the results of what Jesus accomplished for us.

What is heaven like in concrete terms? Scripture uses a variety of pictures to help us understand heaven, such as: wedding party, wine, life, light, peace, paradise, the Father's house. But the real heaven is beyond any picture we can paint of it. ". . . No eye has seen, nor ear heard, nor the heart of man conceived, what God has prepared for those who love him" (*RSV* 1 Cor 2:9).

Seeing God face-to-face in all his glory is an essential aspect of heaven. This is called the "beatific vision." To make this possible God must reveal himself and give us the capacity to behold him.

Purgatory

Those who die in the state of grace and friendship with God, but are not fully purified from their sinfulness, are assured of their eternal salvation. They must undergo a purification to obtain the holiness needed to enter heaven. This is purgatory. In the Liturgy of All Souls, the Church remembers this teaching and recommends Eucharist, prayer, charitable giving, and works of penance on behalf of the departed.

Hell

Hell is eternal separation from God. It is impossible to be united with God if we refuse to love him. When we sin seriously against God, neighbor, or self, we have failed to love God. The great Last Judgment scene in Matthew (25:31-46) reminds us that we will go to hell if we fail to meet the serious needs of the poor and helpless. Freely chosen, self-exclusion from communion with God is called hell.

Immediately after death, the souls of those who die in a state of mortal sin go to hell. The principal suffering of hell is absolute and eternal separation from God. While images of fire are used to portray hell, the reality exceeds our ability to describe the pain which truly comes from rejecting God's love.

Scripture and the teaching of the Church regarding heaven and hell emphasize a call to personal responsibility by which we use our freedom, aided by divine grace, to affect our eternal destiny. There is always an urgent call to conversion and repentance. "God predestines no one to go to hell [Cf: Council of Orange II (529): *DS* 397; Council of Trent (1547: 1567]" (*CCC* 1037), only a free turning away from God in mortal sin and persistence in this attitude leads to hell. The Church prays everyday in her liturgy for the conversion of her members. "The Lord . . . is patient with you, not wishing that any should perish but that all should come to repentance" (2 Pet 3:9).

The Last Judgment

"The Last Judgment will come when Christ returns in glory. Only the Father knows the day and the hour; only he determines the moment of its coming. Then through his Son Jesus Christ he will pronounce the final word on all history. We shall know the ultimate meaning of the whole work of creation and of the entire economy of salvation and understand the marvellous ways by which his Providence led everything towards its final end. The Last Judgment will reveal that God's justice triumphs over all the injustices committed by his creatures and that God's love is stronger than death [Cf. *Songs* 8:6]" (*CCC* 1040).

New Heaven and New Earth

Once the Kingdom of God arrives in its completion at the end of time there will be a renewal of the universe itself in Christ. Scripture uses many images to describe this mysterious reality. There will be a new heavens and a new earth. ". . . creation itself will be set free from its bondage to decay . . ." (*RSV* Rom 8:21). The holy city will descend from heaven to earth. We do not know when or how this will happen. But we do believe that God will make this happen. At the end of time, ". . . the universe itself, which is so closely related to man and which attains its destiny through him, will be perfectly re-established in Christ *[LG*, 48; cf. *Acts* 3:21; *Eph* 1:10; *Col* 1:20; 2 *Pet* 3:10-13]" (*CCC* 1042).

Catechism Reflection

1. How are the souls in purgatory helped by us?

"By virtue of the 'communion of saints,' the Church commends the dead to God's mercy and offers her prayers, especially the holy sacrifice of the Eucharist, on their behalf" (*CCC* 1055).

2. What happens at the Last Judgment?

" 'The holy Roman Church firmly believes and confesses that on the Day of Judgment all men will appear in their own bodies before Christ's tribunal to render an account of their own deeds' [Council of Lyons II [1274]: *DS* 859; cf. *DS* 1549]" (*CCC* 1059).

3. What will the full kingdom of God be like?

"At the end of time, the Kingdom of God will come in its fullness. Then the just will reign with Christ for ever, glorified in body and soul, and the material universe itself will be transformed. God will then be 'all in all' (*1 Cor* 15:28), in eternal life" (*CCC* 1060).

Connecting to Our Family

In earlier times when people died at home, death was a part of life and people possessed a host of customs for adapting to death and caring for loved ones. In our time, with the aged and dying cloistered in nursing homes and factory-like hospitals, the family fumbles with awkwardness when coping with the crisis of dying.

In the old days, when one died at home, one could hear and smell meals being cooked and children playing and being soothed by the familiar rhythm of life. Grandparents could see grandchildren at any hour. Friends and relatives would stop in as a matter of course. The great warm womb of life was around them as the dying passed their final days.

Nothing tests the family's capacity to love more than experience of caring for a dying member. The dying person is still mom, pop, grandma, grandpa, son, daughter, brother, or sister. The heart that loved you when it was well still loves you and pleads for love in return.

The family should listen to the dying as they teach us how to love and care. The dying speak with insight and conviction because they are going through an experience from which to instruct. They can show the family how to love them, as long as the family learns to notice and is alert to the precious moments allowed.

Thus, losing someone close can be life's greatest lesson in love. Since the lesson is so hard won, would anyone really want to miss it?

1. How does our belief in the immortality of the soul affect your acceptance of death? Similarly, how does our faith in the resurrection of the body give us a sense of hope that death is not the end, but a transition to new life?

2. In our dying moments, the Church loves us by giving us absolution, anointing, and viaticum. Why is it so important to have these events of faith in our last moments? How do they help us overcome the fear of dying

and the dread of judgment? If we have loved our family, friends, and those in serious need, what does that tell us we will hear at our judgment?

3. What are some inspiring stories of dying that give you the courage to face your own inevitable death? How can you begin to experience heaven on earth so that at the hour of death you look forward to union with perfect love in Christ?

Family Prayer

Father of life, you have called us to eternal life after our faith journey on earth. You want us to have perfect joy after the troubles of this life. We commend to you those who are seriously ill in our family, among our friends, and those who have no one to pray or care for them. Help us to live today with love, compassion, and sympathy for others so that when we arrive at our own death, our last moments will be filled with those virtues that make life worth living and death a friend that takes us to glory. Amen.

Glossary

Immortality: Means the soul lives on after death. It will be reunited to the resurrected body at the second coming of Jesus.

Resurrected Body: By God's power our bodies will rise again, transformed by the Spirit, at the resurrection of the dead. Read First Corinthians 15.

Four Last Things: The four last things are death, judgment, heaven, and hell.

Purgatory: Those who die in God's friendship, but are not completely purified from sinfulness, undergo a purification in purgatory to prepare them for heaven.

Particular Judgment: Immediately after death we are judged by God as to whether we go to heaven, hell, or purgatory.

Last Judgment: Scripture teaches that there will be a final judgment in which God makes visible for all to see the victory of Jesus over sin. The Kingdom of God will arrive in its fullness. The world will be transfigured and the just will reign with Christ in glory.

Chapter Two
The Christian Mystery

The Holy Family
— by Raphael

Lesson 12

Liturgy: The Celebration of the Christian Mystery

Resource: *CCC* paragraphs 1066-1209

Fling wide the portals of your heart
Make it a new Temple set apart,
Adorned with prayer and love and joy.

— George Weissel

The Parable of the Ant Keeper

A long time ago there was an ant keeper who had a beautiful garden. Two winged ants, male and female, flew about the garden, enjoying its beauty and food. The ant keeper — also known as the gardener — gave them the freedom of the garden, but forbade them to eat of the plant at the top of the hill. One day a witch from the swamp came to them and urged them to eat of the forbidden plant.

"Then you will be like the gardener."

They heeded her malicious advice and flew to the plant, not realizing it was a Venus Fly Trap. Caught in it, they cried for help. The gardener came and released them. "I am sorry you did this. I regret what happened to you." You see, they lost their wings.

Then the ants multiplied, red, black, all kinds. The witch came again and said, "Life is too boring for you. Make war on each other. Red ants against black. Slave against master. Husbands against wives." And so it was.

The gardener, dismayed, sent his son to stop this. The son walked down the hill, lay down on the ground and wrapped himself in an egg-like cocoon. The ants came and unwrapped the cocoon, finding a new ant, whom they welcomed to their world.

The new ant had a message different from the witch. "Love one another. Keep your promises. Make peace." This angered the witch, who stirred up her followers to destroy him. A mob of hostile ants rushed on him and killed him. A leaf fell from a tree and covered his body.

Three days later, the ants who believed in him came to take away the leaf and look at his body. Suddenly they beheld the ant keeper and his son. The son showed his hands to his father. Scars glowed from the middle of his palms. The believers sang alleluias. They were even happier when they noticed they had been changed. . . .

They were wearing wings.

Liturgy Makes the Paschal Mystery Present

The parable of the ant keeper retells the death and Resurrection of Jesus in folk language. It reminds us of the central act of our religion, the paschal mystery of Jesus Christ, which we celebrate in the liturgy of the Church.

Part Two of the *Catechism* lays out for us the basic teachings about the liturgy in section one. In this lesson we will meditate on section one. In future lessons we will study Part Two, section two — the sacraments.

At Pentecost the Holy Spirit inaugurated the time of the Church. The Spirit made salvation present and communicated it through the liturgy, which is ultimately the work of the Trinity:

- The Father, source and goal of the liturgy, blesses us.
- The Son, at the heart of the liturgy, redeems us.
- The Spirit, the soul of the liturgy, sanctifies us.

The Father Blesses

In the liturgy we associate the work of the Father with blessing. The Father blesses us from the liturgical hymn of creation in Genesis to the songs of the heavenly Jerusalem in the Apocalypse. The Father blessed Adam and Eve, Noah, Abraham, and Moses and the holy people of Israel in the exodus, temple, exile, and return. Israel's liturgies used the Torah, the prophets, and the Psalms to think of the Father's blessings and thank him.

All Christian liturgies are directed to the Father. United with Jesus and dependent on the Spirit, we assemble as the Church to praise God from whom all blessings flow.

The Son Redeems

At the liturgy Jesus acts in the events of the sacraments to communicate grace-divine life to us. Jesus enacts his paschal mystery, his dying and rising, so that we may share more deeply in salvation. Some people behave as though Jesus is an audience and the worshipers are the actors "doing something to Jesus." It is quite the opposite. Jesus is the agent who acts on and in us. It is Jesus who baptizes, confirms, and offers the Eucharistic sacrifice through his visible ministers. At the Last Supper and on Easter night, Jesus gave to the Apostles the power of sanctification and apostolic succession. All the worshipers are expected to participate actively in liturgy.

The Spirit Sanctifies

The Spirit teaches the faith to God's people and is the artist of God's masterpieces, the sacraments. The Spirit makes the mystery of Jesus present and real. The Spirit is the Church's living memory, reminding us of the teachings of Scripture and Tradition which we tend to forget. The Spirit does more than put the teachings before us; it also gives life to the liturgical acts of proclamation, gestures, and symbols. At Eucharist the priest begs the Holy Spirit to come and change the bread and wine into the Body and Blood of Christ. A medieval poet said it this way:

> Come Holy Spirit,
> Bake this bread in your holy fire,
> Cook this wine in your holy flame.
>
> — Matthew of Riveaulx

The work of the Spirit at the liturgy may be summarized this way:
- To prepare the assembly to encounter Christ.
- To manifest Jesus to the faith of the assembly.
- To make Christ's saving work present and active.
- To make the gift of Communion bear fruit in the Church.

The Sacraments of Salvation

The Church makes the sacraments. The sacraments make the Church. What are sacraments? They are:

(1) *Efficacious signs of grace,* which means they accomplish what they signify. Baptism washes away all our sins. Confirmation anoints us with the oil of the Spirit to strengthen us. Eucharist feeds us with the eternal life of Jesus.

(2) *Instituted by Christ*, which means it is Jesus who originates the sacraments and who acts in them today.

(3) *Entrusted to the Church,* which means we have seen already that the Church is the sacrament of salvation. By Christ's will the Church oversees and celebrates the sacraments.

(4) *To give us divine life*, which means the sacraments are the divinely appointed events of salvation from sin and sources of divine life for us.

The sacraments of initiation are Baptism, Confirmation, and Eucharist. The sacraments of healing are Reconciliation and Anointing. The sacraments that build up the community of the Church are Matrimony and Holy Orders.

What is the purpose of the sacraments?
- To call us to worship God.
- To make us holy.
- To build up the Church.
- To deepen our faith.
- To train us to pray.
- To incorporate us into the Church's Tradition.

God works primarily through the sacraments, though God is not limited by the sacraments (cf. *CCC* 1257). God also works through prayer, catechesis, evangelization, spirituality, good works, and social ministry. These activities orient us toward the Eucharist and help us to participate more vitally in that celebration. The liturgy is not entertainment. The liturgy is more like dieting, exercise, or the energies demanded by our professional lives. Liturgy is *work*!

82

Who Celebrates?

The whole Body of Christ celebrates the liturgy. Jesus, our high priest, Mary, the angels, and the saints are present at our liturgy. When we gather for liturgy we are an ordered and structured community. The *Catechism* gives us this powerful passage on the dignity of the liturgical assembly: "Forming 'as it were, one mystical person' with Christ the head, the Church acts in the sacraments as 'an organically structured priestly community [*LG* 11; cf. Pius XII, *Mystici Corporis* (1943)].' Through Baptism and Confirmation the priestly people is enabled to celebrate the liturgy, while those of the faithful 'who have received Holy Orders, are appointed to nourish the Church with the word and grace of God in the name of Christ' [*LG* 11 § 2]" (*CCC* 1119).

Hence we have a hierarchical model of the liturgy which respects the varying roles and responsibilities of those at the liturgy.

There are "diverse liturgical traditions or rites, legitimately recognized, [which] manifest the catholicity of the Church, because they signify and communicate the same mystery of Christ" (*CCC* 1208).

How Do We Celebrate?

We use signs and symbols, such as candles, water, and fire in our celebration. We take these symbols from creation which reflects the Creator. We relate them to our human life, so at the liturgy we wash sins away and eat and drink the Body and Blood of Christ. We relate these symbols to the history of salvation. Hence, at Baptism we recall God's liberation of the Israelites from political slavery at the crossing of the Red Sea, and see ourselves liberated from spiritual slavery by the power of Christ as we cross over the waters of redemption.

These cosmic elements, human rituals, and memorial gestures become vessels of Christ's saving actions. During the liturgy, notice the rich texture of signs: The *words* of Scripture, prayers, and homilies. The *deeds* of hands upraised in prayer, processions, reverential kneeling, silence, bowed heads, and Signs of the Cross. The *arts* of colored glass, sculpture, architecture, music, songs, and statuary. These liturgical symbols form a coherent symphony that appeal to the senses, the heart, and the soul as well as the mind. They reflect a divine artistry.

When Do We Celebrate?

One liturgical musician put it this way. She played the organ at three consecutive Masses on Sundays. She wanted to make sure that her work did not become routine. The organ happened to be in the sanctuary area. Just as she left the sacristy she removed her watch, which tells human clock time so that she could remind herself that she was entering "God's time," liturgical time.

At the heart of liturgy lies the Christian Sunday. It recalls the Resurrection of Jesus, summons the Christian people to worship, and ideally should be a family day and a time of rest from our busy work. There is also the liturgical year — Advent, Christmas, Lent, Easter, Pentecost, Trinity, Corpus Christi, and Ordinary Time. This year of grace unfolds for us the mystery of Christ.

The most solemn part of the liturgical year is the *Sacrum Triduum* — Holy Thursday, Good Friday, and Easter Vigil. Chronologically these are three days. Liturgically they are One Day unfolding the unity of Christ's paschal mystery.

Next, we have the memorials and feasts of the Blessed Mother and the saints. These events hold before us their example of Christian living and also invite us to seek their intercession on our behalf.

Every day we can join the Church in the Liturgy of the Hours. Seven times each day we can join the universal Church in praising God at the Office of Readings, Morning Prayer, Daytime Prayer (three sessions), Evening Prayer, and Night Prayer. The Liturgy of the Hours prolongs the celebration of the Eucharist, flowing from the Mass and flowing back to it.

Thus liturgical time consecrates and sanctifies human time and opens us to the flood of divine graces available to us every hour, day, week, and year.

Where Do We Celebrate?

Sacred acts make sacred places! We worship in our parish churches, our diocesan cathedrals, monastery chapels, and shrines of our Blessed Lady and the saints. These buildings are visible images of the heavenly Jerusalem to which we are journeying and where we:

• Worship God
• Pray to God
• Hear Scripture
• Offer Christ's Sacrifice
• Sing God's praises
• Center ourselves on God's Presence

Jesus is the true Temple of God and by his love we are Temples of the Holy Spirit and living stones of the Church. All the visible richness of the "things" associated with places of worship are meant to minister to the building up of the holy community of love and faith.

The Liturgy Is Eschatological

We will celebrate the liturgy until Jesus Christ comes again. The communion of saints in heaven celebrates with us. Read the Book of Revelation and note how often St. John takes us right to heaven to hear the choirs of angels and saints praising and adoring God. He told his people to read these words at their liturgies and to sing those hymns so that they might realize the intimate connection between the worship in heaven and that which took place at their Sunday Eucharists. Sacraments refer to eternal life as well as life here.

In a way, time "collapses" at liturgy. The Eucharist celebrates the Passover of the Old Testament, the Christian paschal mystery, and the future coming of Jesus. All these joyful events are "made present" by the power of the Holy Spirit at each Mass and other sacramental celebrations. This is why the pulse of incredible happiness surges at the liturgy, for the joy of heaven itself is present. And it is enjoyed by those who have eyes to see, ears to hear — a possibility given to us by the grace of faith.

Catechism Reflection

1. What are the sacraments?

"The sacraments are efficacious signs of grace, instituted by Christ and entrusted to the Church, by which divine life is dispensed to us. The visible rites by which the sacraments are celebrated signify and make present the graces proper to each sacrament. They bear fruit in those who receive them with the required dispositions" (*CCC* 1131).

2. What does Sunday mean for us?

"Sunday, the 'Lord's Day,' is the principal day for the celebration of the Eucharist because it is the day of the Resurrection. It is the pre-eminent day of the liturgical assembly, the day of the Christian family, and the day of joy and rest from work. Sunday is the 'foundation and kernel of the whole liturgical year' (*SC* 106)" (*CCC* 1193).

3. How is unity maintained among varied liturgical traditions?

"The criterion that assures unity amid the diversity of liturgical traditions is fidelity to apostolic Tradition, i.e., the communion in the faith and sacraments received from the apostles, a communion that is both signified and guaranteed by apostolic succession" (*CCC* 1209).

Connecting to Our Family

The Christian Sunday provides the opportunity for family gathering. In quieter times Sunday was not only a time for Sunday Mass, but also for Sunday dinner and a time when family members would enjoy one another's company. In today's culture, the family meal is too often a rarity. From a Christian perspective, the family meal is central to family life.

If there is going to be a family meal, the time must be agreed to and the members must make sacrifices to make it happen. The spiritual impulse to community that occurs at Eucharist needs to find a practical application in the most natural setting for any community experience, the family. If Sunday is not the right day for a family gathering because of other duties and obligations, then pick another time. Observing the Christian Sunday means nourishing God's covenant love with family members as well as those in the wider community. At a family meal, "The blessings that were never bought or sold are centered there, and are better than gold."

1. When you bring your children to your parish church, how do you explain the numerous signs and symbols to them? The altar, the Cross, the

windows, the statues, the lectern, the sacred books, the vestments of the priest, the candles, the music, the shrines, the incense, the processions, etc.?

2. Take the questions — who celebrates, when do we celebrate, how do we celebrate, and where do we celebrate — and put the answers in language your children will understand.

3. How might you have home festivals that reflect the liturgical year? This is easy for Christmas and Easter, but how might you create domestic echoes of Advent, Lent, Pentecost, Corpus Christi, and the feasts of Our Lady and the saints?

Family Prayer

Father, we believe that at the liturgy we experience your blessings, the redemption of Jesus, and the power of the Spirit making present your wonderful works of salvation. Our faith also tells us that the Holy Trinity, Mary, the angels, and saints are present at our worship. Give us eyes to see, ears to hear, and hearts to experience this heavenly worship intimately joined to our parish celebrations. Awaken us to the joys of the liturgical year where the mystery of Christ is unfolded. May we continually die to sin and grow in divine life through these sacramental experiences. We praise you for these gifts of grace so abundantly available to us.

Glossary

Heavenly Liturgy: The books of Hebrews and Revelation describe acts of worship in heaven by means of various images. This heavenly liturgy is invisibly present at our earthly one.

Liturgy: The term comes from the Greek word meaning "people's work." By Baptism all the faithful are called to offer a sacrifice of praise. The ordained priest acts in the person of Christ to make Christ's saving action present by the power of the Spirit.

Paschal Mystery: Liturgy is a mystery because it is the divine act of the Father, Son, and Spirit. It is paschal because it makes present the dying and rising of Jesus Christ.

Liturgical Year: The Church's year which unfolds the mystery of Christ. It includes Advent, Christmas Season, Lent, Easter Season, Pentecost, Trinity, Corpus Christi, Ordinary Time, and the feasts and memorials of the Blessed Virgin and the saints.

Liturgy of the Hours: Seven times a day the Church praises God at the Office of Readings, Morning Prayer, Three Daytime Hours, Evening Prayer, and Night Prayer. These prayers prolong the celebration of the Eucharist, flowing from it and back to it.

Lesson 13
The Sacraments of Baptism and Confirmation

Resource: *CCC* paragraphs 1213-1321

Sacraments are 'powers that come forth' from the Body of Christ, [Cf. *Lk* 5:17; 6:19; 8:46] . . . They are 'the masterworks of God' in the new and everlasting covenant (*CCC* 1116).

Crying Out Like a Madman

In his letters to St. Ignatius, St. Francis Xavier, priest, writes:

"We have visited the villages of the new converts who accepted the Christian religion a few years ago. No Portuguese live here — the country is so barren and poor. The native Christians have no priests. They know only that they are Christians. There is nobody to say Mass for them; nobody to teach them the Creed, the Our Father, the Hail Mary, and the Commandments of God's Law.

"I have not stopped since the day I arrived. I conscientiously made the rounds of the villages. I bathed in the sacred waters all the children who had not yet been baptized. This means that I have purified a very large number of children so young, that, as the saying goes, they could not tell their right hand from their left. The older children would not let me say my Office or eat or sleep until I taught them one prayer or another. Then I began to understand: 'The kingdom of heaven belongs to such as these.'

"I could not refuse so devout a request without failing in devotion myself. I taught them, first the confession of faith in the Father, the Son, and the Holy Spirit; then the Apostles' Creed, the Our Father and Hail Mary. I noticed among them persons of great intelligence. If only someone could educate them in the Christian way of life, I have no doubt they would make excellent Christians.

"Many, many people hereabouts are not becoming Christians for one reason only: there is nobody to make them Christians. Again and again I have thought of going around the universities of Europe, especially Paris, and everywhere crying out like a madman, riveting the attention of those who have more learning than charity: 'What a tragedy: how many souls are being shut out of heaven and falling into hell because of you!'

"This thought would certainly stir most of them to spiritual realities, to listen actively to what God is saying to them. They would forget their own desires, their human affairs, and give themselves over entirely to God's will and his choice. They would cry out with all their heart: 'Lord, I am here! What do you want me to do? Send me anywhere you like — even to India!' " (*Office of Readings*, December 3).

Baptize Them!

This excerpt from the letters of St. Francis Xavier gives us a good introduction to the subject of Baptism, if for no other reason that he baptized so many people during his missionary days that sometimes he could scarcely raise his arm one more time for another Baptism because of weariness. The other things to notice in this letter are his zeal for souls and his love of teaching prayers to children.

The *Catechism* tells us the sacraments of initiation are Baptism, Confirmation, and Eucharist. We will deal with the first two sacraments in this lesson and with Eucharist in the next one.

Just before his Ascension into heaven, Jesus gave the Apostles the Great Commission to preach the Gospel and baptize the converts. "Go therefore, and make disciples of all nations, baptizing them in the name of the Father, and of the Son, and of the holy Spirit" (Mt 28:19).

The word *Baptism* comes from the Greek word that means to "plunge into water." The immersion in water symbolizes our death to sin. We die with Christ and are reborn in him. Early Christians liked to call Baptism the "enlightenment" because the revelatory teaching that accompanies the sacrament gives the light of Christ to our minds and hearts.

Jesus voluntarily submitted himself to the Baptism of John the Baptist, intended for sinners, "to fulfill all righteousness" (Mt 3:15). Jesus did this to manifest his self-emptying (cf. Phil 2:7). The Spirit who had hovered over the waters at the first creation, descended on Christ as a prelude of the new creation, and the Father revealed Jesus as his "beloved Son" (Mt 3:16-17; See also *CCC* 1224).

Through his saving death and resurrection, Jesus gave Baptism a new meaning. Though Baptism remains a Baptism of repentance for the forgiveness of sins, repentance is now seen as a turning to Christ, and the forgiveness of sins occurs on the authority of Christ and by his power through the ministry of the Church.

The Liturgy of Baptism

The rite of Baptism has varied throughout history, but six essential elements have always been present: (1) The proclamation of the Word; (2) a religious conversion that included acceptance of the Gospel; (3) the profession of faith; (4) the Baptism itself; (5) the receiving of the Holy Spirit; and (6) admission to Eucharist.

In the early Church the candidacy for adults involved a number of stages that included religious instruction and various rituals. In the case of babies, such a process was impossible beforehand, so there was need for a catechetical explanation after the child was old enough to understand. Vatican II has restored the "catechumenate," the process for initiating converts into the Church. It is called the Rite of Christian Initiation of Adults (RCIA).

The meaning of Baptism is best seen through the ceremonies by which it is celebrated. There are six rituals that teach us Baptism's significance:

(1) Sign of the Cross. The imprint of the Cross on the candidate reminds us of Christ's sacrifice by which he saved us. Baptism is a sacrament of salvation.

(2) Readings from Scripture. God's revealed Word is spoken to the candidate with the purpose of asking for a faith response, a faith that implies conversion to Christ and obedience to his Word. Baptism is a sacrament of faith.

(3) Exorcism and anointing. Jesus is about to liberate the candidate from evil. An exorcism prayer is recited to loosen the candidate from the power of Satan. The celebrant anoints the candidate with the oil of catechumens. The candidate explicitly renounces Satan and professes the faith of the Church.

(4) The essential rite of Baptism. The candidate is either immersed three times in water, or water is poured three times upon the head. The celebrant says, "N., I baptize you in the name of the Father, and of the Son, and of the Holy Spirit." This brings about death to all sin, original and personal, and entry into the life of the Trinity through identity with Christ's paschal mystery.

(5) Anointing with chrism. The celebrant anoints the newly baptized with oil of chrism to symbolize the person's internal anointing and reception of the Holy Spirit.

(6) White garment and candle. The white garment shows that the baptized has put on Jesus and risen with him. The candle symbolizes the light of Christ which now shines in the baptized.

These ceremonies are teachers of the meaning of Baptism. Not just the words that are spoken, but also the nonverbal elements as indicated above. Now the newly baptized is an adopted child of God in union with Jesus and able to pray, "Our Father."

Who Can Be Baptized?

Adults who have not been baptized are welcome to the sacrament after the proper preparation. This is clear enough in mission countries, but also true in the United States where many millions have not been baptized.

Infants are also to be baptized. The custom of baptizing babies goes back to New Testament times when whole households were brought into the faith (Acts 16:15). The newborn come into the world with a fallen nature and original sin. They need a new birth in Baptism.

The faith that brings us to Baptism must not stop there. Growth in faith should be a lifelong process. This should happen in one's personal relationship with Christ and also must involve lifelong development in understanding the teachings of Christ as proposed and understood by the Magisterium of the Church.

How Necessary Is Baptism?

Jesus taught that Baptism is necessary for salvation. He commanded his Apostles and disciples to proclaim the Gospel to all nations so that everyone would hear the Word, respond in faith, and be baptized. But for those who have never heard of Christ, the *Catechism* makes a crucial distinction. *"God has bound salvation to the sacrament of Baptism, but he himself is not bound by his sacraments"* (*CCC* 1257).

"Every man who is ignorant of the Gospel of Christ and of his Church, but seeks the truth and does the will of God in accordance with his understanding of it, can be saved. It may be supposed that such persons would have *desired Baptism explicitly* if they had known its necessity" (*CCC* 1260).

People who die for Christ, though not yet baptized, are baptized by their death for the sake of Christ. Candidates who desire Baptism, but die before actual reception are considered to be saved by their "Baptism of desire."

What about children, babies, and the unborn who die without Baptism? The Church entrusts them to the love and mercy of God. Since God wills that all people be saved and since Jesus said, "Let the children come to me" (Mk 10:14), we have a hope that there is a way of salvation for children who die without Baptism.

Effects of Baptism

In Baptism all sins are forgiven, original sin and all personal sins as well as any punishment due to sin.

But the consequences of sin remain in the baptized, such as illness, death, character weaknesses, and an inclination to sin.

Baptism welcomes us into membership in the Church — the Body of Christ, the Temple of the Spirit, and the People of God. This brings with it the responsibilities and rights of communion with the Church. By Word and sacrament and by the prayers and the witness of the believing community, each new member is nourished, strengthened, and sustained for the journey of faith. Baptism also unites us with other baptized people who are not yet in full communion with the Catholic Church. This serves as a bond with them as we work toward the unity of all believers desired by Christ.

Baptism confers on us a "seal," an indelible spiritual "mark or character" that signifies our belonging to Christ. No sin can annul this. Once we are baptized we stay baptized. The sacrament should not be repeated.

Catechism Reflection

1. What are the major effects of Baptism?

"The fruit of Baptism, or baptismal grace, is a rich reality that includes forgiveness of original sin and all personal sins, birth into the new life by which man becomes an adoptive son of the Father, a member of Christ and a temple of the Holy Spirit. By this very fact the person baptized is incorporated into the Church, the Body of Christ, and made a sharer in the priesthood of Christ" (*CCC* 1279).

2. How necessary is Baptism?

"Baptism is a birth into the new life in Christ. In accordance with the Lord's will, it is necessary for salvation, as is the Church herself, which we enter by Baptism" (*CCC* 1277).

The Sacrament of Confirmation

The second sacrament of initiation is Confirmation.

The Old Testament prophets foretold that the Spirit of God would rest upon the future Messiah. Jesus was conceived by the Spirit in the womb of Mary. At his Baptism in the Jordan, the Spirit descended upon him to testify he was the expected Messiah. Jesus promised the Spirit to his followers. This happened first on Easter night and then most dramatically at Pentecost (Jn 20:22; Acts 2:1-4). The Spirit, once given to the Messiah, is now poured out upon the messianic people.

The Apostles, after baptizing the new converts, laid hands upon them to impart the gift of the Spirit who completes the grace of Baptism. This imposition of hands is recognized by Catholic Tradition as the origin of the sacrament of Confirmation. Early in the life of the Church an anointing with perfumed oil (chrism) was added to the laying on of hands.

Anointing connects the person with the title "Christian" because the word *Christ* actually means "anointed one." In Scripture, oil is a sign of abundance and joy. It was used as a cleansing agent at one's bath and was employed by athletes to limber up their muscles. Doctors used oil to heal and soothe wounds. Kings, priests, and prophets were anointed with oil as a sign of their consecration to God.

All these symbols explain the use of oil at Confirmation and the effects of the sacrament. The oil marks the person with the seal of the Spirit, signifying one's belonging radically and permanently to God. Hence, Confirmation cannot be received again. We are enrolled in Christ's service forever. While we may reject our covenant with Christ, he never withdraws his commitment to us while we live.

The essential rite of Confirmation is conferred by the anointing with chrism on the forehead which is done by the laying on of the hand along with the words, "Be sealed with the gift of the Holy Spirit."

Catechism Reflection

1. What are the effects of Confirmation?

". . . the effect of the sacrament of Confirmation is the special outpouring of the Holy Spirit as once granted to the apostles on the day of Pentecost.From this fact, Confirmation brings an increase and deepening of baptismal grace:

— it roots us more deeply in the divine filiation which makes us cry, 'Abba! Father!' [*Rom* 8:15];

— it unites us more firmly to Christ;

— it increases the gifts of the Holy Spirit in us;

— it renders our bond with the Church more perfect [Cf. *LG* 11];

— it gives us a special strength of the Holy Spirit to spread and defend the faith by word and action as true witnesses of Christ; to confess the name of Christ boldly, and never to be ashamed of the Cross [Cf. Council of Florence (1439): *DS* 1319; *LG* 11; 12]" (*CCC* 1302-3).

2. Who may be confirmed?

"A candidate for Confirmation who has attained the age of reason must profess the faith, be in the state of grace, have the intention of receiving the sacrament, and be prepared to assume the role of disciple and witness to Christ, both within the ecclesial community and in temporal affairs" (*CCC* 1319).

3. How is Confirmation celebrated in the Eastern Church?

In the East, Confirmation is administered immediately after Baptism and is followed by participation in the Eucharist; this tradition highlights the unity of the three sacraments of initiation.

Connecting to Our Family

The fact that Baptism and Confirmation both give us an indelible character speaks to us about God's call to permanent fidelity to him. This should be especially evident in the marriage promises and loyalty to friends.

Some years ago in London a host of British VIPs, including Prime Minister Winston Churchill and his wife, Lady Clementine, attended a banquet. It was a tradition at this particular banquet to play some kind of little game before the main address by the guest speaker. The game that night was, "If you couldn't be who you are, who would you like to be?"

All the guests answered the question in their own way. The audience was intrigued as to how Churchill would respond. After all, a Churchill would not want to be a Caesar or a Napoleon. When Churchill, the ranking member of the occasion, arose as the last speaker, he said, "If I can't be who I am, I would most like to be, . . ." the seventy-eight-year-old Churchill said, turning to his wife and taking her hand, "Lady Churchill's second husband."

The charm of this story lies in its tribute to marital fidelity, publicly reaffirmed amid a cluster of friends in the warmth of a traditional dinner party. We have seen that Baptism and Confirmation join us to Jesus in a permanent way, so much so that the sacraments cannot be repeated. They signify that Jesus is determined to be covenanted with us — and that we should resolve to be covenanted with him. The stability of the family is linked to the fidelity and loyalty all members show to one another.

1. It is common enough to celebrate our birthdays in our family setting. How could you celebrate the baptismal days of your family members? Recall that you have your baptismal candles which could be part of the event.

2. Baptism unites you to Jesus and the Church. How have you taken an active part in your parish life as an application of your baptismal commitment?

3. Confirmation gives us the graces to be courageous Catholics. What are some ways you have witnessed your faith in difficult circumstances? How comfortable are you in sharing your faith with others? How could you be more forthright about your Catholicism?

Family Prayer

Jesus, Mary, and Joseph, come to our family and help us renew the promises made in our Baptism and Confirmation. Show us how to profess our faith with all the freshness that marked the first time we gave ourselves to Christ and the Church. Holy Spirit, breathe in us once more the fire we need to be visible and loving witnesses of our faith. Take away our fears and fill us with your divine love. Amen.

Glossary

Baptism: The first of the sacraments of initiation in which we are immersed in water three times or have water poured on us in the name of the Father, Son, and Holy Spirit. We are freed from all sin, original and personal, and the temporal punishment due to sin. We are filled with divine life and enlightened by Christ's revelation.

Confirmation: The second of the sacraments of initiation. Confirmation perfects the grace of Baptism. We receive the Holy Spirit, who roots us more profoundly in the divine filiation, incorporates us more deeply into Christ, renders us more solidly linked with the Church, associates us with the Church's mission, and helps us witness Christ by words and deeds.

RCIA: The initials for the Rite of Christian Initiation of Adults. This is a process for bringing converts into full Communion with the Catholic Church through the sacraments of Baptism, Confirmation, and Eucharist.

Catechumenate: Another name for the RCIA process.

Indelible Character: A spiritual mark of identity with Christ received in the sacraments of Baptism, Confirmation, and Holy Orders. The character signifies the permanence of our covenant with Christ and means these sacraments can only be received once.

Lesson 14
The Sacrament of the Holy Eucharist

Resource: *CCC* paragraphs 1322-1419

I taste in you my living Bread
And long to feast upon you still.
I drink of you my Fountainhead
My thirsting soul to quench and fill.
— St. Bernard of Clairvaux

What Happened on Holy Thursday?

What did the Apostles see and experience when they entered the Upper Room on Holy Thursday night? They saw the table prepared with the traditional foods for a Passover meal. It was as familiar to them as a Thanksgiving feast is for us. They would remember once again how much God loved their people when he delivered them centuries before from slavery in Egypt.

Salad bowls held endive, a tart-tasting herb to remind them of the bitterness of slavery in Egypt. Plates of unleavened bread rested next to dishes containing a dip made of crushed apples, dates, and nuts flavored with cinnamon, which gave this mix a brick coloring to remind them of the bricks their ancestors were forced to make in the Egyptian slave camps.

Crowning the center of the table was the roast lamb, a portion of which had been sacrificed at the Temple. Four cups of wine stood at each place setting. Jesus and the Apostles sat on cushions on the floor around a low table.

Jesus opened the meal with a blessing, praising God for all the gifts of creation and salvation. Then the youngest Apostle told the story of the Exodus, stopping at certain points in the narrative so the community could sing hymns of praise for God's merciful love. At the conclusion of the story, Jesus took the first cup of wine, raised it and toasted God for his love and graces. The group joined him and drank their wine.

As the host of the banquet, Jesus took a platter of unleavened bread, blessed it and broke it. Normally he would have distributed the bread in silence, but he broke with tradition and said these words, "Take and eat. This is my Body which will be broken and given for you." Scripture remains silent about their thoughts and feelings as they shared the Bread of Life for the first time in history.

After this the group took the second cup of wine and ate the paschal meal in a spirit of joy and deep community. After the meal Jesus took the third cup of wine, customarily consumed while post-dinner conversation continued. Instead he added new words to this moment. "Take and drink. This is my Blood which will be poured out for you." Again Scripture preserves no immediate reaction of theirs to this second mysterious event at the Last Supper.

Then they lingered at table with one another savoring every moment. They talked and sang. This is the only time Scripture reports Jesus singing — just before his Passion and death. As the Last Supper came to a close, they raised the fourth cup, drank it, and with a sense of both joy and foreboding, left the Upper Room.

Eat This Bread — Drink This Cup

The Holy Eucharist completes the sacraments of initiation. Jesus instituted the Eucharistic at the Last Supper. In a mysterious manner it contains the sacrifice of his Body and Blood and enables that sacrifice to continue in history until he comes again. He entrusted the Eucharist to his Church. It remembers and makes present his saving death and Resurrection for our salvation. The Eucharist is a sacrament of love, a sign of unity, a paschal meal in which we consume Jesus, have our minds filled with grace, and receive the pledge of eternal life.

What are the names we use for this sacrament?

The *Catechism* gives us ten names traditionally associated with this sacrament:

- We call it *Eucharist* because it is act of *thanking* God for creation, salvation, and sanctification.
- We name it the *Last Supper* because that is when Jesus instituted the Eucharist.
- We recall it as the *Breaking of the Bread* because that is what Jesus did in the Upper Room, and how he revealed himself to the disciples at Emmaus, and it was the phrase the early Christians used for Eucharist.
- We view it as the *Eucharistic assembly* since we celebrate it in community as a visible expression of the Church.
- We know it as the *memorial* of Christ's Passion, death, and Resurrection. Not just a memory of the past, but making it present by the power of the Spirit and the ministry of the priest.
- We celebrate it as the *Holy Sacrifice of the Mass* because it makes present the one sacrifice of Jesus Christ.
- We participate in it as the *Holy and Divine Liturgy* because it is the center and most intense expression of all Christian worship.
- We adore the Eucharist as the *Most Blessed Sacrament*, reserved in the tabernacle for our continued worship and devotion.
- We take the Eucharist as *Holy Communion* wherein we are united to Christ and shaped by him into the Body of Christ, the Church.

- We witness Eucharist as *Holy Mass* a word that comes from the Latin "to send." At the end of Eucharist the priest sends us forth to love and serve the Lord and one another and do God's will in our daily lives. (See the *CCC* paragraphs 1328-1332 for a fuller coverage of these names.)

Not one of these ten names says it all about the Eucharist, but together, they give us a tapestry of the broad richness of what the Eucharist means.

Scriptural Background

The origins of the principal elements of Eucharistic celebration lie deep in the mists of Israelite history. The key may be found in the celebrations that followed three harvests: wheat, wine, and lambs. People naturally thanked God for the harvests and went on to have a party.

When the wheat was gathered, they thanked God and celebrated the feast of the Unleavened Bread.

As the bushels of grapes filled their yards, they made wine, danced for joy before God, and celebrated the feast of Tents, in which they lived while harvesting the grapes.

When they saw their flocks of new lambs, they praised God and rejoiced in the feast of Passover.

In the beginning these were mainly agricultural holidays associated with pagan worship. In Israel they took on a new religious meaning as they were associated with the historical experience of the true God's mighty works of salvation, especially in the Exodus from Egypt, the pilgrimage in the desert, the covenant at Sinai, and the entry into the Promised Land.

Their most solemn annual feast was Passover, which combined unleavened bread, ceremonial wine, and the sacrificial lamb. Jesus transformed the old Passover into the new pasch. Jesus himself became the Lamb of Sacrifice and changed the bread and wine into his Body and Blood.

In the Gospels the wine miracle and the bread miracle (occurring five times) foreshadowed the Eucharist. The Gospels of Matthew, Mark, and Luke, and Paul's first letter to Corinth recount Christ's institution of the Eucharist. While John does not contain this narrative, he devotes chapter six to a Eucharistic explanation of the multiplication of the loaves.

The scriptural narratives of the Last Supper, the words of institution of the Eucharist, the breaking of the bread at Emmaus, and the other references to the breaking of the bread by the early Christian community provide abundant revelatory testimony about the Eucharist.

The Essential Elements of Eucharistic Celebration

In the second century, St. Justin Martyr wrote to the pagan emperor, Antoninus Pius, around the year 155, to explain what Christians did at

Eucharist. His description contained the outline of celebration which we use today in all our great liturgical rites. There are five essential movements in all Eucharists:

(1) *The gathering.* Christians gather in one place for the worship. Jesus, our high priest, presides invisibly over the celebration. The bishop or priest is the visible presider, acting in the person of Christ, preaching the homily, receiving the offerings and saying the Eucharistic prayer. All the worshipers actively participate: readers, those who bring the offerings, the extraordinary Eucharistic ministers — and the whole assembly whose "Amen" signifies their participation;

(2) *Liturgy of the Word.* There are readings from the Old Testament, the Letters of the Apostles, the Acts, the Apocalypse, and the Gospels. This is followed by the homily and the intercessory prayers. This proclamation and explanation of the Word is meant to call us to a deeper faith and prepare us for the next part of the Mass;

(3) *The presentation of the offerings.* Normally, on Sundays there is a procession with the bread and wine to the altar. This commemorates Christ "taking the bread and wine" and changing it into his Body and Blood. From the beginning there have always been gifts for those in need. Hence the collection for the parish needs happens at this time.

(4) *The Eucharistic prayer.* This part of the Mass has five parts:

• Preface. We thank the father through Christ in the Spirit for the gifts of creation, salvation, and sanctification.

• Epiclesis (Invocation). We ask the father to send the Spirit to change the bread and wine into Christ's Body and Blood.

• Institution Narrative. The acts of Christ and the Spirit give power to the words spoken by the priest to transform the bread and wine into Christ's Body and Blood. Only validly ordained bishops and priests may do this.

• The Remembrance. We remember the Passion, Resurrection, and glorious return of Christ.

• Intercessions. We celebrate with the whole Communion of Saints in heaven and on earth — with all of God's people.

(5) Communion. After the Lord's Prayer, and the breaking of the bread, we receive the Body and Blood of Christ.

Real Presence — Holy Communion

The Mass is both a holy sacrifice and a holy meal. The Eucharist is a sacrifice because it makes present the sacrificial act of Jesus at Calvary. The same Jesus who once offered himself in a bloody manner on the Cross to save us from our sins and give us divine life now offers himself on our altars in an unbloody manner. This sacrifice becomes the offering of the whole Church. At Mass, we unite ourselves with Jesus and identify with his Cross — an act that leads us to his Resurrection where we rise with him.

The Mass is also a holy meal, a sacred banquet where we partake of the Body and Blood of Christ. We speak here also of the Real Presence of Jesus. Jesus is present to us in many ways: in the Scriptures, in the Eucharistic assembly, in the poor and the sick and those in prison, in the sacraments, in the priest. But above all, in the Eucharist.

"This presence is called real — by which is not intended to exclude other types of presence as if they could not be real too, but because it is presence in the fullest sense: that is to say, it is a substantial presence, by which Christ, God and man, makes himself wholly and entirely present" (Paul VI, *Mystery of Faith*, 39).

At Mass we adore the real presence of Jesus in the Eucharist by genuflecting or by bowing deeply. And we adore the reserved presence of Christ in our tabernacles. "Because Christ himself is present in the sacrament of the altar, he is to be honored with the worship of adoration. 'To visit the Blessed Sacrament is . . . proof of gratitude, an expression of love, and a duty of adoration toward Christ our Lord' " (Paul VI, *Mystery of Faith*, 66).

The celebration and reception of the Eucharist should have an impact on our lives. As we finish Mass we always hear the priest tell us to love and serve the Lord. This is done practically by acts of love, justice, and mercy to one another, especially the poor.

> "You have tasted the Blood of the Lord,
> yet you do not recognize your brother . . .
> You dishonor this table when you do not judge
> worthy of sharing your food someone judged
> worthy to take part in this meal . . .
> God freed you from all your sins and invited you here,
> but you have not become more merciful"
> (St. John Chrysostom, Homily on 1 Cor, 27, 40).

Catechism Reflection

1. What happens at the consecration in the Mass?

"By the consecration the transubstantiation of the bread and wine into the Body and Blood of Christ is brought about. Under the consecrated species of bread and wine Christ himself, living and glorious, is present in a true, real, and substantial manner: his Body and his Blood, with his soul and his divinity (cf. Council of Trent: *DS* 1640; 1651)" (*CCC* 1413).

2. What is an essential preparation for Communion?

"Anyone who desires to receive Christ in Eucharistic communion must be in the state of grace. Anyone aware of having sinned mortally must not receive communion without having received absolution in the sacrament of penance" (*CCC* 1415).

3. What are the benefits of Holy Communion?

"Communion with the Body and Blood of Christ increases the communicant's union with the Lord, forgives his venial sins, and preserves him from grave sins. Since receiving this sacrament strengthens the bonds of charity between the communicant and Christ, it also reinforces the unity of the Church as the Mystical Body of Christ. The Church warmly recommends that the faithful receive Holy Communion when they participate in the celebration of the Eucharist; she obliges them to do so at least once a year" (*CCC* 1416-17).

Connecting to Our Family

The strength of the Catholic family comes both from the love that binds the members and the grace of Christ, especially as it is found in the Eucharist. Family and local parish should be closely linked. At the center of the parish church stands the altar, the great Welcome Table for all parishioners.

Some years ago a motherly black woman founded a Baptist church in Washington, D.C. for new, poor migrants who had traveled north to find work and hope. She called herself Bishop Jones and became successful enough to have a Sunday morning radio broadcast from her church.

One of her sermons explored the theme of the church as a welcoming community gathering around Christ, the host. In her maternal way she said, "Children, remember how hard it was when you worked on the farm. At the end of the day, your back was sore. Your arms ached. Your head throbbed. But then you heard your mother come out on the porch and say, 'Come on in. It's time to eat.' And as you sat and ate, your aches and pains melted away and peace filled your heart.

"Now next Thursday is Holy Thursday. Christ will come out on the porch and say, 'Come on in and eat.' And when you do, he will take away the ache in your heart and the sorrow in your soul. He will fill you with peace, love, and forgiveness. . . . And an even greater day will come, the day of your death. Then Christ will come out on the heavenly porch and say, 'Children, come on in and eat. I have an eternal banquet for you. Welcome home.' "

What Bishop Jones told her poor black congregation is definitely true for those of us who have the privilege of participating in the Eucharist in which is contained the entire treasure of the Church, Christ himself. Take your family to celebrate at the Welcome Table where Jesus calls all of us home.

1. What are some ways your family prepares for Mass? How often do you look over the readings and prayers of the Eucharist before going to church?

2. How do you teach your children to have a reverence for the Eucharist? How do you help them to pray to Jesus after receiving Communion?

3. How often do you stop in and make visits to the Blessed Sacrament? Is there adoration of the Blessed Sacrament at your parish? How solemnly are Corpus Christi and Holy Thursday celebrated?

Family Prayer

Loving Jesus, we thank you for the gift that makes it possible for us to celebrate the Holy Eucharist. We pray that your divine love will flow into us so that we can share that with one another in our families and with those in need. Just as you transform bread and wine into your Body and Blood, please transform us more and more into yourself. We praise you for this great gift and adore you for your immense generosity to us by saving us from our sins and giving us divine life.

Glossary

Eucharist: The sacramental celebration in which the Word of God is proclaimed and responded to in faith; the priest consecrates the bread and wine which is turned into the Body and Blood of Christ by the power of the Spirit; the assembly, in union with the priest, offers this sacrifice to the Father to thank him for creation, salvation, and sanctification; the worshippers receive Communion at the sacred banquet.

Sacrifice of the Mass: The Holy Eucharist makes present the redeeming sacrifice of Jesus at Calvary and his saving Resurrection at Easter.

Real Presence: After the bread and wine are consecrated at Mass, they become the Body, Blood, Soul, and Divinity of Christ. We know this with faith. The Real Presence of Jesus is reserved in the tabernacles of our parish churches for our adoration, devotion, and Communion for the sick.

Transubstantiation: Refers to the process of changes of substances that takes place in the bread and wine at Mass when they become the Real Presence of Jesus.

Lesson 15

The Sacraments of Reconciliation and Anointing

Resource: *CCC* paragraphs 1420-1532

Though often foolishly I strayed,
Yet in your love you sought me
You taught me to be unafraid,
And home again you brought me.

— Henry Baker

I Have Sinned

In 1945 a nineteen-year-old man made his girl friend pregnant. He told her to get an abortion, which she did. Then he dropped her. Ten years later he made another woman pregnant. This time, as a doctor, he aborted the child himself. He proceeded to open an abortion clinic in New York City. Through the years he performed or presided over 75,000 abortions. His name is Dr. Bernard Nathanson.

Two events affected him so deeply that he changed his mind completely about abortion. In 1968 he was writing a magazine article about the morality of clinic blockades. He went out to see the demonstrators, did interviews, took notes, and observed the facts. "It was only then," he wrote in his autobiography, *The Hand of God*, "that I apprehended the exaltation, the pure love on the faces of that shivering mass of people, surrounded as they were by hundreds of New York City policemen." They made him wonder about his behavior and about what motivated them.

The second step in his conversion was caused by the invention of ultrasound. It showed that what was in the womb could suck its thumb and do other human-like things. From that time on, Nathanson abandoned abortions altogether. In 1984 he premiered a movie, *The Silent Scream*, which showed an ultrasound of a child being aborted.

From then on he embarked on a spiritual search. "I was looking for a way to wash away my sins. I felt the burden of sin growing heavier and more persistent. I have such heavy moral baggage to drag into the next world that failing to believe would condemn me to an eternity more terrifying than anything Dante imagined in his *Inferno*."

Nathanson was helped by Father John McCloskey, a priest based at Princeton University and a well known adviser to intellectual seekers. Finally, after many years of searching, Dr. Nathanson, at age sixty-nine, converted to the Roman Catholic Church. He stood before the baptismal font and renounced forever the world, the flesh, and the devil.

101

"I am free from sin," he said. "For the first time in my life, I feel the shelter and warmth of faith."

The Confession of Sins

Dr. Nathanson now knows better than most people what St. Ambrose once said of the two kinds of conversion in the Church. "There are water and tears: the water of baptism and the tears of repentance." In this lesson we will study the sacraments of healing: Reconciliation and Anointing. First, let us consider the sacrament of Reconciliation, or Confession as it is popularly known.

The sacraments of initiation bring us new life in Christ. But we carry this life in earthen vessels and are inclined to sin again. Just as Jesus forgave the sins of the paralytic and healed his body, so the Church continues Christ's ministry of healing.

The *Catechism* gives us five ways to speak of the sacrament that forgives our sins:

(1) *sacrament of Conversion*, which is the first step we take back to God after we have sinned;

(2) *sacrament of Penance*, since we are expected to atone for our sins and resolve to avoid them in the future;

(3) *sacrament of Confession*, for we are required to tell our sins to a priest and praise the mercy of God who will forgive us;

(4) *sacrament of Forgiveness*, in which God grants us pardon and peace through the absolution of the priest; and

(5) *sacrament of Reconciliation*, because we are again at peace with God and the Church.

Interior conversion is an essential step in any approach to this sacrament. We like to hear stories of conversion, such as that of St. Peter who denied Christ three times, or St. Augustine who waited many years before turning to Christ. We admire those who join the Church. We forget they must continue their conversion after Baptism, just like ourselves. We should continually turn away from sin and turn towards God.

Real conversion is a grace from God. It is God who pulls our hearts away from sin and draws us longingly to him. All converts testify that their conversion belongs to God. To the Lord alone be the glory.

The major forms of conversion and penance are fasting, prayer, and charitable giving. Spiritual writers give us many paths to conversion: Reconcile yourselves with your enemies. Take care of the poor. Defend what is just and right. Admit your faults honestly like the prodigal son. Examine your conscience. Correct others in a humble and kind manner. Seek spiritual direction. Accept pain and persecution for the sake of the Kingdom. Use the seasons of Advent and Lent for spiritual renewal. Deny yourself. Take up your cross. Follow Jesus.

Sin and Forgiveness

Sin breaks our relationship with God and damages our communion with the Church. Conversion brings us back to God and the Church. This is accomplished liturgically in the sacrament of Reconciliation.

Only God can forgive our sins. Jesus willed that the Church should be the instrument of divine forgiveness. On Easter night the risen Christ imparted to the Apostles his own power to forgive sins. Bishops, who are their successor, and priests, the bishops' collaborators, continue to exercise this ministry. Bishops and priests, by the sacrament of Holy Orders, have the power to forgive all sins, "in the name of the Father, and of the Son, and of the Holy Spirit." Priests must receive the faculty of absolving sins from a church authority.

Through the centuries there have been different concrete forms by which the Church has exercised this power. But beneath the changes the same fundamental structure has remained. There have always been two essential elements: the acts of the penitent and God's action through the intervention of the Church.

The penitent is required to perform three acts.

• Contrition. This involves regret for the sin committed and the resolution not to do it again. Our motives for sorrow should arise from our faith. We may speak of perfect contrition that proceeds from loving God above all else. Such loving sorrow remits venial sins and even mortal sins as long as we resolve to confess them as soon as possible. Imperfect contrition, motivated by fear of damnation and the ugliness of sin, begins the process of withdrawing from sin that with God's grace will be completed in confession.

• Confession. Confession of our sins opens us to reconciliation. We look directly at our sins and take responsibility for them. Confession of sins to a priest is an essential act of the sacrament of Reconciliation. After a diligent examination of our consciences, we must confess all our mortal sins. The Church recommends confessing venial sins too, even though this is not strictly necessary. After the age of discretion, we are required to confess serious sins at least once a year. Children must go to confession before receiving Holy Communion for the first time.

• Satisfaction. Many of our sins injure other people. We should do all we can to repair the harm. For example, this could mean returning stolen goods, restoring the reputation of someone we have undermined, or paying compensation for injuries. Our sins also have a negative effect on our own souls. Absolution takes away the sin, but does not repair the damage done to us. We need to work on recovering our full spiritual health. The penance we receive from the priest is meant to be the first step in our self-improvement. Our return to spiritual health may include prayer, acts of love and service for others, sacrifices, and patient acceptance of the cross we must carry.

After we have confessed our sins to the priest, we are given some encouragement by the priest for our moral and spiritual lives. The priest gives us a penance and asks us to make an act of contrition. Then the priest absolves us from our sins with these words:

God the Father of mercies,
through the death and Resurrection of his Son
has reconciled the world to himself and sent the Holy Spirit among us
for the forgiveness of sins;
through the ministry of the Church may God give you pardon and peace,
and I absolve you from your sins
in the name of the Father, and of the Son, and of the Holy Spirit.

The *Catechism* has this to say about the forgiveness of sins and the remission of temporal punishment due to sin by indulgences. "Individual and integral confession of grave sins followed by absolution remains the only ordinary means of reconciliation with God and with the Church. Through indulgences the faithful can obtain remission of temporal punishment resulting from sin for themselves and also for the souls in Purgatory" (*CCC* 1497-98).

Parishes offer confession face-to-face with the priest or in an anonymous manner when the penitent confesses behind a screen. There are also penance services from time to time during the year when there is a proclamation of the Word, a homily, prayers, and music to help people appreciate the sacrament's purpose. These services are accompanied by individual confession to a priest. In emergency situations, general absolution may be given. If the penitent was in mortal sin, that sin should be confessed at a later time to a priest.

All sacraments bring the participants divine joy and peace. The special happiness received here arises from lifting the burden of sin and guilt. We are released to the freedom of grace. We are restored to the friendship of God, others, and self.

Catechism Reflection

1. What are the main elements of the sacrament of Reconciliation?

"The sacrament of Penance is a whole consisting in three actions of the penitent and the priest's absolution. The penitent's acts are repentance, confession or disclosure of sins to the priest, and the intention to make reparation and do works of reparation" (*CCC* 1491).

2. What are the spiritual effects of the sacrament of Penance?

"The spiritual effects of the sacrament of Penance are:

— reconciliation with God by which the penitent recovers grace;

— reconciliation with the Church;

— remission of the eternal punishment incurred by mortal sins;

— remission, at least in part, of temporal punishments resulting from sin;
— peace and serenity of conscience, and spiritual consolation;
— an increase of spiritual strength for the Christian battle" (*CCC* 1496).

The Sacrament of the Anointing of the Sick

The second sacrament of healing is the sacrament of the Anointing of the Sick. The problem of pain, experienced in old age and illness, is one that bothers all of us eventually. Serious illness makes us think of our deaths. We feel powerless. We experience our limits. Sickness makes some people angry — even with God. They turn in upon themselves and tend to despair. For others, being ill matures them and draws them to God.

Jesus had a preferential love for sick people and even identified himself with the suffering. "I was sick and you visited me" (*RSV* Mt 25:36). Jesus healed the whole person, body, mind, and soul. He cured the paralytic's physical disability as well as his moral one when he forgave him his sins. Jesus often touched people when he healed them. In the sacrament of Anointing, Jesus touches the sick to heal them — always from sin, but sometimes even from the physical ailment.

Jesus did not heal all sick people. His cures were signs of the arrival of the kingdom of God. They were meant to tell us of a more basic healing, the conquest of sin and death by his death and Resurrection. In the sufferings of the Cross, Jesus assumed the full weight of evil and took away the sin of the world of which illness is an effect. He gave a new meaning to pain. We are now able to unite our suffering to his redemptive Passion.

The Church continues Christ's compassion for the sick and a healing ministry in three ways:

(1) Most frequently this is seen in the many religious orders that were founded to provide hospital care, originally for the indigent poor and then for others. Church-sponsored hospice care is a new form of this ministry of healing. We also think here of all the relatives and friends who show compassion for the sick among them.

(2) Some people have the "charism" or gift of healing. They manifest the power of the risen Lord. We know, however, that prayer does not always heal the sick. Sometimes Jesus calls us to unite our sufferings to his. St. Paul says, ". . . in my flesh I complete what is lacking in Christ's afflictions for the sake of his body, that is, the church" (*RSV* Col 1:24).

(3) Finally, there is the sacrament of Anointing. St. James tells of this. "Is anyone among you sick? He should summon the presbyters [elders] of the church, and they should pray over him and anoint [him] with oil in the name of the Lord, and the prayer of faith will save the sick person, and the Lord will raise him up. If he has committed any sins, he will be forgiven" (Jas 5:14-15).

Who May Receive This Sacrament?

Anyone who is danger of death from sickness or old age may receive the sacrament. If the person recovers and then has another serious illness, he can receive the sacrament again. We may receive this sacrament before a serious operation. Only bishops and priests may minister this sacrament. The sick person receives a special grace to cope in faith with the problems that attend grave illness or old age.

For those sick people who are on their final journey to the next life, this is an anointing unto glory, a sacrament of departure. Baptism began conforming them to the death and Resurrection of Christ. This sacrament completes that work. The sick may also receive the Eucharist, which we call "viaticum." The word *viaticum* means "Christ is with us on the way," through his Eucharistic presence and power.

It is often said that the dying go through stages of death: denial, anger, bargaining, depression, and acceptance. The Anointing of the Sick helps loved ones release the dying to God and assists the gravely ill to accept death should it be God's will for them at this time.

Catechism Reflection

1. How do we celebrate the Anointing of the Sick?

"The celebration of the Anointing of the Sick consists essentially in the anointing of the forehead and hands of the sick person (in the Roman Rite) or of other parts of the body (in the Eastern Rite), the anointing being accompanied by the liturgical prayer of the celebrant asking for the special grace of this sacrament" (*CCC* 1531).

2. What are the effects of this sacrament?

"The special grace of the sacrament of the Anointing of the Sick has as its effects: the uniting of the sick person to the Passion of Christ, for his own good and that of the whole Church; the strengthening, peace, and courage to endure in a Christian manner the sufferings of illness or old age; the forgiveness of sins, if the sick person was not able to obtain it through the sacrament of Penance; the restoration of health, if it is conducive to the salvation of his soul; the preparation for passing over to eternal life" (*CCC* 1532).

Connecting to Our Family

Most of us remember Terry Anderson, the reporter for the Associated Press who was captured by Lebanese radical militants in 1985. For six years, Anderson was held captive and accused of being a spy for the United States. He spent much of that time in isolation chained to a wall. His book, *Den of Lions*, chronicles his captivity, which included meeting Father Martin Jenco, a Servite priest and fellow hostage. When Anderson, a Catholic, heard that his captors also held a priest, he asked them if he could meet the priest to make a confession.

His captors permitted this, and Anderson tells us how he made his first confession in twenty-five years. He told Father Jenco how he had taken his first steps back to the Church before his capture. Now his isolation had given him time to reflect on the mistakes he had made without God as the guiding force of his life.

Finally, Terry confessed his sins, which included adulterous affairs and a prolonged drinking habit. After twenty minutes — twice as long as his captors said they would allow — both he and Father Jenco were crying. Then Father Jenco put his hand on Terry's head, hugged him, and said, "May God give you pardon and peace. I absolve you from your sins in the name of the Father, and of the Son, and of the Holy Spirit. In the name of a gentle, loving God, your sins are forgiven."

This is a good time to reflect on the role of the sacraments of healing in your family life. Let the sacrament of Reconciliation hold an honored place for all members. When the needed time comes, be sure to take advantage of the sacrament of Anointing of the Sick. Jesus once walked through Galilee and Judea healing and forgiving sins. He does this today through the sacraments. Let these holy events renew and rejoice your family.

1. What is the regular practice of your family regarding the sacrament of Reconciliation? Would you say that parental practice gives good example to your children in this matter? If not, how can you change?

2. What are some stories of moral and religious conversion you have heard which inspire you own your own lifelong journey of conversion?

3. What experiences have you had of Anointing of the Sick? What did you learn from them?

Family Prayer

Jesus, healer of our minds, bodies, and souls, we praise you for your compassion toward us in our weakness. Thank you for the gifts of Reconciliation and Anointing by which you continue to heal us today as you once did others in Galilee and Judea. Give us the graces to stay the course in lifelong conversion. Remind us to practice compassion for the sick as well as those whose lives are in need of reconciliation with God and the Church. May our hearts be homes of love, faith, and prayer.

Glossary

Sacrament of Reconciliation: Also called the sacrament of Confession, Penance, Conversion, and Forgiveness, the sacrament of Reconciliation is the sacrament in which the sins committed after Baptism are forgiven. It results in reconciliation with God and the Church.

Acts of the Penitent in Confession: The acts of the penitent in Confession are contrition, confession of sins, and satisfaction for sins.

Perfect and Imperfect Contrition: Perfect contrition means sorrow for sins based on love for God. Imperfect contrition is based on fear of damnation and disgust for sin. The Holy Spirit motivates us in both instances.

Ministers of Confession: Bishops, and their collaborators, priests, are the ministers of the sacrament of Reconciliation.

Sacrament of Anointing: The Church, through anointing with oil and the power of the Spirit, prepares a gravely ill person for the passage to eternal life. Sometimes physical health is restored if it is God's will.

Lesson 16

Called to be a Priest: The Sacrament of Holy Orders

Resource: *CCC* paragraphs 1536-1600

Look, there are those born to sing, those born to write,
those born to play soccer, and those born to be priests.
I was born to be a priest.

— Archbishop Helder Camara

The Priest Has to Find Divine Love

Back in the 1950s a young Father William Nolan faced a dilemma. He was ministering to two hundred Catholic students at Dartmouth College, New Hampshire, while also serving as an assistant at St. Denis parish. The students needed something more than he could give them. He recalls, "I got Cardinal Cushing of Boston to come up and talk to the students at a Communion breakfast. The Cardinal asked me, 'What do you need up here?' We need a Catholic Center at Dartmouth. The Cardinal liked the idea and helped me get permission from the Bishop of Manchester to start the Center."

The dream became a reality in Aquinas House. Father Nolan became a monsignor and served the students at Aquinas House for the next twenty-five years. Today it serves the spiritual and social needs of 1,100 Catholic Dartmouth students. The colonial building houses leisure rooms where students can relax, study, watch films, and have discussions. The chapel is the spiritual heart of Aquinas House.

One of Monsignor Nolan's most remarkable achievements was the fostering of vocations to the priesthood and religious life. During the twenty-five years he was there, he had the joy of seeing forty-five men become priests. One has become a bishop and three women have become nuns.

What was his secret?

"Every life has to have a love in it. It doesn't matter who it is or who you are, one has to have a love. Now the love of a priest is centered around the Blessed Sacrament. And it is the only love that truly satisfies. That doesn't mean that human love isn't beautiful and important — it sure is, no question about that. But the priest has to find divine love. And he does, if God wants him."

Monsignor Nolan retired in 1987. His Aquinas House is one of the most active campus ministries in the Ivy League. God made him an instrument of faith, hope, and love for thousands of Dartmouth students — and an instrument for an unusual number of priestly and religious vocations. Here is a great priest who in his days in pastoral ministry pleased God — moved by the Spirit to respond so generously to the call to priesthood.

109

"The Priesthood is the Love of the Heart of Jesus."
— St. John Vianney

Msgr. Nolan's priesthood inspires us to realize how valuable this gift is for our Church. The *Catechism* groups Holy Orders and Marriage under the Sacraments of Communion *because they minister to the salvation of others.* If they help us with our personal salvation, it is through our service to others. We will devote our attention to Holy Orders in this lesson and Marriage in the next one.

"Holy Orders is the sacrament through which the mission entrusted by Christ to his apostles continues to be exercised in the Church until the end of time: thus it is the sacrament of apostolic ministry. It includes three degrees: episcopate, presbyterate, and diaconate" (*CCC* 1536). Without the bishops, priests, and deacons one cannot speak of Church, for these three orders are organically connected to the Church.

The Church borrowed the word *order* from the Roman empire which used the term to designate a governing body. In this sacrament there are three orders: bishop, priest, and deacon. The rite which makes this possible is called ordination. In the Old Covenant, God's people were called a priestly people. But God chose the tribe of Levi to serve as priests for them. They offered gifts and sacrifices to God on behalf of the people. They prefigured the ordained priesthood of the New Covenant.

The former priesthood finds its perfect fulfillment in Jesus Christ, the one mediator between God and us. Christ's priesthood is made present in the ordained priesthood.

The whole Church is a priestly people. The baptized believers share in the common priesthood of the faithful. The sacrament of Holy Orders confers a special spiritual ministry. Only the ordained priest and bishop may celebrate Eucharist and the sacrament of Reconciliation. Only the bishop can ordain priests and deacons. Only bishops can ordain other bishops.

There are two ways to share in the one priesthood of Christ. The two priesthoods (of Baptism and Orders) differ from each other but are ordered to one another. "Though they differ from one another in essence and not only in degree, the common priesthood of the faithful and the ministerial . . . priesthood . . . are nonetheless interrelated" (*Constitution on the Church*, [LG], 10). Christ calls the common priesthood of the baptized to share in the Spirit's work of sanctifying the world. Christ calls the ordained priesthood to share in the Spirit's work of sanctifying the faithful. Because of his sacred responsibility, the ordained priest has a special obligation to continually and consciously deepen his spiritual life and union with Christ.

The ordained priest acts in the person of Christ as head of the Church: teaching, shepherding, and sanctifying God's people. The priest also acts in the name of the Church, offering the sacrifice of the Body of Christ to the Father for the salvation of God's people and of the world itself. Because the priest represents Christ at worship, he can represent the Church there.

Bishop, Priest, Deacon

The bishop has the fullness of the sacrament of Holy Orders. By it he belongs to the college of bishops and becomes the visible head of the local Church entrusted to him. Bishops are successors of the Apostles. As a college, bishops have responsibility for the mission of the whole Church under the authority of the pope, the successor of St. Peter.

Priests are united with the bishops in sacerdotal dignity. They depend on bishops for the exercise of their pastoral ministry. With the bishop they form a presbyteral community and assume with him the responsibility for the local Church. The bishop appoints priests to parishes or other diocesan ministries.

Deacons receive the sacrament of Holy Orders, but not ministerial priesthood. Deacons may baptize, preach, impart liturgical blessings such as at marriages, and participate in pastoral governance. They exercise their ministries under the pastoral authority of the bishop.

"The *essential rite* of the sacrament of Holy Orders . . . consists in the bishop's imposition of hands on the head of the ordinand and in the bishop's specific consecratory prayer asking God for the outpouring of the Holy Spirit and his gifts proper to the ministry to which the candidate is being ordained [Cf. Pius XII, apostolic constitution, *Sacramentum Ordinis*: *DS 3858*]" (*CCC* 1573).

Only a baptized man may be ordained. Jesus chose only men to be Apostles. In turn the Apostles picked only men to succeed them in ministry. The Church believes that it is bound by the choice made by the Lord himself. For this reason the ordination of women is not possible (cf. *CCC* 1577).

Ordination is not a right; it is a call from God. The man who believes he has a call to priesthood must submit his desire to the Church which has the responsibility to discern whether this call is genuine or not. Normally, it is the role of seminaries to determine this discernment through admissions and screening procedures, followed by a number of years of priestly formation. This process involves human, theological, pastoral, and spiritual training. The seminary presents the candidate to the bishop who must make the final determination about the suitability of the candidate.

In the Latin Church, ordained ministers, with the exception of married deacons, are chosen from the ranks of men of faith who live the celibate life for the sake of the kingdom. Their commitment to celibacy signifies they have resolved to love God and be dedicated to pastoral ministry with an undivided heart. In some cases, married clergy of the Anglican and Lutheran communions, who have converted to Catholicism, have asked to become Catholic priests. After a discernment process, some of them have been admitted to Catholic priesthood and must be re-ordained.

In the Eastern Church, only the bishops must be celibate. Priests and deacons may be married. Still, many of their priests also practice celibacy. In both the East and the West, once a man is ordained, he may no longer marry.

The ordained priest receives an indelible character, similar to the one received in Baptism and Confirmation. This means that the sacrament cannot be received again and also teaches us that Christ is absolutely loyal to the covenant he makes with the priest. It is expected that the priest returns this loyalty to Jesus by making a permanent covenant promise to serve God's people and love them with all his heart, mind, and soul.

The graces of the sacrament of Holy Order are rich and abundant to help the priest keep this commitment. The Holy Spirit offers the priest an ocean of divine love and strength to accomplish this pastoral mission. The Blessed Sacrament is the burning heart of his priesthood, giving him the strength to persevere throughout all his days.

Catechism Reflection

1. What are two ways God's people participate in the one priesthood of Christ?

"The whole Church is a priestly people. Through Baptism all the faithful share in the priesthood of Christ. This participation is called the 'common priesthood of the faithful.' Based on this common priesthood and ordered to its service, there exists another participation in the mission of Christ: the ministry conferred by the sacrament of Holy Orders, where the task is to serve in the name and the person of Christ the Head in the midst of the community" (*CCC* 1591).

2. What are the three degrees of ordained priesthood?

"Since the beginning, the ordained ministry has been conferred and exercised in three degrees: that of bishops, that of presbyters, and that of deacons. The ministries conferred by ordination are irreplaceable for the organic structure of the Church: without the bishop, presbyters, and deacons, one cannot speak of Church (cf. St Ignatius of Antioch, *Ad Trall* 3, 1)" (*CCC* 1593).

Connecting to Our Family

A Christian family that practices the virtues of faith, hope, love, prudence, justice, moderation, and courage and fosters prayer and worship is an ideal setting for opening the hearts of the young to the possibility of priesthood and religious life. The encouragement of a mother and father is immensely helpful in planting the spiritual seeds that might lead to this calling. When children become altar servers and choir singers they become accustomed to the Church's life of worship and breathe it in when their souls are most receptive.

We offer here a testimony of a remarkable priest, Archbishop Helder Camara, retired bishop of Refice, Brazil. He has become world-famous for his love of the poor and his efforts to help them find social and economic justice through prayer, community, and social action. Archbishop

Camara is equally known for his contagious holiness and enthusiasm for the treasures of spirituality. This is what he has to say about being a priest.

Being a Priest

"I can't imagine being anything but a priest. Just think, I consider the lack of imagination to be a crime and yet I haven't the imagination to see myself as not a priest. For me, being a priest isn't just a choice; it's a way of life. It's what water is for a fish, the sky for a bird. I really believe in Christ. Jesus for me is not an abstract idea — he's a personal friend.

"Being a priest has never disappointed me nor given me regrets. Celibacy, chastity, the absence of a family in the way laymen understand it, all this has never been a burden to me. If I've missed certain joys, I have others much more sublime. If you only knew what I feel when I say Mass, how I become one with it! The Mass for me is truly Calvary, and the Resurrection: it's a mad joy!

"Look, there are those born to sing, those born to write, those born to play soccer, and those who are born to be priests. I was born to be a priest. I started saying so at the age of eight and certainly not because my parents put the idea in my head. My father was a Mason, and my mother went to Church once a year.

"I even remember that one day my father got frightened and said: 'My son, you're always saying you want to be a priest. But do you know what that means? A priest is someone who doesn't belong to himself, because he belongs to God and to his people, someone who must dispense only love and faith and charity.'

"And I said, 'I know. That's why I want to be a priest.' "

1. Share the stories of priests and bishops you have known or heard of who have been models of kindness and pastoral sensitivity. If one of your children expressed an interest in being a priest or a religious, what would your reaction be?

2. What are some of the positive reactions you have had to the clergy and bishops whom you have experienced in your Church life? If you wanted your son to be a priest, what would you do about it?

3. If you have ever been to an ordination, what was the experience like for you? How would you make your home life favorable to the growth of a vocation to the priesthood?

Family Prayer

Jesus, our high priest and heavenly mediator, we glorify you for your compassionate intercession on our behalf as you stand before the Father to obtain blessings and graces for us. We thank you for sharing your priesthood with us in our Baptism so we become members of the common priesthood of the faithful. We praise you for sharing your priesthood with our parish priests, diocesan bishop, and the pope in the sacrament of Holy Orders by which they become members of the ministerial priesthood. As they give us the Eucharist to unfold the potential of our Baptisms, we are filled with gratitude for your infinite affection for us. We pray with the whole Church for an increase of vocations to the priesthood and religious life so that an army of laborers will go out to gather the great harvest.

Glossary

Sacrament of Holy Orders: By the imposition of hands and a prayer of consecration, the Holy Spirit is invoked to ordain bishops, priests, and deacons for the sanctification of God's people.

Two Ways of Sharing in the One Priesthood of Christ: The baptized share in Christ's priesthood and become the common priesthood of the faithful for the sanctification of the world. Those ordained for Holy Orders share in Christ's priesthood in a uniquely different way and become the ministerial priesthood to serve the Communion of the Church and the sanctification of her members.

Lesson 17

Hearts of Love — Hands of Prayer: Marriage

Resource: *CCC* paragraphs 1601-1666

Some enchanted evening,
When you find your true love, . . .
Then fly to her side. . . .
Once you have found her,
never let her go.

— Oscar Hammerstein

The Story of Ruth

The biblical story of Ruth begins on a farm near Bethlehem. Crop failures force Naomi and Elimelech and their two sons to migrate to neighboring Moab which offers them a chance for survival. They worry about being strangers in a different culture with people who have another religion.

The Moabites prove to be friendly. They welcome the newcomers, sell them land, and even arrange to have Naomi and Elimelech's sons marry Moabite women, Orpah and Ruth.

Ten prosperous and happy years pass. Then, an epidemic strikes the family, killing off the male members and leaving three grieving widows. Naomi feels frightened and alone. She does not want to be a burden to her daughters-in-law who are still young enough to seek new husbands. Naomi is homesick. Good times have returned to Bethlehem. She has relatives there who will care for her. She resolves to go home.

Naomi tells her plans to Ruth and Orpah and wishes them good luck in the homes of their future husbands. Dutifully, the young women protest they should go back with her to Bethlehem. Naomi appreciates their offer, but reminds them she has no other sons to offer them. They must look out for themselves and find husbands in Moab. Orpah kisses Naomi good-bye and goes away.

Ruth loves Naomi too much to abandon her. She holds the aging Naomi tightly in he arms and utters a canticle of commitment that inspires us to this day. "Do not ask me to abandon or forsake you! for wherever you go I will go, wherever you lodge I will lodge, your people shall be my people, and your God my God. Wherever you die I will die, and there be buried" (Ruth 1:16-17).

Small town gossip assails the two women upon their return to Bethlehem. Naomi first abandoned her homeland — now she returns with this pagan! Such coldness makes Naomi bitter, but Ruth ignores this hostility. To keep them from starving, Ruth goes to the barley fields to pick up the leftovers behind the reapers.

One day she attracts the attention of a rich farmer named Boaz. It is a case of love at first sight. He gives her permission to reap in the best field and shares his noon meal with her. That evening she tells Naomi about her good luck. Naomi praises God and devises a plan that will bring Boaz to marry Ruth. When Boaz settles down to sleep, Ruth should go to his tent, turn back the covers and lie at his feet until Boaz tells her what to do.

Boaz is enormously touched that Ruth should show interest in him and place herself in so vulnerable a position. He realizes she wants him as a husband. So "Boaz took Ruth. When they came together as man and wife, the LORD enabled her to conceive and she bore a son. . . . They called him Obed" (Ruth 4:13, 17). Thus Ruth became part of God's plan for a Savior, for Obed became the father of Jesse, who sired David, of whose family was born Jesus Christ, the Savior of the world.

Marriage in God's Plan

Ruth's fidelity reflected God's fidelity in his covenant with us. Ruth achieved little in worldly terms. She was a wife and a mother on a moderately prosperous farm in an obscure part of the world. Yet she was privileged to be part of the family tree of Jesus. We remember her because her promise keeping gives us a glimpse of the grandeur of God's fidelity — an essential ingredient of his plan for marriage.

The Bible begins with the Lord's creation of man and woman who become two in one flesh and ends with a vision of the marriage feast of the Lamb. Scripture constantly speaks of marriage, its "mystery," its history, its problems and its renewal in the covenant Jesus made with the Church.

God created marriage. It is not a purely human institution, despite the changes it has experienced in different cultures and social situations. We should be more aware of the common and permanent features of marriage.

All cultures sense the greatness of marriage, even if not with the same perceptiveness. Most of the world's peoples believe that a healthy marriage is important for a wholesome society and the human and Christian good of the individual.

Marital love should be an image of the absolute and unfailing love God has for every human being. Scripture teaches that man and woman were created for each other. "It is not good for the man to be alone" (Gen 2:18). The woman is his counterpart and his equal. Jesus repeated the teaching of Genesis when he declared that marriage ought to be an unbreakable union, for man and woman are no longer two, but one flesh (cf. Mt 19:6).

But all of us experience the impact of original sin. We are radically flawed — and radically redeemed. We all suffer tendencies to infidelity, disorder, jealousy, and conflicts that can cause hatred and separation. The first sin ruptured our relation with God and negatively affected the original communion of man and woman. Domination and lust can spoil and ruin a marriage. God offers his grace to married couples to overcome these wounds of sin.

The Old Testament describes the evolution of people's consciences toward the ideal of the unity and indissolubility of marriage under God's guidance. God's covenant with Israel taught the people about permanent commitment and love. The books of Ruth and Tobit witness the ideals of marriage, describing the fidelity and tenderness that should exist between the spouses. The Song of Solomon pictures a human love that mirrors God's love, a love as strong as death which "deep waters cannot quench. . ." (Sg 8:7).

Jesus brought this divine plan for marriage to full awareness. At the beginning of his public ministry, Jesus performed his first miracle at a wedding in Cana of Galilee. Jesus confirmed the goodness of marriage and made the sacrament of Marriage an efficacious sign of his presence.

Jesus unequivocally taught the indissolubility of marriage (Mt 19:1-12). Many today think this is an impossible ideal. Even his first disciples thought so too. "If that is the case of a man with his wife, it is better not to marry" (Mt 19:10). But Jesus argued that he has come to restore the original order of creation disturbed by sin. He will offer couples the graces they need in the new world of the reign of God to stay faithful to each other until death.

In the Latin Church, the celebration of marriage normally takes place at Mass because all sacraments have a connection to the paschal mystery of Christ. Moreover, all Christian life reflects the spousal love of Jesus for the Church. In marriage, the couple witness this truth in the most vivid manner. St. Paul writes, "Husbands, love your wives, even as Christ loved the church. . . . This is a great mystery, but I speak in reference to Christ and the church" (Eph 5:25, 32).

In the Latin Church the spouses, as ministers of Christ's grace, confer on each other the sacrament of Marriage by expressing their consent before the Church. In the Eastern liturgies the minister is the priest or bishop who "crowns" the bride and groom after receiving their vows.

The sacrament of Marriage bonds the man and woman to each other forever. A Church Father, Tertullian, dwelt on this joy of marriage:

How can I ever express the happiness of a marriage joined by the Church, strengthened by an offering, sealed by a blessing, announced by angels and ratified by the Father? How wonderful the bond between two believers, now one in hope, one in desire, one in discipline, one in the same service! They are both children of one Father and servants of the same Master, undivided in spirit and flesh, truly two in one flesh. Where the flesh is one, one also is the spirit (*Ad Uxorem* 2, 8, 6-7).

The Goods of Marriage

The *Catechism* teaches that Christ's graces in the sacrament of Marriage protects three blessings or goods: (1) Unity and indissolubility; (2) the fidelity of conjugal love; and (3) openness to fecundity and the welfare of the children.

Unity and Indissolubility

The unitive aspect of marriage deals with all that conjugal love between the spouses implies. This involves the mutual attractiveness of the bodies of the spouses, their emotional lives, their spiritual growth, and their wills. All of these elements go into the whole gift of the persons of the spouses to one another. Love includes it all. They are to form one heart, mind, soul, and body with each other. While these elements are part of all natural conjugal love, they are elevated by the sacrament to the expression of Christian values.

Because of the sacrament, the spouses not only enter into communion with each other, but also with Jesus Christ who deepens their common faith, and in the Eucharist, nourishes and perfects their profound love for each other. The indissolubility of their union affects their whole married life because they are forever two in one flesh.

Fidelity of Conjugal Love

The second good of marriage, which the sacrament protects, is their marital fidelity to each other. This human covenant is raised to a divine level by the sacrament where it shares in the power of Christ's covenant. By this he enables husband and wife to participate in his powerful fidelity to the Church. Just as Jesus is the bridegroom of the Church and will never let her down, so the spouses gain entrance into a similar covenant because of Christ's graces to them. Marital love is meant to be forever, not just "until further notice."

The goods of unity and fidelity are destroyed by divorce. In obedience to the sixth and ninth commandments, and to the very nature of marriage itself, the Church teaches that these goods require that sexuality be confined to the married state. Hence, adultery, fornication, and homosexual acts are forbidden. The bond between unitive-faithful love and procreative love is meant to be unbreakable.

Openness to Children and Their Welfare

"Children are really the supreme gift of marriage and contribute very substantially to the welfare of their parents. . . . The true practice of conjugal love, and the whole meaning of the family life which results from it, have this aim: that the couple be ready with stout hearts to cooperate with the love of the Creator and the Savior, who through them will enlarge and enrich His own family day by day" (*Church in the Modern World*, [*GS*], 50).

118

By its nature, marriage is directed to the procreation and education of children. Parents should oversee the moral, spiritual, and supernatural growth of their children, as well as seeing to their physical, intellectual, and emotional development. Parents are the principal and first educators of their children.

The home is the first school of Christian life and a school for human enrichment. In this domestic church, the members learn love, the joy of work, perseverance, how to forgive, how to pray, and to participate actively in divine worship.

Once again, we should say that the bond between the unitive-faithful aspect of marriage and the procreative one is meant to be unbreakable. At the same time, it should be noted that spouses who have not received the gift of children from God can still have a married life full of meaning in human and Christian terms.

Jesus obviously has blessed married life. He also blessed virginity. Consecrated virginity and celibacy do not devalue married life. The fidelity of married people encourages those with a celibate commitment. Conversely, the faithful celibate witness enriches marital commitment.

Pastors should have a special solicitude for single people, many of whom have no opportunity to marry and some of whom have no family to whom they can turn. The Christian community should open its heart to these people and welcome them in to a circle of friendship.

Catechism Reflection

1. What are the graces of the sacrament of Marriage?

"The sacrament of Matrimony signifies the union of Christ and the Church. It gives spouses the grace to love each other with the love with which Christ has loved his Church; the grace of the sacrament thus perfects the human love of the spouses, strengthens their indissoluble unity, and sanctifies them on the way to eternal life (cf. Council of Trent: *DS* 1799)" (*CCC* 1661).

2. What is the role of public consent and celebration for marriage?

"Marriage is based on the consent of the contracting parties, that is, on their will to give themselves, each to the other, mutually and definitively, in order to live a covenant of faithful and fruitful love. Since marriage establishes the couple in a public state of life in the Church, it is fitting that its celebration be public, in the framework of a liturgical celebration, before the priest (or a witness authorized by the Church), the witnesses, and the assembly of the faithful" (*CCC* 1662-63).

3. What is the status of divorced and remarried Catholics?

"The remarriage of persons divorced from a living, lawful spouse contravenes the plan and law of God as taught by Christ. They are not separated from the Church, but they cannot receive Eucharistic communion.

They will lead Christian lives especially by educating their children in the faith" (*CCC* 1665).

Connecting to Our Family

Our culture swings between ideal and pessimistic visions of marriage and the family. Today it would claim that all families are "dysfunctional," afflicted by divorce, single-parent situations, spousal abuse, kids taking drugs, and other woes. But fifty years ago the culture dwelt on the ideal family. Who can forget "Ozzie and Harriet?" From 1952 to 1966 we enjoyed the stories of an American family where mothers and fathers and children lived happily together.

Ozzie and Harriet lived in an imaginary small town where there were never any politics, contentions, or heartbreaks. Everyone was well fed, lived in a nice house, and had the same heart and the same values. In the show they lived in perpetual harmony. Their problems were simple. Will Ozzie play Ping-Pong in the father-and-son tournament with David or Ricky? Is David old enough to have his own key to the house? Should Harriet change her hair style?

Critics of that vision argue that it gave a false vision of life. It ignored the ugliness of the oppression of women and minorities, domestic violence, sexual harassment, and a host of other abuses and injustices.

But is all family life sunk in the abyss of such problems? Is not family life today often a succession of simple events not unlike those of Ozzie and Harriet? The dog still gets lost. There are daily hellos and good-byes and hellos again. We still have little league in addition to the new "soccer moms." We still get colds, enjoy the small ones looking for Santa Claus, cry on the first day of school, play games on car trips, and keep a plentiful supply of peanut butter and jelly. The beloved Erma Bombeck reminded us of the humor of family life, the numerous small decisions that bind us together.

Today it is popular to look only at the miseries that beset families and ignore the good things that happen. Ozzie and Harriet may have stood at the other end of the spectrum, but they were closer to the perennial values that make family life work.

Jesus gives husbands and wives, mothers and fathers the graces to overcome the inevitable problems of family life. Jesus knew there was evil in the world. But he was not morbidly fixed on sin, for he came to overcome sin and its effects by his suffering, Passion, and Resurrection. He offers the married couple the blessings of unity, indissolubility, fidelity, and openness to children. These gifts make wholesome family life possible. The Christian family can thus be a true domestic church.

1. What helps you to practice fidelity to one another? Why is family loyalty such an important virtue? What do you see around you that challenges your ability to be faithful to your spouse?

2. What are the benefits of focusing on the ideal side of family life? What do you learn from an honest appraisal of the realistic aspects of marriage and family?

3. What spiritual activities help your family to grow closer together? How do your help one another to pray? Why is faith a strong bond for your family? How does religion help you to have a happy family life?

Family Prayer

Lord, we thank you for the three blessings of our married life: unity and indissolubility, fidelity, and openness to children and their welfare. We yearn for and welcome the graces you promise us and give us in such abundance. Help us to face with courage and faith the challenges to our marriage and family that the world around us presents from day to day. Open our eyes to see the small but important courtesies which make everyday family life a joy. Fill our hearts with love and our wills with determination so that we can be a warm domestic church, a haven in an often heartless world and a light of welcome to all around us.

Glossary

Unitive Aspect of Marriage: God willed that husband and wife be committed permanently to one another in a communion of love. This communion of persons reflects the community of the Trinity.

Procreative Aspect of Marriage: God willed that marriage have a parental dimension in which husband and wife procreate and educate children. The bond between the procreative and unitive aspects of marriage may not be broken.

Goods of Marriage: The three goods or blessings of marriage are: (1) unity and indissolubility; (2) fidelity to conjugal love; and (3) openness to fecundity and the welfare of children.

Virginity and Celibacy: Consecrated virginity and celibacy, normally lived in the priesthood and religious life, are a call from God to witness the reality of the kingdom of heaven and our supernatural life and destiny.

Chapter Three
Life in Christ

The Transfiguration
— by Raphael

Lesson 18

The Catholic Basis of the Moral Life

Resource: *CCC* paragraphs 1691-2051

If I can stop one heart from breaking,
I shall not live in vain;
If I can ease one life the aching
Or cool one pain,
I shall not live in vain.

— Emily Dickinson

The Smile Button

The shortest distance between two people is a smile. In December 1963, the State Mutual Life Assurance Company was having a morale problem because of a merger. They asked an artist, Harvey Ball, to draw a smile to be used as a button to cheer up the people in the office. He should just paint a smile, nothing else, no eyes, no nose.

"I had a choice," Ball said, "I could have used a compass and made it as neat as possible, but I drew it freehand to give it some character." He liked his slightly crooked smile — but there was a problem. "A smile upside down is a frown." So he added two eyes and colored it yellow. The insurance company initially made one hundred buttons. Ball made $45 for the job. Everyone was happy.

But a few years later, two novelty manufacturers married the words "Have a nice day" to the smiley face, and the rest is history. An estimated fifty million buttons have been made since 1971. Harvey Ball never trademarked the smiley face, so he never made any more money on the button.

"It doesn't bother me that I never made a lot of money on it. Money isn't everything. You can only drive one car at a time; you can only eat one steak at a time."

Recently, Harvey celebrated his seventy-fifth birthday. He has learned that happiness is not a birthday cake nor making millions on a cultural icon. "You have to put it into perspective. My life changed on Saturday, April 21, 1945, at 4 p.m. on the island of Okinawa. Bingo! A Japanese mortar shell exploded right in front of me. It killed my two buddies to the left, it killed the guy in front of me, and wounded the guy to my right. I was unhurt. That changes your attitude. I was happy to be alive. I think doing the best you can and living responsibly will make you happy" (adapted from "Are We Happy Yet?" by Stan Grossfield, *Boston Globe Sunday Magazine*, January 19, 1997, pp. 14-15, 66).

Catholic Morality Is Life in Christ

The World Database on Happiness lists 2,475 titles — books, journal articles, dissertations, conference papers — on the topic of happiness. Among their findings, they conclude: (1) Close relationships, including a happy marriage and religion, are the most important elements in achieving happiness; (2) physical attractiveness doesn't guarantee subjective well-being; and (3) happiness is more desired by people than are cherished social goals such as peace and equality.

Part Three of the *Catechism* is about the Catholic moral life, which it calls "Life in Christ." Section one lays down the foundations of the moral life. Section two deals with each of the Ten Commandments. It is clear from the text that living morally brings the much-desired human fulfillment and happiness that we all hunger for. In this chapter we explore the basics of the moral life. Subsequent chapters will deal with each of the Ten Commandments.

The *Catechism* lays out nine basic "building blocks" which form the conditions for the moral life and the happiness which results from it.

Images of God

The building blocks of morality begin with understanding ourselves as images of God. What does it mean to be an image of God?

• I have a mind that can know the truth, including the ultimate truth of God and the faith realization that God is truth.

• I have a will that can love the good in the world and the absolute good which is God.

• I have received the gift of freedom. I am free to do what I should and not just whatever I please.

• I have been wounded by original sin. This means I have a difficult time knowing the truth and must struggle for it. I notice a conflict in my will. I often choose what I shouldn't — and fail to choose what I should. I am inclined to evil in the exercise of my freedom.

• I have new life in the Holy Spirit, due to my Baptism and my participation in the sacraments. These graces help me not just to "be" an image of God, but also to "act" as God's image and overcome the difficulties posed by original and actual sin.

• I am destined for the life of glory in heaven.

It is because I am an image of God that I even have the possibility of happiness. The capacity to know and love in a properly free manner opens me to the only permanent source of joy, an enduring relationship with God.

I Am Called to Happiness

The second building block is found in the Beatitudes (Mt 5:3-12). In his eight Beatitudes, Jesus calls us to be happy and shows us the way to it. True happiness, following the Beatitudes, is the best motivator for being moral. God has planted in me a natural desire to be happy. I should discover that God alone will satisfy me. "How is it then that I seek you, Lord? Since in seeking you, my God, I seek a happy life, let me seek you so that my soul may live, for my body draws life from my soul, and my soul draws life from you" (St. Augustine, *Confessions*, 10, 20).

"The Beatitudes teach us the final end to which God calls us: the Kingdom, the vision of God, participation in the divine nature, eternal life, filiation, rest in God" (*CCC* 1726).

God has put us in this world to know, love, and serve him and to be with him in paradise. The Beatitudes help us to live this vocation. The Ten Commandments, the Sermon on the Mount, and the Church's teaching office (the Magisterium) show us how to live the life of the Beatitudes. Because of our sinful inclinations, we cannot be completely happy on earth. But in heaven we will have perfect joy.

Human Freedom and Responsibility

The third building block of Christian morality is the responsible use of our freedom. God made us rational beings. Our human dignity as persons means we can initiate and control our own acts. We are not robots controlled by some outside force or inner compulsion. It is true that there are outer social pressures and, in some cases, inner psychological drives that sometimes overwhelm us. Normally, we are basically free to act. Our freedom is rooted in our intelligence and will.

"The imputability or responsibility for an action can be diminished or nullified by ignorance, duress, fear, and other psychological or social factors" (*CCC* 1746).

The more we do the good, the more free we become. The more we do evil, we become slaves of sin, and lose our freedom. Freedom makes us responsible for our behavior. The right to exercise our freedom, especially in moral and religious matters, is an inalienable part of our dignity as a human person. Freedom does not mean the right to say or do anything we please — only what we should, according to God's will. People who are truly free, in the sense meant here, have the best chance for happiness.

The Morality of Human Acts

How can we tell what goes into a truly moral act? Our fourth building block addresses this question. There are three parts to the moral act: (1) The act itself; (2) the subjective motive; and (3) the situation or circumstances. All three parts must be good for the act to be good. Moral laws can help us tell whether the act is good or bad. Rape is wrong. So is abortion. Some acts are clearly, always, wrong — intrinsically evil. This is the objective part of a moral act.

The second part of the moral act is the intention. What are some morally wrong intentions? Hate, greed, lust, envy, sloth, malice, despair. This is the subjective side of a moral act.

The third part of a moral act is the situation or the circumstance surrounding the act. Circumstances contribute to increasing or diminishing the moral goodness or badness of the act (such as the amount of a theft). The circumstances diminish or increase the moral responsibility of the agent (such as acting out of a fear of death).

To have a morally good act, all the parts must be good: the act itself, the intention of the doer, and the circumstances. But the end does not justify the means. We may not do evil so that good may come of it.

Moral Conscience

The fifth building block of Christian moral teaching is the development of a proper moral conscience. What is conscience?

"Conscience is a judgment of reason by which the human person recognizes the moral quality of a concrete act" (*CCC* 1796).

A good conscience requires lifelong training and formation. The Word of God is a major light for informing our consciences. We must assimilate it in faith and prayer and put it into practice. Our conscience is also enlightened by the prudent advice of others, their good behavior, and the authoritative teaching of the Church. Regular examination of conscience, aided by the gifts of the Spirit, will help us develop a morally sensitive conscience.

A well-formed conscience makes judgments that conform to reason and the real good willed by the wisdom of God. Any time we face a moral choice our consciences can make a correct judgment according to reason and God's law, or, on the contrary, make an erroneous judgment that contradicts reason and divine law.

"A human being must always obey the certain judgment of his conscience. Conscience can remain in ignorance or make erroneous judgments. Such ignorance and errors are not always free of guilt" (*CCC* 1800-01). Readers are encouraged to read *CCC* 1790-94.

Practice Virtues

If we want to be happy, we must be moral. If we want to be moral, we must practice the human and theological virtues. This is our sixth building block. Human virtues are habits of mind and will that govern our behavior and control our passions. These virtues guide our conduct according to faith and reason. What are some of these virtues? They include self-discipline, compassion, responsibility, friendship, work, courage, perseverance, honesty, and loyalty. Traditionally, we group them around the "cardinal" virtues of prudence, justice, temperance, and fortitude.

How do we acquire these virtues? First, by hearing stories of virtuous people that inspire us to practice them. Second, by the good example of others who motivate us to imitate them. Third, by education in the value of virtues and ways to acquire them. Fourth, by formal, repetitive acts —

doing them over and over until they are grooved into our character and behavior. Fifth, with determination to have them and perseverance in their quest. Sixth by prayer, especially to the Holy Spirit for the seven gifts to help us: wisdom, knowledge, understanding, courage, counsel, piety, and fear of the Lord.

We also should practice the *theological virtues* of faith, hope, and charity. They are direct gifts from God and dispose us to have a vital relationship with the persons of the Trinity. They are called theological because they explicitly direct us to faith and hope in God and a loving surrender to his divine plan for us. Theological virtues affect all the moral virtues, elevating them to the divine level and increasing their stability and effectiveness in our lives.

Understanding Sin

To talk about morality and avoid a discussion of sin would be absurd. An understanding of sin is the seventh building block of the *Catechism*'s teaching about morality. For a long time there was a denial of sin in our culture. This led psychiatrist Karl Menninger to write a book, *Whatever Became of Sin?* He wrote that there was a time when people admitted their sins, went to a priest, and obtained absolution. Then sin became a crime, which was presented to the judge and punished by imprisonment or execution. Finally, sin became a neurosis or psychosis, which was "confessed" to a psychologist and treated by therapy.

He exploded this myth and argued that this confusion should be clarified. Yes, mentally ill people should see a therapist and criminals should go to a courtroom. But sinners should admit their spiritual guilt to a proper authority and receive absolution and forgiveness.

The *Catechism* couldn't agree more. The recovery of a sense of sin is an act of moral realism that both gives us an honest assessment of self as well as the opportunity for redemption. If there is no sin, then why would Jesus be called a Savior and why did he suffer so much for us on the Cross? Why did he rise from the dead to give us new life and the graces that would help us avoid sin?

What is sin? It is any word, thought, deed, or desire that is against God's law and breaks our relationship with him as well as people. It is an act of disobedience to God. Sin is an act that is opposed to reason. Sin corrupts our nature and harms our communion with people.

When we commit a mortal sin, we knowingly and willingly do something that is gravely contrary to the divine law and opposed to our ultimate destiny. Mortal sin destroys the love that we need for eternal happiness. If we do not repent a mortal sin, we will suffer eternal death.

A venial sin is a moral disorder that can be overcome by the charity which it allows to remain in us. Repeated sins, even venial ones, open us to vices, especially the capital ones: pride, envy, lust, anger, sloth, gluttony, and greed. (Read the *Catechism* 1846-76 and our chapter on the sacrament of Reconciliation as well as the material on original sin again to supplement what is said here.)

A Sense of Community and Social Justice

The eighth building block for a Christian moral life is an appreciation of our human community with all peoples and our call to work for Christ's Kingdom of love, justice, and mercy. The Holy Trinity is a communion of persons, bound by absolute love. On earth we are called to form a community among all human beings, a communion of love that, in a certain manner, reflects the inner life of God.

Connected to this should be a profound respect for the dignity of each human person. All governments and other social institutions should serve and enhance the integrity and dignity of persons. It is the responsibility of society to create a situation that favors the growth of virtue and a hierarchy of values which give the primacy of spiritual values over physical and instinctual ones.

The state and its authority are based on human nature and so belong to an order established by God. Political authority must be used for the common good of society. To reach such a goal this authority should use morally acceptable means. This will involve establishing the social conditions that allow the citizens the proper exercise of their freedom. All of this is meant to promote the common good.

"The common good comprises 'the sum total of social conditions which allow people, either as groups or as individuals, to reach their fulfillment more fully and more easily' (*GS* 26§1)" (*CCC* 1924).

Social justice demands that people be allowed to form associations to achieve their goals. This will include genuine human rights and human equality which flow from an understanding of the dignity of the human person. Each of us should consider the other as "another self." The quest for social justice will seek to reduce excessive social and economic inequalities. Solidarity with all people is a form of communion of persons and is a Christian virtue. God calls us to share both spiritual and materials goods with one another.

Law and Grace

God's plan of salvation through law and grace constitutes the ninth building block of the Christian moral life. In the divine law, God teaches us the way to heavenly happiness and the ways of evil that must be avoided. The natural law is our way of participating in God's goodness and wisdom. It expresses our human dignity and forms the basis for rights and duties. Because it is a participation in divine law, the natural law is a changeless presence in history. It continues to serve as the bedrock of moral and civil law.

The Old Testament contains the first stage of revealed law and this is summarized in the Ten Commandments. This law prepared the world for the Gospel. We call the new law the grace of the Holy Spirit which is received by us through faith in Jesus Christ. Its major expression is found in Christ's Sermon on the Mount (Mt 7-9). We receive these graces by active participation in the sacraments.

Because of the salvation won for us By Jesus Christ in his death and Resurrection, the Holy Spirit makes us sharers in the life of God. In the application of Christ's saving work, the Spirit can move us away from sin and toward God. This salvation is also called justification, which includes the forgiveness of sins and the sanctification of our inner lives.

We cannot stress enough that our salvation and justification have been won for us by the paschal mystery, the death and Resurrection of Jesus Christ. Our Christian moral lives are made possible by this supreme act of love and mercy, willed by the Father, accomplished in Christ, and made available to us by the activity of the Spirit in the Church and sacraments. The popular hymn "Amazing Grace" touchingly reminds us that sin is not the primary focus of the moral life despite its powerful and unfortunate presence and influence in the world. The *Catechism* correctly raises our eyes to the throne of divine mercy from which flows sanctifying grace. This grace enfolds us, precedes, prepares, and elicits our free response to God's love. God gives us this grace in total freedom because he loves us.

Hence we merit salvation only because God decided to involve us in this work of grace. Merit belongs in the first place to the grace of God and second to our collaboration with it. At the same time it must be said that we do not merit the initial grace of conversion. This is a gracious and free act of the Holy Spirit.

Catechism Reflection

1. How does the Church give us assured moral guidance?

"The Roman Pontiff and the bishops, as authentic teachers, preach to the People of God the faith which is to be believed and applied in moral life. It is also incumbent on them to pronounce on moral questions that fall within the natural law and reason. The infallibility of the Magisterium of the Pastors extends to all elements of doctrine, including moral doctrine, without which the saving truths of faith cannot be preserved, expounded, or observed" (*CCC* 2050-51).

2. Why are correct moral decisions necessary for salvation?

"The way of Christ 'leads to life'; a contrary way 'leads to destruction'[*Mt.* 7:13; cf. *Deut* 30:15-20]. The Gospel parable of the *two ways* remains ever present in the catechesis of the Church; it shows the importance of moral decisions for our salvation: 'There are two ways, the one of life, the other of death; but between the two, there is a great difference [*Didache* 1, 1: SCh 248, 140]'" (*CCC* 1696).

3. What are major elements that help us form our consciences?

". . . the conscience of each person should avoid confining itself to individualistic considerations in its moral judgments of the person's own acts. As far as possible conscience should take account of the good of all, as expressed in the moral law, natural and revealed, and consequently in the law of the Church and in the authoritative teaching of the Magisterium on moral questions. Personal conscience and reason should not be set in opposition to the moral law or the Magisterium of the Church" (*CCC* 2039).

Connecting to Our Family

All family life is always somehow involved in moral education and personal moral growth, spouse to spouse and parents to children. Helping each other to become Christian moral persons is the best route to fulfillment and happiness here and perfect happiness in heaven. Keep in mind that:

- We are images of God.
- Desire for happiness is a great motivator for being moral.
- Virtue acquisition is essential.
- Belief in God's mercy and Christ's saving work liberates us from sin in the sacrament of Reconciliation.
- Conscience formation always includes living by the natural and revealed law and willingness to be guided by the Church's teaching authority.
- Faith, prayer, and the action of the Spirit make the "yoke light and the burden easy."

In a special way, the life of the virtues should be a priority. Helping each other grow in virtue is as important as lifelong learning and crossing the street safely. The moral life is an adventure, exhilarating in the journey and satisfying in the achievement. We do not do it ourselves. The Holy Spirit is living and active in our quest and does more than we dream of to assure our moral progress.

1. What does the *Catechism* tell you about being an image of God? Why is this important for moral living? Why can we say that the need to be happy is an excellent motivator for becoming a moral person?

2. What is your idea of sin? How do you relate this to God's mercy and Christ's salvation? How well do you take advantage of the sacrament of Reconciliation?

3. How do you examine your conscience? What have you done about forming a correct conscience? What forces in the culture militate against being moral?

Family Prayer

Loving and merciful Father, you gave us the Ten Commandments at Sinai to be moral guides for our lives so that our relationship with you can grow and mature. Your Son, Jesus, gave us the Sermon on the Mount to show us the full meaning of your new law which is meant to fulfill us and lead us to partial joy here and perfect happiness in heaven. We pray that you send your Holy Spirit to our family to lead us away from sin and toward the life of virtue which conforms us to Christ and prepares us for our eternal destiny with you. We praise you for this great gift and pray that we remain always responsive to you.

Glossary

Human Virtues: Human virtues are habits of mind and will that govern our behavior and control our passions.

Cardinal Virtues: These are prudence, justice, temperance, and fortitude. These human virtues guide our conduct according to faith and reason.

Theological Virtues: The theological virtues are faith, hope, and charity. They are gifts of the Holy Spirit. They are directed to believing and hoping in God and our loving surrender to him. They elevate and perfect the cardinal virtues.

Lesson 19

O God, You Are My God: The First Commandment

Resource: *CCC* paragraphs 2052-2141

There never was found in any age of the world, either philosopher or sect, or law or discipline, which did so highly exalt the public good as the Christian faith.

— Francis Bacon

Beyond the Stars — God

Scene: A bookstore specializing in the occult.
Characters: Jill (owner of the bookstore); Jack (a customer).

Jack: I want a book on the stars.

Jill: Were you born under a lucky one?

Jack: Perhaps. I'm a Saggitarian, but I want to have a better idea of how my life is shaped by the stars. I'm supposed to be an optimist according to my horoscope.

Jill: I happen to be a Gemini, the sign of the twins. It fits me well. At times I feel like two people inside me.

Jack: The two faces of Eve? Or two-faced? Or a split personality?

Jill: Don't be flippant. The struggle is often fierce within me. I wonder who will win.

Jack: Why don't you take charge?

Jill: I try. Then I give up and play with the Tarot cards. Would you like me to tell your fortune?

Jack: No, I'll stay with the stars and my rock music and meditation.

Jill: Is that how you get your high?

Jack: Sometimes. My horoscope helps me so long as I block out the world with rock and breathing exercises. Then I feel pulses from the stars.

Jill: (Sings) "When the moon is in the seventh house and Jupiter aligns with Mars . . ."

Jack: (Sings) ". . . Then peace will guide the planets and love will steer the stars."

Jill: This looks like the dawning of a sale. Here's a book for you. *Looking for the Soul*. Does religion interest you?

Jack: I may just do that. My friend, Glenda, likes to talk about God and Jesus. I look up and just see stars. She breaks into, "Praise Jesus! I love you Father, Spirit! Stay!"

Jill: I feel I may lose this sale.

132

Jack: Not yet. She hasn't convinced me. But . . . she knows about my hunger to hear music from the heavens.

Jill: Stop! This is where I get off. Are you sure you wouldn't like this Zodiac medal? It has a Saggitarius on it.

Jack: Sold. I'll take the book too.

Jill: How about something for Glenda?

Jack: Okay. She's a Virgo, though she may be moving me to Trinity.

Faith in a Real God

Our dialogue between Jack and Jill shows that young people look for God, but some of them settle for less. Jack has a taste for the spiritual, but has not gone far enough. Glenda has found faith in a real God and, with patience, she may move Jack to authentic faith. The first commandment tells us that God has revealed himself to us because he loves us. In return, God asks us to have faith in him, the real God.

Purpose of the Commandments

Any discussion of the commandments should begin with the scene at Sinai where God gave them to us. Read Exodus 19:3-6; 20:1-17. The first event is a covenant experience. God tells Moses how much he has loved the Israelites, is delivering them from slavery by "raising them up on eagles' wings," and is bringing them to freedom. God then offers them a binding covenant of love. He will be their only God and they will be his chosen people. It's like a marriage experience, an exchange of vows between God and Israel.

The next section shows God telling them how to live out the love they have pledged. He gives them the Ten Commandments as the means to live the covenant, to express the love they have promised. The *Catechism* points out that the Ten Commandments are privileged expressions of the natural law, made known to us by reason as well as Divine Revelation. We are obliged in obedience to observe these laws of love, both in serious and light matters. Love is in the details as well as the large matters. We must remember that what God has commanded, he makes possible by his grace.

Jesus set the tone for understanding the importance of the commandments. When a rich young man came to him and asked him what he should do to enter eternal life, Jesus replied, "If you wish to enter into life, keep the commandments" (Mt 19:17). In another case, someone asked him which were the greatest commandments, Jesus replied, "You shall love the Lord, your God, with all your heart, with all your soul, and with all your mind. This is the greatest and first commandment. The second is like it: You shall love your neighbor as yourself" (Mt 22:37-39). The first three commandments deal with Christ's call to love God with all our being. The last seven commandments show us how to love our neighbor as we love ourselves.

First Commandment

The first commandment summons us to have faith in the true God, to hope in him and love him enthusiastically with mind, heart, soul, and will. This is our response to the God who has revealed himself to us, created and redeemed us, and looks after us caringly in his providence.

Every commandment calls us to a virtue and forbids certain kinds of behavior. The commandments are not uniformly negative, even the ones that begin with a "Thou shalt not." There is always a twofold aspect to them, the positive value and the negative injunction. The positive invitation of the first commandment deals with faith, hope, love, and the virtue of religion. In the virtue of religion we respond to God's generosity with acts of adoration, prayer, and fidelity in keeping our promises to God.

The negative injunction of the first commandment forbids superstition, idolatry, magic (not the entertainment kind), sacrilege, simony (sale of church position), and atheism.

Faith

Social observers such as George Gallup, Jr. report that most Americans believe in God. The majority believe they will face God on judgment day and confess that they sometimes feel very aware of God's presence. Generally, Americans have a religious worldview.

But there are many who do not believe in God, or seriously doubt his existence. Some hesitate to believe because they cannot overcome objections to faith, or do not know how to handle the mystery. Some baptized Catholics lapse into heresy when they formally and consciously deny a truth that is held as a matter of faith by the Church. We use the term *apostasy* to describe those baptized who repudiate the faith. Schismatics are those Christians who refuse to acknowledge the authority of the pope.

Hope

When God revealed his plan to save us, he offered us the gift of hope which gives us confidence that God will bless us here and give us heaven hereafter. When we refuse this gift, we lapse into either the sin of presumption or the sin of despair. Those who practice the sin of presumption think they can be saved by their own efforts without grace, or they simply expect God's grace without their taking the trouble to live a moral life. Presumers do not need to hope, or so they think. Those who fall into the sin of despair think they are so evil that God cannot forgive them. They have lost hope in God's mercy. Despairers do not think they have any reason to hope.

Love

God loves us with an everlasting love. He invites us to respond with love in return. The *Catechism* teaches that we sin against this call to love through indifference, ingratitude, lukewarmness, sloth, or outright hatred. Read the *Catechism* 2093-94.

Sins Against the First Commandment

Scripture teaches that idolatry is the worship of false gods, who have eyes that do not see, ears that do not hear, and feet that do not walk. Today idolatry takes new forms. We have discovered fresh ways to adore creatures instead of God. Many today are willing to worship Satan — i.e. in satanic cults, money, power, pleasure, race, even the state. Many martyrs died rather than worship the "beast."

Belief in God is weakened by taking seriously the promises of those involved in astrology, palm reading, interpretation of omens, clairvoyants, mediums, and others who claim to know the future and to have control over time and history.

Atheism

Atheists deny the existence of God. Atheism comes in different forms. Some atheists put all their hope in materialism. Some are called atheistic humanists because they place man in absolute control of himself, his history, and the world. Others look for human liberation through radical economic and social reform. They reject religion because they argue it gets in the way of such improvement of the social and economic order.

The guilt of these atheists may be significantly diminished by their intentions and the circumstances. ". . . believers can have more than a little to do with the rise of atheism. To the extent that they neglect their own training in the faith, or teach erroneous doctrine, or are deficient in their religious, moral, or social life, they must be said to conceal rather than reveal the authentic face of God and religion" (*Church in the Modern World*, [*GS*], 19, 3).

Another form of evading the call of the first commandment is *agnosticism*, a word that means, "I don't know." Some admit there is a God, but we cannot know anything about him. Others say it is impossible to know whether there is a God. Some honest agnostics are looking for God. Others are merely too lazy to try developing a moral conscience, or they are indifferent to ultimate questions. Many are practical atheists.

Is religious art permissible?

When God gave the first commandment, he included the injunction not to make "graven images." The point was that God is greater and more mysterious than any artistic representation of him. The rule also was meant to keep the Israelites from carving idols like the pagans. Nonetheless, God did permit Israel to make images that symbolically pointed to the coming Incarnate Word. Hence they did have the bronze serpent, the ark of the covenant, and the golden cherubim.

In early Church history some of the Christians of the East decided that religious icons were against God's law. They proceeded to smash them and eliminate them from their churches. They were called "Iconoclasts." To correct them, the seventh Council of Nicaea (787) justified the veneration of icons using the doctrine of the Incarnate Word. The Fathers judged that we could venerate images of Jesus, the Mother of God, angels, and saints.

When the Son of God became a visible human being, he introduced the basis for making such images for fostering faith. Whoever venerates a holy image honors the person portrayed. This honor is a respectful veneration, not the adoration due to God alone. We do not venerate the things (statues, paintings, stained-glass windows), but the holy persons portrayed by these images.

Catechism Reflection

1. What are the acts of the virtue of religion?

"Adoring God, praying to him, offering him the worship that belongs to him, fulfilling the promises and vows made to him are acts of the virtue of religion which fall under obedience to the first commandment" (*CCC* 2135).

2. How are covenant and commandments related?

"The Commandments take on their full meaning within the covenant. According to Scripture, man's moral life has all its meaning in and through the covenant. The first of the 'ten words' recalls that God loved his people first. . . . The Commandments properly so-called come in the second place: they express the implications of belonging to God through the establishment of the covenant. Moral existence is a *response* to the Lord's loving initiative" (*CCC* 2061-62).

3. What is the call of the first commandment?

"The first commandment summons man to believe in God, to hope in him, and to love him above all else" (*CCC* 2134).

Connecting to Our Family

The best way to practice the call of the first commandment is to keep growing in the love of God. We know we should love people. Some of us forget we should also love God with all our hearts. If we stop loving God we will love people less. We will also lose our faith and hope in God. The easiest way to have faith in God is to love him. St. Teresa of Ávila urges us, "Habitually make many acts of love of God for they set the soul on fire and make it gentle."

Our love for God is often shown in the simplest manner.

The artist Norman Rockwell once did a painting reminding us to pray and thank God for the food we eat. The scene is a restaurant at a truck stop. He depicted a grandmother sitting at a table across from a small boy. They are saying the blessing before they eat. At the other tables are truck drivers and other men wearing hard hats. These men are watching the grandmother and the boy say their meal prayer. The men look happy. They are remembering that they, too, had grandmothers who always said the blessing before a meal was eaten. A few of the men have taken off their hats and are sitting quietly until the prayer is finished. The love of God touches everyone.

When Jesus performed the miracle of the loaves, he blessed and praised God for the food before it was distributed. Recall that originally there had not been enough food to feed everyone, but then Jesus provided food in abundance. There were even baskets of bread left over! Just as bread is multiplied in the giving, so is love expanded in the loving. Plant the love of God in your family and it will multiply with every act.

1. In what ways is the love of God practiced in your family? What holy images are on the walls or tables of your home that draw you to think of God and revere him?

2. Why can we say that acts of love for God will also deepen your faith in God? Have members of your family lost their faith in God? What can you do to reawaken their faith in God?

3. What is going on in our culture that erodes faith in God? What positive steps can we take to overcome this?

Family Prayer

O God, you are God. For you we long, for you we desire your love and your glory. Increase our love for you that we may always be aware of your presence. Awaken faith in our hearts that we may share you with our family, friends, and others. Show us how to spread faith in you among those who have yet to know and love you. Remove all traces of discouragement from our hearts and make us resolve to be with you now and always.

Glossary

Sacrilege: Disrespect in word and act toward the sacraments and liturgical actions as well as to persons, things, or places consecrated to God.
Simony: The buying or selling of spiritual things (cf. Acts 8:9-24).
Agnostic: The agnostic says one cannot know whether God exists.
Atheist: The atheist denies God's existence.
Secularist: The secularist appears not to care whether God exists.

Lesson 20

The Art of Reverence:
The Second Commandment

Resource: *CCC* paragraphs 2142-2167

> O Lord my God! When I in awesome wonder
> Consider all the works thy hands have made.
> I see the stars, I hear the rolling thunder,
> Thy works throughout the universe displayed.
> — Stuart Hine

Isaiah's Diary

I was born into a middle-class Jewish family in 762 B.C. My parents were deeply religious people who practiced what they preached. They were determined that I should have a moral conscience and a reverence for God and all God's creatures. They created in me a sympathy for the poor, the widow, the alien, and the orphan.

"Never forget, young man, the needs of the poor. Defend them against oppression by powerful people who have no morals."

They told me about vicious loan sharks. They showed me how some businessmen cheated the poor with false weights and measures. I still recall the many family discussions we had about bribery at King Uzziah's court, the corruption of some priests, and the helplessness of the poor.

Mother would look at me and say, "Many of the rich and powerful live by a double standard, one for themselves and one for the powerless. God wants us to be aware of this and to cure both the symptoms and causes of injustice."

We studied God's Word together. My father loved to dwell on passages that spoke of the covenant God established with Israel.

"My son, God loved us. We must return that love by care and compassion for others."

On my twenty-first birthday I received an invitation to the coronation of King Jotham, successor to the recently deceased Uzziah. It took place on the front steps of the Temple building. The purple-robed king arrived in a procession of soldiers, government officials, his family, several choirs, an orchestra of musicians playing lutes, harps, drums, and resounding trumpets. Clouds of incense filled the air with sweetness and lent a mystical look to the event. People packed every inch of temple courtyard.

It was then I had my life-changing vision. The king's throne faded from my eyes and seemed to become the Ark of the Covenant with a host of angels bowed in adoration before God enthroned above the Ark. Angel choirs replaced the earthly musicians and sang heartily of the holiness of God. Incredibly, I saw God. I felt the holiness and purity of God. In a moment that seemed to roll on forever, I grasped the sacredness of all creation. I never before realized how reverence should really feel.

My own imperfection and sinfulness overwhelmed me. Who am I compared to such glory? God sent an angel, who took a burning coal and placed it on my lips. It was a fire that purified me but did not consume me. I burned with holy joy.

That day God gave me a mission to preach and witness his holiness and the sacredness of all people and creation itself. I would prophesy to kings and the mighty that God's holiness shines in the hearts of the poor and powerless. They should be treated with reverence and justice. "Comfort, comfort my people." I did this for fifty years and then slept in the Lord.

Respect God and You Will Respect People

Isaiah's vision of God's holiness shows us what is behind the second commandment's call to reverence God and all his creatures. In his preaching, Isaiah enshrined for us a powerful title for God as the "Holy One." The positive value upheld by the second commandment is the virtue of reverence for the holiness of God and the God-given sacredness of people, places, and things. In our culture, we often hear, "Is there nothing sacred anymore?" The questions reflect an instinct people have that God has planted his holiness in the world and the human capacity to celebrate it.

The commandment says we should respect God's name. His name reveals his personhood, who he is and what he plans to do in creation. When we meet new people, we ask them their names. The name reveals the humanity of the person. We admire people who remember our names because that is a sign they respected us enough to take the trouble to remember. As we hear someone's name, we notice distinguishing characteristics about the person: height, hair color, the look in their eyes, posture, weight, the sound of their voice, the quality of their handshake, clothing style, and so on. The name leads us to the person.

This is just as true of God's name. We could not know God's name unless he told us. We would never know about God's thoughts, plans, and attitudes toward us if he had not revealed these secrets of his inner, mysterious life. God respected us enough to tell us his name. God expects our respect in return, both to himself and to one another and creation itself.

In any introduction there is usually a process that goes from fear to love. Meeting a new person has elements of apprehension. Will he or she like me, accept me for who I am, treat me respectfully, enjoy my presence, and be friendly to me? So the opening moments of a new relationship has elements of unease, uncertainty, and yes, even fear.

If the new acquaintance is a powerful authority figure, a celebrity, a person of great wealth — a president, pope, actor, billionaire — then the fear of rejection or clumsy self-presentation on our part enters the picture. "Will I be loved?" That causes our initial fears. If acceptance and affection is offered, we relax and feel at home with this new person who has entered our lives.

It is the same with relating to God. The first encounter causes us fear, mixed with awe. God always puts us at ease. Think of how often God the Father in the Old Testament or Jesus in the New Testament says to frightened people, "Do not be afraid." When we move from fear to love of God, we spontaneously break out into words of praise and glory for God. We both kneel and bow our heads in adoration and stand, throwing up our arms and exclaiming, "Then sings my soul, my Savior God, to thee — How great thou art!" Adoration of God — exultation in his presence — becomes customary for us.

The more we respect God, the more we will reverence ourselves and others. The reason our culture is so coarse and tawdry is the loss of the practice of adoration and reverence for God. Once we undermine the source of the sacred, we vulgarize the rest of life. The "word pollution" in our conversations, TV and films, talk radio and novels is an inevitable outcome of losing touch with the fountain of holiness. It used to be said, that "All that is, is holy." That dream is gone. We now say, "All that is — *should* be holy."

Sins Against the Second Commandment

The second commandment forbids the wrong use of God's name. In our parishes, the Holy Name Society was founded to spread reverence for God's name and to eliminate curses and blasphemies that use the names of God and Jesus Christ in a callous, scornful, and improper way.

Blasphemy is an act that speaks against God in words of hatred and defiance. It is blasphemous to use God's name to justify criminal practices, the enslavement of peoples, torture, and murder.

We are also forbidden to use God's name to witness a perjury or a false oath and thus use God to approve our lie.

Wrong use of God's name has been used to justify wars, slaughter enemies, and impose unlawful power over others. Tragically, many have used the God of love to impose hatred, the God of trust to enhance betrayal, and the God of mercy to support acts of cruelty. Critics of religion have a field day dramatizing the sins of hypocritical Christians who have made the wrong use of God's name.

At our Baptism we were initiated into the Church, "in the name of the Father, and of the Son, and of the Holy Spirit." God's name sanctified us and we were given a personal name, one taken from a canonized saint. The Church names us after a disciple of Christ who has led an exemplary life. This model of Christian love will also be a special saint to intercede for our needs. God calls us by name. Our name is sacred, a revelation of our personal dignity. We deserve respect and we are obliged to respect others.

Catechism Reflection

1. What is the positive call of the second commandment?

"The second commandment enjoins respect for the Lord's name. The name of the Lord is holy" (*CCC* 2161). "Like the first commandment, it belongs to the virtue of religion and more particularly it governs the use of speech in sacred matters" (*CCC* 2142).

2. What are some deeds forbidden by the second commandment?

"The second commandment forbids every improper use of God's name. Blasphemy is the use of the name of God, of Jesus Christ, of the Virgin Mary, and of the saints in an offensive way. False oaths call on God to be witness to a lie. Perjury is a grave offence against the Lord who is always faithful to his promises" (*CCC* 2162-63).

3. What is the value of our baptismal name?

"In Baptism, the Christian receives his name in the Church. Parents, godparents, and the pastor are to see that he be given a Christian name. The patron saint provides a model of charity and the assurance of his prayer" (*CCC* 2165).

Connecting to Our Family

Here is a testimony from a father who wants his family to practice the second commandment:

"I'm so mad at Hollywood that I wouldn't even consider going to a movie where they take God's name in vain, something almost all PG, PG-13, and R-rated movies do repeatedly. My God has been so good, so faithful, and so giving that I refuse to support an industry that cuts him down. I'm mad at the television set that repeatedly curses God and portrays Christians as wimps or bigots. Ted Turner, owner of CNN and TNT, said, 'Christianity is for losers.' Because our kids feel the same, they have agreed to watch only one or two carefully selected TV shows a week.

"Anger can be a sin — but certainly not when God's reputation is as stake. Today our God is being dishonored at every turn. The money changers are everywhere. People take his name in vain repeatedly (Jesus Christ!) to sound cool or fit in with the crowd. Some don't care. Some use the church or the TV church to get rich. Anyone who loves God would be angered at such disrespect.

"Love your enemies and pray for those who persecute you. Loving God means being concerned for his honor and doing what you can to see that he is exalted, not mocked" (Dr. Joe White, Page 180, *Faith Training*, Focus on the Family Publishers, 1994).

1. How would you rate the language used in your family? Is it talk that

honors the human dignity of each member and the sacredness of God? Or does the quality of your speech share in the culture's vulgarity and blasphemy?

2. If you and your children have caught the contagion of the culture coming to you from the entertainment world (films, TV, cable, the anger and coarseness from some talk radio, and some periodicals) how can you create a process that brings you to your senses and Christian courtesy that becomes your dignity?

3. What are some initiatives you have undertaken to make your home a civilized environment and your neighborhood a wise place to raise your children? What can we all do to make our culture be a better reflection of our faith and the honor of God?

Family Prayer

Jesus, hold before us the beauty of your holy family where you and Mary and Joseph lived in the purity of an environment of faith, hope, and love. Help us to hear the tone of dignity, cheerfulness, and care with which you spoke to one another. Visualize for us the prayer that permeated your lives. Convince us that such a lovely family can exist not just at Nazareth but in our own neighborhoods. Show us how to make that possible. Deluge us with the graces that will strengthen us in this process. Remind us that your family ideal will lift us out of the present apathy and move us into the dynamic future that corresponds to your divine plan for us.

Glossary

Awe and Wonder: Awe and wonder are attitudes that draw us to God and cause us to reverence his holiness. This respect for God then flows into our reverence for the dignity of people and the sacredness of creation.

Blasphemy: Blasphemy is a wrong use of God's name, a disdain for God, and a rejection of God's love for us. We make wrong use of God's name when we perjure ourselves, take a false oath or justify cruelty, torture, enslavement, or use any form of injustice in the name of God.

Lesson 21

Eat This Bread, Drink This Cup:
The Third Commandment

Resource: *CCC* paragraphs 2168-2195

We remember how you loved us — to your death,
And still we celebrate for you are with us still.
And we believe that we will see you — when you come
In your glory Lord. We remember. We celebrate. We believe.

— Marty Haugen

Marcellino's Gift of Bread and Wine

Spanish monks of the Middle Ages loved to tell the story of *Marcellino Pan y Vino*, Marcellino of the Bread and Wine. Abandoned as a baby at the door of a monastery, Marcellino proved to be a ray of sunshine amid the gray stones and black robes of the monks. As he grew into a lively little boy, he specialized in mischief.

He tied a goat's tail to the Abbey bell. He put lizards in the salad and a frog in the cook's bed. Brother cook corrected the boy and said threateningly, "See that stairway? Never go up there. The Big Man will get you."

Naturally one day Marcellino had to go up the stairs to see who this Big Man was. He found him in a dark attic. He saw the Big Man on a Cross. The Big Man had thorns on his head, nails in his hands and feet, and pain in his face. At first Marcellino was scared, but then he became more at ease. As he gazed on the figure, he said, "You look hungry."

That night he took bread and wine from the kitchen and brought it to the Big Man. A light appeared from the Big Man's right hand. Smiling, he reached out and took the food and drink. On cold, stormy nights Marcellino brought him blankets and comforted him.

One day the Big Man came down from the Cross and sat on a chair. He took Marcellino in his arms. "What would you like to see most in all the world?" the Big Man asked. "To see my mother," said the boy. "Then you must go into a deep sleep. Close your eyes, Marcellino."

The next day, the monks looked in vain for the little boy. The cook figured it out. "He must be upstairs." Up they went. Slowly they opened the door. The room was flooded with light. Their beloved child had gone home to see his mother.

Body of Christ, Be Thou My Saving Guest

The legend of Marcellino brings home to us the connection between our celebration of the Eucharist and the practical love that should result from it. Marcellino offered Jesus bread and wine as a way of saying, "I love you and I want to take care of you." For us, his Body and Blood is Jesus' way of saying to us, "I love you and I want to take care of you."

The third commandment calls us to keep holy the Sabbath day. This is Sunday, the day Jesus rose from the dead. The Church asks us to keep Sunday holy by actively participating in the Mass. Celebrating the Eucharist is an essential way of observing Sunday.

At the Last Supper, Jesus instituted the Eucharistic sacrifice of his Body and Blood. By his divine power he made it possible for the sacrifice of the Cross and its saving graces to be present for us at every Mass. Not only the Cross, which saves us from our sins, but also the Resurrection, which gives us divine life communicated to us in the active presence of the Holy Spirit. At the Eucharist we can experience a sacrament of perfect love. In this paschal banquet, we consume Christ, are filled with grace, and receive a pledge of future glory.

In a magnificent passage, the Fathers of Vatican II tell us why we should celebrate Eucharist on Sunday (or its beginning on Saturday evening):

"The Church, therefore, earnestly desires that Christ's faithful, when present at this mystery of faith, should not be there as strangers or silent spectators. On the contrary, through a proper appreciation of the rites and prayers, they should participate knowingly, devoutly, and actively. . . . By offering the Immaculate Victim, not only through the hands of the priest, but also with him, they should learn to offer themselves too. Through Christ the Mediator, they should be drawn day by day into ever closer union with God and each other, so that finally God may be all in all" (*Constitution On the Sacred Liturgy, [SC],* 48).

Hence the Eucharist is more than a passive experience of the acts of the priest and the music of the choir. It should be an active event in which we pour out our love to God and to the members of the worshiping community. The more we concentrate on what we bring to it, the more we worship in spirit and truth and benefit from the ocean of graces that flow from the altar to our souls.

The *Catechism* begins its teaching about the third commandment with the biblical explanation of the Sabbath. In Exodus (20: 8-11), we read that the Sabbath was the seventh day on which the Lord rested after the work of creation on the previous six days. Deuteronomy chapter five, verse twelve, stresses that the Sabbath is a day to renew our covenant with God. In other words, the Sabbath is linked both to creation and covenant, two major events in the history of salvation.

The idea that God rested on the Sabbath is more than a quaint picture of God being exhausted after a tough work week, just as we are after our weekday exertions. This is a faith insight. Creation is the first act of the process of salvation. Once the work of creation was over, God began his love affair with us.

If all we do is work we shall have no time to love one another or love God. If God did nothing but work, he would (in a symbolic way of speaking) have no time to have a love relationship with us. We need a day off to nurture our love of God — and with the bonus result of renewing ourselves and our love of our family and friends.

The biblical history of Sabbath observance shows that it was a day of worship, joy, and relaxation with one's family. "Then (on the Sabbath) you shall delight in the Lord, and I will make you ride on the heights of the earth" (Is 58:14). God intended that people enjoy their day off. They should include worship in their renewal process. God wanted some "love time" with them. During their liturgies, the people looked back on their history and family roots. They praised and thanked God for his love and renewed their covenant faith. They considered their whole day holy because it reminded them of God's gifts.

As time passed the religious leaders added numerous burdens for the Sabbath. The *Book of Jubilees* forbade the marital act, lighting a fire, or preparing food on this day. The *Mishna* listed thirty-nine kinds of forbidden activities. In Christ's time the Pharisees forbade people to carry a bed, nurse a sick person, or pick a few ears of corn on the Sabbath. Jesus rejected this legalism. He preached that care for people was more important than joyless rules. "The sabbath was made for man, not man for the sabbath" (Mk 2:27). Still, Jesus respected the holiness of the Jewish Sabbath. He declared that the Sabbath was a day to love and care for others (Mk 3:4).

Sunday

Jesus rose from the dead on Sunday. That is why we make it the Christian Sabbath. Because it is so special, Sunday is called the "eighth day" — a day signifying eternity. Sunday fulfills and completes the meaning of the Sabbath because it signifies our eternal rest in God. The Sabbath recalls the first creation. Sunday remembers the "new creation in Christ." Our Sunday celebration implements our inner moral drive to give God visible, public, and regular worship. It also carries forward the Old Testament tradition of Sabbath worship, only now we adore our Creator and Redeemer. Sunday Eucharist is at the heart of the commemoration of the Lord's Day.

The practice of the Christian assembly celebrating Sunday Eucharist dates from the beginning of the Apostolic times. "We should not stay away from our assembly, as is the custom of some, but encourage one another . . ." (Heb 10:25).

The Catholic parish, shepherded by the priest under the authority of the diocesan bishop, is the ordinary setting for Sunday worship. Here we are initiated into the Church's liturgical life. We hear the saving teachings of Christ, offer Jesus to the Father, and take his saving Body and Blood into our bodies and souls. We are then missioned to love and serve the Lord and all peoples.

Not only is Sunday a day to pray, it is also a day to "play." This means it should be a day that we take time to be with one another in meals, conversation, and the deepening of family life. We all need leisure, mental, and emotional refreshment. Our batteries need to be recharged. It is also a day to uplift the spirit by acts of generous service to the sick, the old, and the needy.

Catechism Reflection

1. What does the Church require of us on Sunday?

" 'Sunday . . . is to be observed as the foremost holy day of obligation in the universal Church' (CIC, can. 1246 § 1). 'On Sundays and other holy days of obligation the faithful are bound to participate in the Mass'(CIC, can. 1247)" (*CCC* 2192).

2. What about work on Sundays?

" 'On Sundays and other holy days of obligation, the faithful are bound . . . to abstain from those labors and business concerns which impede the worship to be rendered to God, the joy which is proper to the Lord's Day, or the proper relaxation of mind and body' (CIC, can. 1247)" (*CCC* 2193).

3. How should Sunday be a day of personal renewal?

"The institution of Sunday helps all 'to be allowed sufficient rest and leisure to cultivate their familial, cultural, social, and religious lives' (*GS* 67 § 3). Every Christian should avoid making unnecessary demands on others that would hinder them from observing the Lord's Day" (*CCC* 2194-95).

Connecting to Our Family

For a long time there was a myth that the more modern a nation became, the less its people would go to religious worship. This is true for all modernized countries — except the United States. Sixty percent of Americans attend religious services regularly — a statistic that has not changed since the 1950s. The total number of Catholics attending Mass on a single weekend is greater than all the fans who go to major league baseball games in an entire season.

Studies show that Americans' voluntary giving to houses of worship amounts to $38 billion annually, a figure exceeding the gross national product of many nations. There are proportionately more houses of worship in the United States than in any other nation, one for every nine hundred Americans.

One-third of the baby boomers have remained faithful to religion since the 1960s. Of the remaining two-thirds, many dropped out of organized religion. But now more than a third of them have returned, meaning that 43 million baby boomers attend churches or synagogues. Most are married with children. For many of them, the experience of having children awakened their religious impulses and their desire to foster moral values in their children.

What are some guidelines to help families with Sunday Worship?

• Consider the Mass obligation a privilege more than a law. If we love the Mass it will cease to be a burden. Love will mean giving ourselves to the celebration more than worrying what we get out of it. We receive joy and graces in proportion to our giving of ourselves to the worship.

• The best way to love the Mass is to live the Mass. What did Jesus do at Eucharist? He took, blessed, broke, and gave us the bread and wine, made of his Body and Blood. Then on Good Friday and Easter Sunday, Jesus let the Father take, bless, break, and give him to the world. We live the Eucharist when we allow God to take, bless, break, and give us to each other and to our neighbors.

• Get a Sunday Missal and prepare the Sunday liturgy in a family setting. Go over the readings and prayers and ask each other how these beautiful texts make our lives worth living. How can we become the living words expressed by the Spirit-composed texts of Scripture?

• Go to Mass with generous hearts. Lighten up. Adopt an attitude which says, "It is a joy to sing and pray before the Lord in union with the faithful members of the community." Urge the pastor to have liturgies for children as well as those for teens. This adaptation to youth needs helps them to have a setting where their hearts can expand in a manner suited to their life stages.

• Set aside individualism and privatized ideas of religion. Catholicism is a community religion. Notice how often the pope speaks of *communio*, the Latin for community. Our faith is ignited by contact with other fervent believers. A believing assembly is more than a collection of individuals, more than the sum of the number there. Transcendence occurs. We surpass, by the power of the Spirit, mere numerical presence. Join in and form a community of faith and praise.

• Come to Mass with the idea and attitude that you are going to pray. The Mass is the greatest prayer of the Church. In times of persecution, Catholics have always said, "Nothing compares to the sense of prayer we have than at Eucharist." A prayerful attitude is one that reflects our hearts open to God and filled with a longing for him.

1. What is regular Mass attendance like in your home? If it needs improvement, what steps do you believe could be taken? If there was a decline, how did it happen? How could you use the above suggestions?

2. What are examples of Masses in your life which have brought you great joy? What helps you most to make the Mass an experience of faith and prayer? Why is Eucharist the supreme form of worship in your life?

3. How could the Sunday family meal be restored? How does your family makes Sunday a day of relaxation and renewal?

Family Prayer

Jesus, our High Priest, we love you for providing us with the celebration of the Eucharist. In faith we see you at the heavenly liturgy, as the Lamb slain and risen, standing before the Father to offer the one eternal sacrifice. In that same faith we see you at our parish church, through the presence and action of our priest, continuing on earth that one supreme act of death and Resurrection so we can be forgiven our sins, be filled with divine life, and look forward to eternal life with you. Fill us with enthusiasm for the Mass and move us to practice its message in a mission of love, service, justice, and mercy.

Glossary

Sabbath: The biblical seventh day on which God's people were expected to rest from work and praise God for the gifts of creation and covenant.

Sunday: Sunday carries forward and completes the meaning of Sabbath. Relaxation should be accompanied by participation in the Eucharist to praise and thank God for the gifts of creation and redemption and begin to savor the eternity prepared for us.

Lesson 22

All in the Family: The Fourth Commandment

Resource: *CCC* paragraphs 2196-2257

The most important thing a father can do for his children is to love their mother.

— Rev. Theodore Hesburgh

Don't Forget to Brush Your Teeth

One Sunday afternoon I looked up over the newspaper I was reading and noticed a rather distraught, unhappy look on the face of six-year-old Jonah.

"What's wrong, buddy?'

"Oh, nothing."

"You sure?"

"Yeah."

I looked back to the newspaper, but my mind wasn't on the words. I was thinking of yesterday afternoon — the soccer game and the miserable little kid who had called Jonah a "klutz."

I put down the paper and pulled Jo up on my knee.

"You know, buddy, I've been thinking a lot lately about some things you are extra good at."

"Me?"

"Yes. Do you know that you're incredibly good at being friendly to other kids?"

I went on telling him things he was extra good at. The list included, "making baby laugh," "saying your 'r's' clearly," and "remembering to brush your teeth." Jonah's whole demeanor changed before my eyes. His posture changed, his expression changed to a glow. His eyes took on a sparkle. He soaked up the praise like a dry sponge.

"Dad, let's write these down."

"Write what down?"

"Write down those things I'm good at." He wanted to preserve them, to lay claim to them.

"Where?" I said, glancing around for a piece of paper.

"Here," he said, "right here on my hand. Write with your pen on my hand all the things I'm good at."

And I did. And he didn't wash his hand until his mom made him. (Excerpted from Richard Eyre, *Teaching Your Children Values*, Simon and Schuster, NY, 1993, pp. 33-4.)

149

Honor Your Father and Your Mother

Little Jonah's father knew the child craved attention. Dad knew that all too often parents give attention to negative behavior and ignore positive deeds. The tendency is to spend all our time correcting what is wrong. Jonah's dad turned that around and caught his six-year-old "doing something right." We turn now to the fourth commandment that deals with family life.

The first three commandments explain how to love God with all our minds, hearts, and strengths. The next seven commandments show us how to love our neighbors as we love ourselves.

The fourth commandment shows us that, after God, our parents are next, in the divine order of charity, to be the focus of our love. The following commandments deal with other aspects of family life as well as relationships to our neighbor: respect for life, the role of marriage, attitudes to material goods, and the proper use of speech. Taken together, these establish the foundation of the Church's social teachings.

The fourth commandment lays out the duties of children to their parents as well as the responsibilities of adult children toward their older parents. It also refers to all those who exercise authority: teachers, leaders, judges, and all those who govern the community.

A man and a woman, bound by their marriage vows, together with their children, form a family. God is the author of marriage and the family. The institution of the family exists before any other institution. The family precedes the state, which is obliged to recognize and support it.

The Christian family is expected to be a community of faith, hope, and love. When these virtues are practiced by the parents and children, the family begins to realize its spiritual quality as a "domestic church." This family, becoming a community of love, is an image of the loving communion of the Father, Son, and Holy Spirit.

The Family and Society

The family is the basic unit of society. A healthy family means a healthy society. Family virtues, such as authority, stability, and loving relationships, are essential for a society that desires a life of freedom, security, and community awareness. Successful societies need citizens who are honest, respect one another, are disciplined, trustworthy, peaceable, faithful, chaste, loyal, dependable, loving, just, merciful, and have faith in God. All these virtues can and should be taught and practiced in the family.

The family is the school of the virtues. Society can help families achieve these goals, but society needs families that already do so. Weakened family life is a threat to society. Hence society and the state should do everything possible to provide the family with the means to achieve what families have been designed by God to accomplish.

To guide governments and other institutions of society (media, business, education, etc.), the Church has outlined a Bill of Rights for the family.

"The political community has a duty to honor the family, to assist it, and to ensure especially:

— the freedom to establish a family, have children, and bring them up in keeping with the family's own moral and religious convictions;

— the protection of the stability of the marriage bond and the institution of the family;

— the freedom to profess one's faith, to hand it on, and raise one's children in it, with the necessary means and institutions;

— the right to private property, to free enterprise, to obtain work and housing, and the right to emigrate;

— in keeping with the country's institutions, the right to medical care, assistance for the aged, and family benefits;

— the protection of security and health, especially with respect to dangers like drugs, pornography, alcoholism, etc.;

— the freedom to form associations, with other families and so have representatives before civil authorities [cf. *FC* 46]" (*CCC* 2211).

Family Duties

(1) Respect your parents. They gave you life, loved you, worked for your well-being, and helped you grow to maturity. "With you whole heart, honor your father; your mother's birthpangs forget not. Remember, of these parents you were born; what can you give them for all they gave you?" (Sir 7:27-28).

(2) Children, obey your parents. During the years of growing up, children should obey parents and accede to what is for your good and that of the family. Anticipate your parents' wishes, seek their advice, and accept their just admonitions. When you are grown up your obligation to obey ceases, but your duty to respect and revere your parents never stops. This attitude is rooted in one of the gifts of the Holy Spirit, the fear of the Lord — fear meaning reverence for the sacred bond that ties you to your parents.

(3) Become responsible grown children. Do all you can to give your parents the support they will need in their old age, be it moral or material, especially when your parents are sick or lonely.

(4) Promote family harmony. Be energetic in reducing rivalries, angers, hostilities, and hurts among brothers and sisters. Fill your home with light and warmth. Establish the possibilities of the flow of love between the generations. Support one another with patience and charity. Draw strength from the graces of your Baptism, the Eucharist, your faith, and your life in the Church.

Parental Duties

(1) Raise your children conscientiously. It is not enough simply to give birth to children. They need a lengthy nurture period — physically, spiritually, intellectually, emotionally, and morally. Care for their souls as well as their bodies. Give them every opportunity you can for a wholesome education. Oversee their moral training with diligence. All this takes a great deal of personal time on the part of both father and mother, but it means giving proper example to your children. Parental witness is a powerful form of child rearing.

(2) Emphasize the virtues. It will be hard to keep the commandments without the acquisition of virtues — grooved habits that incline the person to virtuous behavior. Children need training in virtues, through storytelling that inspires them to virtue, through good parental example, and finally through repetitive acts of virtue which ingrain these acts into their behavior and attitudes. Virtues also become the source of self-fulfillment. Children need to acquire virtues such as self-discipline, compassion, responsibility, friendliness, work, courage, perseverance, honesty, loyalty, and faith.

(3) Focus on faith. Teach your children to pray from their earliest years. Share with them the lives of the saints. Bring them to Church. Help them to feel at home in the liturgy. Encourage them to go to Confession. Emphasize the positive side of faith and help them be forgiving of the weaknesses of the Church's members. Show them how to be in touch with the Blessed Mother, the angels, and the saints and to have a personal relationship with Christ.

Civil Authorities

Civil authorities should consider their powers in terms of service to the people. Decisions should be in harmony with God's plan for humanity, the natural law, and the dignity of each person. Government leaders must do what they can to promote freedom and responsibility in the citizenry. They ought to be defenders and protectors of the family. They ought to dispense justice in a humane manner and be especially fair when dealing with the poor.

Citizens should collaborate with civic authorities for the common good of society. Submission to authority and co-responsibility for society make it morally obligatory to pay taxes, vote, and defend the country. When the governing authorities require behavior that is against the moral order, then the citizens have a moral obligation in conscience not to obey such a law. There is a distinction between serving God and the political community. ". . . repay to Caesar what belongs to Caesar and to God what belongs to God" (Mt 22:21).

Catechism Reflection

1. What is the basis of the fourth commandment?

"The conjugal community is established upon the covenant and consent of the spouses. Marriage and family are ordered to the good of the spouses, to the procreation and the education of children" (*CCC* 2249). "Children owe their parents respect, gratitude, just obedience, and assistance. Filial respect fosters harmony in all of family life" (*CCC* 2251).

2. What are the duties of parents?

"Parents have the first responsibility for the education of their children in the faith, prayer, and all the virtues. They have the duty to provide as far as possible for the physical and spiritual needs of their children. Parents should respect and encourage their children's vocations. They should remember and teach that the first calling of the Christian is to follow Jesus" (*CCC* 2252-53).

3. What are some principles that govern the relationship of citizens and society?

"Public authority is obliged to respect the fundamental rights of the human person and the conditions for the exercise of his freedom. It is the duty of citizens to work with civil authority for building up society in a spirit of truth, justice, solidarity, and freedom" (CCC 2254-55). " 'The well-being of the individual person and of both human and Christian society is closely bound up with the healthy state of conjugal and family life' (*GS* 47 § 1)" (*CCC* 2250).

Connecting to Our Family

A twelve-year-old girl came home from school one day and asked her mother, "Mom, why don't they hand out prizes for being nice?" The mother repeated her daughter's question to several of her friends. From those discussions, she put together these rules of thumb:

- Remember that child-rearing is child-loving, not a performance evaluation.
- Never ignore or belittle a child's attempt to be considerate and loving.
- Don't suggest that love is conditional upon the accomplishments of the child.
- Praise who a child is as well as what a child does.
- Scold the mischief, not the mischief-maker.
- Expect worthy standards of behavior and be lovingly firm in setting limits.

These are commonsense guidelines. They need to be supplemented with faith training. If we raise children who love Jesus, we will have a richer child-rearing approach. Faith does not get passed on like blue eyes or freckles. It must be handed from person to person, consciously and devotedly from generation to generation. Every child of God must grasp it and run the race that cannot be run by anyone else. ". . . stir into flame the gift of God. . ." (2 Tim 1:6). That is what St. Paul said to his spiritual son, Timothy. When he knew his time on earth was giving out, Paul lived and died to put the truths of faith deep into Timothy's heart, so that he could carry the fire into the next generation.

1. How would you evaluate the way the fourth commandment is a living and positive influence in your family? What areas need improvement — duties and responsibilities of children and parents? What virtues have priority in the training of your children and your own parental witness?

2. What secrets of building family community have you learned along the way? Which ones did you receive from your parents? What has been the most successful approach in building up your family?

3. When it comes to faith training, how would you grade yourself? Where do you find the most resistance? What could you do to change this?

Family Prayer

Jesus, Mary, and Joseph, we are inspired by the family witness you gave us from Nazareth. The simplicity, faith, and love you demonstrated is just what we are looking for today. The prayer that filled your home is exactly what we need now. The moral behavior that you show us is a goal that we can realize with divine help. Jesus, give us the grace of family values so that we may live out the mystery of your salvation by which you free us from our sins and flood us with divine graces. We praise you Lord, now and forever.

Glossary

Bill of Rights: A list of rights for support of the family for families, published by the Synod of Bishops in 1980. It dramatizes the highest priority the Church gives to defending and protecting the family.

Communion of Persons: The Trinity is the supreme model of the communion of persons where absolute unity and love exist. The family needs to be such a community, striving for the highest ideals of love among the members.

Lesson 23

Culture of Death; Gospel of Life:
The Fifth Commandment

Resource: *CCC* paragraphs 2258-2330

No one can arbitrarily choose to live or to die. The absolute master of such a decision is the Creator alone, in whom 'We live and move and have our being' (Acts 17:28).

— John Paul II, *Gospel of Life*

The Woman Who Gave Up Her Life for Her Baby

Margie Janovich delayed her cancer treatment during a pregnancy so that her daughter could be born a healthy infant. The mother died after a twenty-month struggle against her illness.

Margie died at age forty-four. She was five months pregnant when she was diagnosed with thyroid cancer. Her doctor told her that her treatment could end her pregnancy, so she put it off until the birth of her ninth child. She gave birth to a healthy child and so began chemotherapy, but doctors said that her unusually aggressive cancer had already spread to her breasts and the lining of her lungs. A number of different treatments failed to work.

"I would much rather give up my life for my baby," Janovich said in an interview. "Any good mother would do the same. I know there's a lot of them out there."

Until she was hospitalized for the last time, she continued looking after her six sons and three daughters, ranging in age from twenty-one-year-old Nick to fifteen-month-old Mary Beth. She taught three of her children at home.

Her husband said that someday he'll tell Mary Beth what her mother gave up so she could live.

"I'll just tell her the whole story the way it was," Ron Janovich said. "If there was a saint on earth it was she."

Love Makes the World Safe for Life

Margie Janovich's love for her unborn child protected the life of her infant and witnessed the truth of God's words in the book of Isaiah: "Can a mother forget her infant, / be without tenderness for the child of her womb?" (Is 49:15).

This is a witness to the sacredness of life so eloquently defended by Pope John Paul II in his encyclical, *The Gospel of Life*. When Jesus was born, a choir of angels filled the sky over Bethlehem and sang praises to the glory of God. An angel proclaimed that Christ's birth was an event of great joy. The source of this joy was the birth of our Savior. Christmas also reveals the meaning of every human birth. The birth of the Messiah heralds the joy we have for every child born into the world.

Jesus preached the heart of his salvation message when he said, "I came so that they might have life and have it more abundantly" (Jn 10:10). He was referring to the eternal life to which we are called by the Father, won for us by the Son, and given to us by the power of the Spirit. This eternal life bestows meaning on all the stages of human life.

The Father calls us to divine life, a vocation that reminds us how precious is our human, earthly life. Had we not received the gift of life here, we would not know the possibility of divine life hereafter. Our human lives are sacred. We must live them with responsibility and with a love for all people. With the light of reason and the hidden reality of grace, all people can come to know their personal dignity and final destiny in God.

Vatican II teaches that "By his incarnation, the Son of God has united himself in some fashion with every human being" (*Modern World*, 22). Because of this, our human lives are precious from beginning to end on earth and we have the right to have our lives respected.

This same Council document lists threats to human life forbidden by the fifth commandment. Its powerful words deserve to be quoted in full:

> "Furthermore, whatever is opposed to life itself, such as any type of murder, genocide, abortion, euthanasia, or willful self-destruction, whatever violates the integrity of the human person, such as mutilation, torments inflicted on body or mind, attempts to coerce the will itself; whatever insults human dignity, such as subhuman living conditions, arbitrary imprisonment, deportation, slavery, prostitution, the selling of women and children; as well as disgraceful working conditions, where men are treated as mere tools for profit rather than free and responsible persons; *all of these things and others like them are infamies indeed"* [emphasis added] (*Church in the Modern World*, [*GS*], 27).

All of these acts are attacks on the dignity of human beings. Worse yet, public opinion often approves of such behavior and justifies crimes against life. Some governments have decided not to punish these practices against life — and have even made them legal. *Choices that were once considered criminal have become socially acceptable.* This is a serious sign of moral decline in our modern world. Connected to this is the gradual darkening of human conscience so that increasingly, people cannot tell the difference between good and evil.

In this brief chapter we can only underline the major life issues that confront us today. We urge you to study the *Catechism's* treatment of the fifth commandment and the superb exposition of the Church's teaching on

156

life in Pope John Paul II's *Gospel of Life*. There are five life issues that command our attention: murder, abortion, euthanasia, war and the death penalty. Let us examine each of these in turn.

Murder

The biblical account of Cain's murder of Abel reveals the presence of anger and envy in all human beings. These negative attitudes have been the consequences of original sin from the dawn of human history and often lead to murder. Scripture forbids murder. ". . . do not slay the innocent and the righteous" (*RSV* Ex 23:7). Jesus forbade murder and also inner attitudes of anger, hatred, and revenge that can lead to murder. He asked us to turn the other cheek and love our enemies. Remember, at the beginning of his Passion he did not defend himself and told Peter to put away his sword.

The murder of a human being offends the dignity of the person and the holiness of the Creator. At the same time, self-defense against an unjust aggressor is permitted. In fact, self-defense is a moral duty for whoever is responsible for the lives of others and the common good.

Abortion

Ever since *Roe* v. *Wade*, no moral issue has engaged our attention more than the legalization of abortion. From the very beginning of Christianity, the Church has condemned abortion. "You shall not kill the embryo by abortion" (*Didache* 2, 2 — written about 60 A.D.). This teaching has never changed and it will not change. Abortion is ever and always contrary to the moral law. Formal cooperation in an abortion is morally wrong.

At the same time, the Church extends Christ's gift of mercy to those who have had an abortion. *Project Rachel* is a ministry extended to those mothers who have had abortions and mistakenly believe they have committed the unforgivable sin. Psychologically and spiritually, many such mothers believe they have no recourse to God's mercy. *Project Rachel* reaches out to them to restore their unity with God and to offer them whatever counseling that may be needed.

The Pro-Life movement has developed a range of services to pregnant women to help them save their child, offering them options for adoption or for raising the child themselves.

The Church teaches that the embryo "should be treated as a person from conception, . . . defended in its integrity, cared for, and healed like every other human being" (*CCC* 2323).

Euthanasia

Intentional euthanasia is murder. It is morally unacceptable. The publicity given to Dr. Jack Kevorkian's version of physician-assisted suicide and to the experiments with euthanasia in Holland appears to justify this behavior. But many state and federal courts have been ruling against the constitutional right to die. Judge Noonan of the Ninth Circuit Court over-ruled a May 1994 decision of Judge Barbara Rothenstein in *Compassion in Dying* v. *Washington State.* Judge Noonan cited five special reasons why this is wrong. Following is a paraphrased summary of his argument:

(1) We should not have physicians in the role of killers of their patients. It would perversely affect their self-understanding and re-duce their desire to look for cures for disease if killing instead of curing were an option.

(2) We should not subject the elderly and infirm to the psycho-logical pressures to consent to their own deaths.

(3) We should protect the poor and minorities from exploitation. Pain is a significant factor in the desire for doctor-assisted suicide. The poor and minorities often do not have the resources for the alle-viation of pain.

(4) We should protect all the handicapped from societal indiffer-ence and antipathy and any bias against them.

(5) We should prevent abuses similar to what has happened in the Netherlands, which now tolerates both voluntary and involuntary eu-thanasia.

Catholic moral tradition has always taught that we can discontinue medical procedures that are burdensome, extraordinary, or disproportion-ate to the outcome. The use of painkillers to alleviate the sufferings of the dying, even at the risk of shortening their lives, is morally permissible so long as death is not willed or intended.

Suicide is contrary to justice, hope, and charity and is forbidden by the fifth commandment. Serious psychological disturbances, anxiety, fear of suffering, or torture can diminish the responsibility of the one committing suicide. Can suicides achieve eternal salvation? Only God knows, the God who can provide the opportunity for repentance. The Church prays for those who have taken their lives.

War

The *Catechism* begins its treatment of war by emphasizing the need to safeguard peace. We must cherish peace in our hearts and abandon the anger and hatred that leads to wars. Peace is more than the absence of war. Peace is a process that eliminates the causes of war. Real peace is the work of justice and the effect of love. Peace can happen when we protect human rights and respect the dignity of all peoples. We need to disarm our hearts if we wish to disarm the world. " 'The arms race is one of the greatest curses on the human race and the harm it inflicts on the poor is more than can be endured' (*GS* 81 § 3)" (*CCC* 2329).

Historically, the Church has tried to mitigate the evils and horrors of war. Just because a war has started does not mean that the moral law has stopped. Genocide and ethnic cleansing are evil. Destruction of cities and their inhabitants is wrong. Wounded soldiers and prisoners of war deserve humane treatment. In paragraph 2309, the *Catechism* outlines the strict conditions for legitimate defense by military force. It concludes by saying "The power of modern means of destruction weighs very heavily in evaluating this condition" [for a just war].

When Christ rose from the dead, his first words were about peace. "Peace be with you. As the Father has sent me, so I send you" (Jn 20:21). Ultimately, peace is a gift from God. Humanly speaking, we must do all we can to achieve it. Divinely speaking, we must never stop imploring God with fervent prayer for the gift of peace.

Death Penalty

The *Catechism* teaches that governmental authority has the right and duty to punish criminals by means of suitable penalties, "and does not exclude recourse to the death penalty . . ." (*CCC* 2267). Pope John Paul II's *Gospel of Life* gives this passage of the *Catechism* a very restrictive interpretation. He says the death penalty is an extreme solution that should only be used when it would be otherwise impossible to defend so-called society. "Today, in fact, as a consequence of the possibilities which the state has for effectively preventing crime, by rendering one who has committed an offense incapable of doing harm . . . the cases in which the execution of the offender is an absolute necessity 'are very rare, if not practically non-existent' (*Gospel of Life*, 56)" (*CCC* 2267). The revision of the Catechism reflects the Pope's teaching.

The pope asks us not to dwell on a legal argument about the death penalty against the background of danger and revenge, but in the positive light of building a culture of life.

Catechism Reflection

1. Why is human life sacred?

"Every human life, from the moment of conception until death, is sacred because the human person has been willed for its own sake in the image and likeness of the living and holy God. The murder of a human being is gravely contrary to the dignity of the person and the holiness of the Creator" (*CCC* 2319-20).

2. Why is abortion wrong?

"From its conception, the child has the right to life. Direct abortion, that is, abortion willed as an end or as a means, is a 'criminal' practice (*GS* 27 § 3), gravely contrary to the moral law. The Church imposes the canonical penalty of excommunication for this crime against human life. Because it should be treated as a person from conception, the embryo must be defended in its integrity, cared for, and healed like every other human being" (*CCC* 2322-23).

3. What is our teaching about euthanasia?

"Intentional euthanasia, whatever its forms or motives, is murder. It is gravely contrary to the dignity of the human person and to the respect due to the living God, his Creator" (*CCC* 2324).

Connecting to Our Family

Mike Barnicle, a columnist for the *Boston Globe*, wrote a story in March 1997 about a woman who worked at the same abortion clinic as the woman who was slain by John Salvi. While she worked there she sterilized the trays and instruments after the abortions. The tray would have the instruments they used as well as a plastic container which was filled with formaldehyde and what they liked to call "the product of conception."

She told Mike that they were not supposed to perform abortions after twelve weeks, but it happened that some women aborted at sixteen and even twenty weeks. "This happened quite a lot." In these cases, the tray contained blood, tissue, and bone. Asked what she did with this, she said, "I'd dump it in the sink. Just like it was a disposal."

She has since left the clinic. Herself a wife and mother of three, she found her conscience would not permit her to stay there. "Tissue, bone, and blood," the woman remembered. "The first time I saw it, I said, 'Oh, my God!' And then I washed it away down the sink. I'm ashamed I actually did that. I still think about it today. It's why I quit."

Today's families need the preventive moral medicine that keeps all their members from the tragedy of abortion as well as from all the assaults on the dignity of human life, be they suicide, war, euthanasia, or the death penalty. The positive teaching of the *Catechism* about the value of human life, the need to safeguard peace, and the challenge to honor human life from conception until natural death is an inspiring moral challenge. The modern family and the needs of our culture require a wholesome, moral vision of the sacredness of human life. The choice before us is simple and direct. Do we want a culture of life or a culture of death? If there is to be a society of hope where the helpless are defended, then our choice must be for life.

1. How knowledgeable and aware is your family about the Church's teachings on life issues such as abortion, euthanasia, doctor-assisted suicide, and the death penalty? How committed is your family to a culture of life? What practical forms of life witness do you undertake?

2. What happens to a society that tolerates violence? Why did Jesus tell us that not only is murder wrong, but also hatred and revenge?

3. How are we going to evangelize our society back to a culture of life? What is the best way to train children to have a respect for the sacredness of human life?

Family Prayer

Life-giving Father, how often we have heard that we should choose and celebrate life. Yet every day we hear about murders, abortions, wars, and doctor-assisted suicides. We see the growth of the culture of death.

Dear God, help us to rebuild a culture of life. Show us how to reach out to those who would destroy life either at its inception or at its conclusion — or any where in between. May our prayers for life be constant and our efforts on behalf of life be energetic and constant. Thank you for the gift of life and may we show our gratitude by defending it.

Glossary

Abortion: Human life should be protected from the moment of conception. Abortion is the intended destruction of an unborn child and is gravely contrary to the moral law and the holiness of the Creator.

Euthanasia: Direct euthanasia is the intended killing of the sick, the dying, the elderly, or those with disabilities. It is morally unacceptable.

Suicide: Suicide, the taking of one's own life, is contrary to justice, hope, and love. Grave psychological disturbances, anxiety, fear of pain, or torture may diminish the responsibility of the one committing suicide. The Church prays for the salvation of their souls.

Lesson 24

Faithful Spouses: The Sixth Commandment

Resource: *CCC* paragraphs 2331-2400

When the night has been too lonely
and the road has been too long,
And you think that love is only
for the lucky and the strong,
Just remember — in the winter
far beneath the bitter snows,
Lies the seed, that with the sun's love,
in the spring — becomes the rose.

— Amanda McBroom

Who's the Boss?

A farmer's son decided to get married. The father said to his son, "John, when you get married your liberty is gone."

The boy said he did not believe it. The father said, "I'll prove it to you. Catch a dozen chickens, tie their legs together and put them in the wagon. Hitch up two horses to the wagon and drive into town. Stop at every house you come to, and wherever you find a house where the man is boss, give him a horse. Wherever you find the woman is boss, give her a chicken. You'll give away all your chickens and come back with two horses."

The boy accepted the proposition and drove into town. He had stopped at every house and had given away ten chickens when he came to a nice little house and saw an old man and his wife standing out on the front lawn. He called to them and asked, "Who is the boss here?"

The man said, "I am." Turning to the woman, the boy said, "Is he boss?" The woman replied, "Yes, he's boss." The boy asked them to come down to the street. He then explained the reason for asking and told the man to pick out one of the horses. He said he would bring the horse back to him that afternoon. The old man and the old lady looked over the horses carefully, and the husband said, "I think the black horse is the better of the two." The wife then said, "I think the bay horse is in every way the better horse. I would choose him."

The old man took a careful look at the bay horse and said, "I guess I'll take the bay horse."

The boy smiled and said, "No, you won't; you'll take a chicken." (From *Illustrations Unlimited*, James Hewitt, Editor, Tyndale House, Wheaton, IL, 1988, pp 336-7.)

Fidelity Is the Key to Marriage

The humorous story about who is boss in a marriage is from the standard routine in comedy about the "battle of the sexes." It is a way of saying to married people that a loving partnership is a better way of sustaining a marriage rather than striving to control one another. Unresolved friction in a marriage is often the prelude to infidelity by one or both of the spouses. The sixth commandment forbids adultery, which is a sexual act performed by a married person with someone other than one's spouse. The commandment prohibits infidelity.

On the positive side, the sixth commandment summons the spouses to practice fidelity to each other. Fidelity is the marital value that is essential for the success of the marriage. God established marriage and intended that the solemn promises made by husband and wife to be faithful to one another forever should reflect the very covenant which God has made with us.

Just as God is always faithful to his promises, so must the spouses be faithful to one another. The sacrament of Marriage enables the spouses to share in Christ's fidelity to his Church. By their marital chastity, the spouses witness this mystery to the world.

St. John Chrysostom suggests that young husbands say this to their wives:

"I have taken you in my arms and I love you, and I prefer you to my life itself. For the present life is nothing, and my most ardent dream is to spend it with you in such a way that we may be assured of not being separated in the life that is reserved for us. . . . I place your love above all things, and nothing would be more bitter or painful to me than to be of a different mind than you" *(Homily on Ephesians, 20)*.

Chastity

Related to fidelity is the virtue of chastity which is the process by which the spouses integrate their sexuality into their persons. As everyone knows, chastity demands self-mastery, especially in a culture which too often idealizes promiscuity. Chastity brings bodily sex within the broader human reality. It unites bodily sexuality with our spiritual natures so that sex is seen as more than a purely physical act. Sexuality affects every aspect of the person because of the unity of body and soul. In particular it is bonded to our emotional life and our capacity to love and procreate. Jesus is the model of chastity. Every baptized person is called to chastity according to one's state in life.

The *Catechism* places the unitive and procreative aspects of marriage under the topic of chastity. The unitive nature of marriage refers to the bond of love between the spouses. The procreative side of marriage speaks of the openness to having children and raising them spiritually in the faith as well as looking after their physical, emotional, and intellectual development.

The bond between the unitive and procreative should be inseparable and unbreakable. Sexual acts should take place only within the context of marriage. Chaste and faithful spouses will not commit adultery. Similarly, men and women religious, vowed to celibacy and consecrated virginity, must also practice chastity, meaning they must abstain from all sexual acts. Unmarried people observe chastity by continence, that is, abstinence from sexual acts. But chastity is more than that. The virtue of chastity is a form of the cardinal virtue of temperance. Chastity involves self-mastery, which is a long and exacting challenge. Chastity is also a gift from God, a grace by which the Holy Spirit conforms us to the purity of Christ. Chastity involves the gift of self by which the unmarried person can witness to others God's fidelity and living kindness.

The *Catechism* lists the following acts as opposed to chastity:

1. Lust. This is the fostering of disordered desire for sex. Jesus teaches, "You have heard it said, 'You shall not commit adultery.' But I say to you, everyone who looks at a woman with lust has already committed adultery with her in his heart" (Mt 5:27-28).

2. Masturbation. This is a deliberate stimulation of the genital organs to derive sexual pleasure. The explicit use of a sexual organ outside the marital act, for whatever reason, is morally unacceptable. Moral culpability should take into account immaturity, anxiety, habit, or other factors that may diminish responsibility.

3. Fornication. This is sexual union between unmarried men and women. It is wrong because it violates the dignity of the persons and the unbreakable bond between the unitive and procreative aspects of marriage.

4. Pornography. This is the display of sexual acts or fantasies in pictures, films, videos, stories, and other imagery — disconnected from the intimacy of the marriage act. It engenders lust and immoral sexual behavior. It corrupts the participants. Civil authorities should prevent the production and distribution of pornography.

5. Prostitution. Prostitutes sell their bodies for sex. The act degrades both the seller and the buyer.

6. Rape. Rapists and child molesters force sex on unwilling partners. This is always gravely evil and never permitted. Those who rape children (especially in cases of incest) can cause irreparable psychological harm to them.

7. Homosexuality. This is a case of sexual relations between persons of the same sex. Homosexual acts are intrinsically disordered and never permitted. The *Catechism* gives the following guideline for the attitude toward homosexual persons: "They must be accepted with respect, compassion, and sensitivity. Every sign of unjust discrimination in their regard should be avoided" (*CCC* 2358).

Adultery, divorce, polygamy, and "free union" break the promises of fidelity. Some biblical scholars note that the Hebrew word for adultery is similar to the word for idolatry. Since pagan temples in biblical times employed prostitutes, they were havens for adultery. To engage in immoral sexual acts under the sign of a false god was also to enter into a false relationship with another person. Covenant acts take place in the sight of a living and true God. Unfaithful acts occur under the sign of delusion (read *Catechism* paragraphs 2382-86 for the teaching on divorce).

Archbishop Sheen has this to say about marriage in his book *Three to Get Married*: "Fidelity in marriage means much more than abstaining from adultery. All religious ideas are positive — not negative. Husband and wife are pledges of eternal love. Their union in the flesh has a grace which prepares them for union with God. The passing of time wears out bodies, but nothing can make a soul vanish or diminish its eternal value. Nothing on earth is stronger than the fidelity of hearts fortified by the sacrament of Marriage."

Catechism Reflection

1. What did God intend in creating man and woman?

"By creating the human being man and woman, God gives personal dignity equally to the one and the other. Each of them, man and woman, should acknowledge and accept his sexual identity" (*CCC* 2393).

2. What is our teaching about birth control?

"The regulation of births represents one of the aspects of responsible fatherhood and motherhood. Legitimate intentions on the part of spouses do not justify recourse to morally unacceptable means (for example, direct sterilization or contraception)" (cf. CCC 2366-79) (*CCC* 2399).

3. What is implied by the marital covenant?

"The covenant which spouses have freely entered into entails faithful love. It imposes on them the obligation to keep their marriage indissoluble" (*CCC* 2397).

Connecting to Our Family

A father and his twenty-four-year-old son attended a wedding together. The son appeared unaffected by the ceremony until the bride and groom lighted a single candle with their candles and then blew out their own. With that he brightened and whispered, "I've never seen that done before." The father whispered back, "You know what that means, don't you?" The son smiled and said, "No more old flames?"

In *The Art of Loving*, Eric Fromm distinguished between falling in love and staying in love. He meant that the romance which accompanies falling in love does not automatically last when the couple enters marriage. Sooner or later the lover must make a decision to be bound to the beloved. Then lover and beloved must work on their marital relationship. The value of the romance is that it gave the partners a vision of the ideal marital relationship. The value of the marital decision to work on "staying

in love" means that the spouses realize it will take years of daily commitment to attain the ideal first sensed in the romantic days of courtship.

Despite the urgency of sex in a marriage, the central issue finally is
fidelity. What is at stake for staying in love is the person's capacity to be
permanently faithful to a spouse and family responsibilities in a marriage.
This drive to fidelity arises from the love between a man and a woman in
the first romantic beginnings and the "second wind" of marriage.

1. If you were to rate yourself on fidelity in your marriage on a scale of
one to ten, where would you presently find yourself? Are you relatively
satisfied? If not what can you do to change the situation for the better?

2. Why is marital fidelity so important for the stability of your children? What do you notice about the children of divorce? What can be done
to stem the tide of divorce in our country?

3. What are five positive possibilities for helping married couples stay
together and grow in fidelity to each other? Who are some couples you
admire for their fidelity? Why is it working for them? What could you
gain from their witness?

Family Prayer

Father in heaven, you are the author of marriage and willed that the
covenant of husband and wife should reflect the covenant you have established with us. Your beloved Son willed that the covenant of marriage should
reflect his own union with the Church. In these events the virtues of fidelity and chastity are paramount, Christian ideals that assure the stability of
the family and look to the welfare of children. We ask for all the virtues,
gifts, and blessings we need to fulfill these Christian ideals of marriage
and the family. Amen.

Glossary

Adultery: Sex outside of marriage involving a married person.
Fornication: Sex outside of marriage involving two unmarried persons.
Incest: Sex between close family members.
Natural Family Planning: A permissible regulation of births within cer-
tain conditions (cf. *CCC* 2366-72).
Artificial Contraception: The use of a pill or other device to prevent
conception in the marital act.

Lesson 25

Work for the Kingdom: The Seventh Commandment

Resource: *CCC* paragraphs 2401-2463

To tend the earth is our entrusted duty,
For earth is ours to use and not abuse.
Then let us serve as wise and faithful stewards,
While earth gives glory to creation's Lord.
— Omer Westendorf

The Dorothy Day Story

Dorothy Day was born in Brooklyn on November 8, 1897. Her father was a newspaper man who made a definite impression on her life. She chose journalism as a profession. She attended the University of Chicago on a scholarship for two years and enrolled in the Socialist Party because she was greatly troubled by the widespread poverty caused by the Great Depression.

Dorothy moved to New York where she continued her efforts to alleviate the appalling poverty she saw and the conditions that caused it. She took her first job at the Socialist daily paper, *The Call*, where she worked for $5 a week writing a column emphasizing the sordidness of slum living. During this period of her life, she discussed revolution with her friends, walked in picket lines, went on hunger strikes, and was jailed. In order to make a more positive contribution, she worked for a year as a probationer nurse. Disturbed and frustrated by all she saw, Dorothy wandered through Europe, back to Chicago, to New Orleans and, finally, to New York. Here, two important events happened. She joined the Catholic Church and she met Peter Maurin. She and Peter formed the basis of the Catholic Worker Movement.

They founded *The Catholic Worker* newspaper to spread the vision of a society where justice and love were possible. In three years, its circulation increased to 150,000. They also established "houses of hospitality" so that mutual aid could supplant state aid. Peter Maurin believed that charity should be personal and should not be confined to the duties of the government. Thirdly, they created farming communes to provide land and homes for the unemployed.

Peter Maurin died in 1947. He has been called the St. Francis of Assisi of modern times, for he chose to live in poverty all his life.

Under the leadership of Dorothy Day, the Catholic Worker Movement continued to do good for those in need, to give a vision to the working class, and to create a meaningful synthesis of the Gospel and social values.

You Shall Not Steal

Dorothy Day put into practice the social teachings of the Church. She exemplified the Church's teaching that God intended the goods of the earth to be for the benefit of all people. The *Catechism* calls this principle the universal destination of the goods of the earth. God made human beings the stewards of the earth's goods. We also have the right to private property which supports our dignity and freedom and helps families meet their basic needs. This right to private property does not abolish the universal destination of goods.

The *Catechism's* treatment of the seventh commandment deals with the question of stealing and then the broader issue of the Church's social teaching.

It is well known that the seventh commandment forbids stealing. Theft is taking someone's money or property against the reasonable will of the owner. We should acquire the virtues of moderation, justice, and solidarity in order to keep this commandment. Moderation curbs our attachment to worldly goods. Justice helps us respect our neighbor's rights. Solidarity is another name for the Golden Rule, "Do unto others as you would have them do unto you."

In a special way, we should have solidarity with the poor, the alien, the widow, and the orphan. The helpless need us and deserve our compassion. Helping the poor is a witness of love and a work of justice pleasing to God.

We should not steal from one another, cheat in business, pay unfair salaries, or exploit people's weaknesses or distress to make money. Promises and contracts should be made and kept in good faith and with fairness.

Social Teachings

The *Catechism* explains the Church's social teachings in two major sections: in section one of part three, paragraphs 1877-1948 where it reflects on the person and society, the common good, and social justice; and in article seven in section one of part three, the seventh commandment.

Of special note under the seventh commandment are paragraphs 2419-49. Here the *Catechism* teaches that Christian Revelation calls for a deeper understanding of the laws of the social order. The Church has a duty to render a moral judgment on economic and social issues when the fundamental rights of the person and the salvation of souls are at stake. The social teaching of the Church proposes principles for making such judgments and guidelines for social action. The Church must maintain an interest in the temporal common good of every human being because people are destined for God — what happens to people here affects their final goal. We must help all people on their journey to God, honoring and en-abling their dignity here and their destiny hereafter.

The Church makes clear that the moral law opposes any behavior that enslaves human beings or the buying and selling of them as though they were merchandise. Social teachings make a connection between the mineral, vegetable, and animal resources of the earth and the moral responsibility to use them wisely for people today and generations to come.

"Man is himself the author, center, and goal of all economic and social life" (*CCC* 2459). God has intended that the goods of the earth should be available for every person in a just and loving manner. The value of work proceeds from the human person who is both the author of work and its beneficiary. When we work we share in the very processes of creation. When we unite our labors with Christ's intentions for us, our efforts can be redemptive because Christ wills it so.

For more than a century the popes have been active in developing the Church's social teachings in the light of problems caused by the industrial revolution and the technological revolution which is upon us now. Pope John XXIII taught that peace will come more easily when people are treated justly. Pope Paul VI argued that the rich nations of the world have a responsibility to help the poor ones. Pope John Paul II has said that the state has an essential obligation to assure that workers can enjoy the fruits of their labors. While the state has an obligation to protect human rights in the economic sector, the primary responsibility for this belongs to the institutions, groups, and associations that make up a society.

St. Rose of Lima says, "When we serve the poor and the sick, we serve Jesus. We must not neglect our neighbor, because it is Jesus whom we serve."

Catechism Reflection

1. What does the seventh commandment say about stealing?

"Theft is the usurpation of another's goods against the reasonable will of the owner. Every manner of taking and using another's property unjustly is contrary to the seventh commandment. The injustice committed requires reparation. Commutative justice requires the restitution of stolen goods" (*CCC* 2453-54).

2. Why does the Church have social teachings?

"The Church makes a judgment about economic and social matters when the fundamental rights of the person or the salvation of souls requires it. She is concerned with the temporal common good of men because they are ordered to the sovereign Good, their ultimate end" (*CCC* 2458).

3. What is the human dimension in social teaching?

"Man is himself the author, center, and goal of all economic and social life. The decisive point of the social question is that goods created by God for everyone should in fact reach everyone in accordance with justice and with the help of charity" (*CCC* 2459).

Connecting to Our Family

Luke's Gospel (16:19-31) tells the story of a rich gourmet who loved dressing up in expensive clothing and eating splendid meals every day. A homeless man, named Lazarus, sat at the rich man's door hoping to get some scraps that fell from his table. The rich man dried his hands on hunks of bread and threw them on the floor. Lazarus' body was covered with sores and he was too weak to push away the dogs that came to lick his sores and compete for the discarded scraps of bread.

The scene suddenly changes from this world to the next. Lazarus died and went to heaven. The rich man died and went to hell. What was the rich man's sin? He never ordered the unsightly Lazarus to go away. He never did anything explicitly cruel to him. He never grumbled about him.

The rich man's sin was that he never *noticed* Lazarus. The pain of the poor man never touched him. He just took it for granted that he should sit at a table piled with food while a poor man groveled for a bite that might fall from it. The rich man's sin was not what he did, but what *he did not do.* His indifference to human pain cast him into hell.

In a Christian family everyone should acquire a social conscience. This means having compassion for the poor, providing food, money, and clothing for the needy. This also includes political advocacy on behalf of the helpless to see that just laws be passed on their behalf. Third, it means that social institutions — businesses, schools, and hospitals — should generously reach out to help the poor. The family is the first school of generosity. It is in giving that we receive.

At another level, families are places where the other teaching of the seventh commandment should be implemented, namely, the prohibition against stealing. Children need training in moderation, justice, and charity. Moderation tempers attachment to worldly goods. Justice causes respect for other's property and goods. Charity inspires giving rather than taking. Restitution for stolen goods should be taught and accepted.

1. How do you help you family to repudiate all forms of stealing: theft, cheating, burglary, mugging, breach of contracts, etc.? What virtues will help your family remain honest, hardworking people?

2. What forms of generosity to the poor and helpless are regular practices in your family? What opportunities are available to you for volunteering at homeless shelters, food pantries, or similar charitable endeavors?

3. How do you see yourselves responding to the Church's social teachings? What political advocacy have you undertaken on behalf of the poor and helpless? How could you come to know the church's social teachings more adequately?

Family Prayer

Generous Father, you have placed us at the table of abundance which is the goods of the earth. You have taught us that all these goods area meant for the benefit of every human being. You also give us the right to private property so our families can live in human dignity and have the stability we need for achieving proper goals here and eternal life hereafter. At the same time you call our attention to the needs of the poor and helpless. They are our brothers and sisters and need our generosity and concern. Fill us with the courage and wisdom to keep their needs before us and do what we can to help them.

Glossary

Social Teachings of the Church: Refers specifically to the papal teachings about social morality applied to a world where the industrial and technological revolutions raise issues about wealth, poverty, and human dignity. Beginning with Pope Leo XIII's *Rerum Novarum* and into the present, these teachings form a body of developing guidance about social justice.

Universal Destination of the Goods of the Earth: This is a principle of social teachings which states that God has made the goods of creation for the benefit of every human being. People need these goods to maintain their human dignity, to provide for their families, and to achieve fulfilling goals on earth and eternal life hereafter.

Lesson 26

The Truth Shall Make You Free: The Eighth Commandment

Resource: *CCC* paragraphs 2464-2513

Truth is the secret of eloquence and of virtue, the basis of moral authority. It is the highest summit of art and life.

— Henri-Frederic Amiel

If I Stay Silent, I Am Damned

One of the most popular musicals of our times is *Les Misérables*, based on Victor Hugo's great novel. In one scene Jean Valjean, the fugitive and former convict whose life has been changed by the love and generosity of a bishop, learns that another man who resembles him has been apprehended for his crime and is about to go on trial.

The other man is a drifter and lives on the margins of society, while Jean Valjean has become a wealthy and important man on whom many people depend. He sings a song about the agony of his conscience: "If I come forward, I am condemned. If I stay silent, I am damned." Then he steps forward, saving the other man and preserving his own integrity.

A teen boy was asked what he liked best about the show. "The part about the conscience," he said. "Jean Valjean did what was right. He told the truth, and that's the reason everything worked out in the end."

You Shall Not Bear False Witness Against Your Neighbor

The Bible teaches that God is the source of truth. Jesus Christ said, "I am the way and the truth. . ." (Jn 14:6). Jesus embodied truth and always told the truth. At the beginning of his Passion, Jesus was brought before Pilate where the issue of truth came to the fore. In John 18:33 Pilate asked Jesus, "Are you a king?" Jesus replied that his kingdom was a spiritual one, not a political realm.

A born politician always interested in power, Pilate pressed Jesus on the issue of kingship. So Christ's kingdom is spiritual. Does that mean he is king of such a realm? Jesus explained he is the king of truth. His role as king was to witness to the truth.

At the Last Supper, Jesus identified himself with truth. When Jesus spoke of truth, he included the truth of his teachings and his personal fidelity to God and others. Jesus personalized truth. Truth is attainable and it can be taught and learned. The mind can acquire truth from Revelation as well as from using one's intelligence. Truth is truth whether it comes from God or from our minds.

A spiritual kingdom is based on truth. When Jesus witnessed truth, he showed how much he loved us. Truth in the mind is an idea. Truth in the heart is love. A spiritual life is possible for us because it flows from truth. This is why the Church always stresses doctrine — the truth of Christ's teaching — as well as valid philosophy which affirms that the truth can be known.

Relativism in our modern culture claims there is no truth, only opinions that are more or less credible. Is it surprising then that so many people feel free to lie? Is it remarkable that many people, even Church members, downplay or ignore the Church's teachings? If doctrine is just another opinion among many in the "marketplace of ideas," then the truth of doctrine will be avoided. If we undermine the reality of truth, then we will sabotage the reality of the spiritual life. If we deny the possibility of knowing truth, then we will fail to enter Christ's spiritual kingdom which is based on truth.

As Jesus gazed on Pilate he saw a man trapped in pure pragmatism. He'd encountered a ruler whose philosophy was, "To be personal is to be political." Pilate relied on compromise, power plays, ruthless action, pretense, vanity, show, and survival. He politicized his thinking to the point that his brain was virtually dead when faced with the possibility of truth. He could not believe people really lived by truth and would even die to defend it. Pilate would become one of history's best remembered relativists.

Jesus reached out to him and offered him the hope of change. But all Pilate could do was to revert to form and mumble his cynical question, which the world has never forgotten:

"What is truth?" (Jn 18:38).

Christian martyrs know what truth means. They did not shed their blood for a lie. They surrendered their lives to stand up for truth. They showed themselves true in deeds, truthful in words. The last thing that would ever come to their minds would be duplicity, hypocrisy, or deceit. The records of the martyrs form an archive of truth whose text is written in letters of blood.

What Are the Various Ways We Sin Against the Truth?

We have found many paths to lying: ruining the reputation of a neighbor by lies, rash judgment, detraction, perjury, calumny. Liars murder more than truth. Liars kill souls and even bodies. Hitler's book, *Mein Kampf*, proclaimed the value of lying. He argued that big lies work better than small ones. Hitler's lies about the superiority of the Aryan race and the supposed danger posed by the Jews led to the Holocaust and the worst war in history. Lies violate the virtue of truthfulness. Every offense against truthfulness demands reparation.

The right to know the truth is not absolute. Charity and justice govern what may be communicated. People's safety, respect for privacy, and the common good are reasons for being silent or using discreet language about what should not be known. What is told to the priest in Confession may never be revealed by the confessor under any pretext. The seal of Confession is inviolable.

Similarly, professional secrets must be kept. Politicians, soldiers, doctors, lawyers, psychologists, and others in similar positions who receive confidences should preserve confidentiality. The trustworthiness of professional people is at stake as well as the principle of keeping secrets confided under a seal of trust. In our personal relationships, where gossip arises or nosy people want to know more than they should, we should practice reserve and protect others from such intrusion on their personal lives.

The mass media have acquired enormous influence in shaping public opinion. Journalists, editorial writers, and TV personalities such as talk show hosts should remember their responsibilities to justice, charity, and truth. As users and consumers of mass media, we should not mindlessly take in all we are fed. We must be actively engaged in looking for truth and use our critical faculties toward what we read and see. Parents need to protect their children from unhealthy and immoral influences and teach the young how to tell the difference between truth and lies, between fact and propaganda.

Truth works better than lies for the good of the family and society. Journalists and entertainers should get beyond the superficial need to shock, scandalize, and degrade by appealing to sex and violence. Just tell the truth and use imagination to build up the virtues that make for wholesome families and a healthy society. Politicians will lose the trust of people if they persist in half truths, evasiveness, and manipulation of people. Business leaders who want a loyal workforce will succeed more by being honest with employees than by bulldozing them with misinformation. Spouses will have better marriages when they insist on being truthful with each other.

The *Catechism* has an inspiring final section on the eighth commandment dealing with the connection between truth and beauty. Real art is truthful. True art invites us to contemplation of the beauty of God and the divine reflection in creation and human beings. Art expresses beauty in a language that is beyond words. In its best expression, art touches the depths of the human heart, exalts the soul, and opens the person to the mystery of God.

Catechism Reflection

1. What is lying?

"Lying consists in saying what is false with the intention of deceiving one's neighbor. Respect for the reputation and honor of persons forbids all detraction and calumny in word or attitude. An offense committed against the truth requires reparation" (*CCC* 2508, 2507, 2509).

2. Should we preserve confidences?

" 'The sacramental seal is inviolable' (CIC, can. 983 § 1). Professional secrets must be kept. Confidences prejudicial to another are not to be divulged" (*CCC* 2511).

174

3. What is the right of society regarding information?

"Society has a right to information based on truth, freedom, and justice. One should practice moderation and discipline in the use of the social communications media" (*CCC* 2512).

Connecting to Our Family

A young woman was sunning herself on a beach when a little boy in swim trunks came up to her and asked her, "Do you believe in God?" She was surprised by the question, but replied, "Why, yes, I do." Then he asked her, "Do you go to church every Sunday?" Again her answer was, "Yes." He went on, "Do you read your Bible and pray every day?" Once more she said, "Yes." She wondered what he was getting at. The boy smiled and said, "Will you hold my dollar while I go swimming?" He felt he could trust her.

Trust is the social glue that holds us together. We have trust when we experience others consistently telling us the truth. A family must have trustworthy members. That means that all the members must have the virtue of truthfulness. Someone has said, "We are as sick as our secrets." They could add, "We are as sick as our lies." When the ideal of truth penetrates the home, the security of trust is prevalent.

The young need help not only to tell the truth but also to learn how to tell facts from propaganda and truth from lies as they process the flow of information coming to them from TV, the Internet, radio, and newspapers. The quest for truth begets the habit of honesty.

1. What methods do you employ to assure an environment of truth telling in your home? Who is the most honest person you ever met? What was the secret of that person's trustworthiness?

2. When confronted with a lie, what do you do? When invited to share a confidence that should not be communicated, how do you act? What would you do when you came across a confidence betrayed?

3. How do you help your young people be truthful? What can you do to train the young to evaluate TV programs, Internet data, and other sources of information?

Family Prayer

Holy Spirit of truth, give us the gift of honesty. Show us how to tell the truth with simplicity of heart. Remind us that trust is the glue that holds our family together. Help us meditate on Jesus, who both taught the truth and embodied the truth in his life. Instill in us the moral courage that will make truth an act of integrity in our daily behavior.

Glossary

Relativism: Theory that one cannot know truth, only opinions.
Subjectivism: Similar to relativism. The subject is the individual who re-

lies on oneself alone as the source of right and wrong, true and false, good and bad. This person does not subscribe to objective truths whether from Divine Revelation or from reason.

Truth: In the order of Revelation, truth is found in Scripture, Apostolic Tradition, and the Magisterium of the Church — guided by the Spirit. In the human order, truth can be acquired by the light of reason.

Lesson 27

Blessed Are the Pure of Heart:
The Ninth Commandment

Resource: *CCC* paragraphs 2514-2533

Holy in body, simply beautiful in soul.
Pure in spirit, sincere in intelligence,
Perfection in senses, pure of heart and loyal,
Mary possesses all the virtues.

— St. Ephrem of Syria

Susanna's Story

... From the Book of Daniel, Chapter Thirteen

Raised as a devout Jewish daughter, Susanna married a man named Joakim. Two local judges were friends of the young couple and often visited their home. During the afternoon siesta, Susanna, accompanied by two maids, liked to walk in her garden. The judges looked at her lustfully and noted her afternoon custom. At first they kept their unchaste feelings about her to themselves.

One day they left for their separate ways, only to turn back. They met each other in the garden and confessed their lust for the woman. They plotted a means to corner Susanna when she was alone.

The opportunity arose when she decided to bathe in the lake. She disrobed and sent her maids on an errand. When the maids departed the judges approached Susanna. "Look, we are alone with you. No one can see us. Give in to our desires. If you refuse, we will testify against you that you deliberately wanted to be alone so you could have sex with a handsome young man we saw here with you."

Susanna immediately realized her dilemma. Who would believe her rather than these "respectable" judges? If she refused, she would be stoned to death for adultery. If she agreed she would incur spiritual death through the loss of her chastity. She decided her chastity was more important than her life.

The judges aroused the household and accused her of adultery. The trial was held the following day. The judges recited their false story about her and sentenced her to death. Susanna prayed to God in a loud voice, protesting her innocence and begging for deliverance.

Daniel heard her plea and came to her defense. He asked permission to examine the judges. He questioned them separately. "Under which tree did you see Susanna and the young man?" One judge said, "Under a mastic tree." The other said, "An oak tree." Daniel reported their contradictory testimony and exposed them as liars.

The people praised God for protecting Susanna and her chastity. They stoned the judges to death for their lust and deceit.

You Shall Not Covet Your Neighbor's Wife

The real issue in the Susanna story is the state of the heart — purity in her case, lust in that of the judges. The sixth commandment deals with external acts of fidelity, chastity, adultery, and allied sins. The ninth commandment looks to the internal attitudes of the human heart in areas of purity and lust.

The state of the human heart determines the morality of the person. Jesus taught that "out of the heart come evil thoughts, murder, adultery, fornication. . ." (*RSV* Mt 15:19). The sixth beatitude emphasizes the need for a pure heart for personal happiness. "Blessed are the pure in heart, for they shall see God" (*RSV* Mt 5:8).

God's holiness demands that our minds and wills should excel in charity, chastity, and the love of truth that includes the content of faith. There is an essential connection between purity of heart, body, and faith. Those enslaved by a lustful heart and impure behavior will find it hard to accept the truths of faith. This is the wisdom contained in the conversation between a penitent and a confessor: "Father, I'm having problems of faith." "What is her name, my son?" There is often a moral cause for a doctrinal doubt. Sin in the heart can beget disbelief in the mind.

The Modern Struggle for Purity

Some people connect concupiscence exclusively with the rebellion of the sexual passions against the dictate of right reason. But concupiscence is a general movement of all passions and emotions toward some created good without respect for — or subordination to — reason. Catholic faith tells us that man was created exempt from concupiscence. Original sin removed this exemption. The Council of Trent taught that concupiscence is not of itself sinful, but results from and inclines us toward sin. One experience of concupiscence is what St. Paul called the war of the flesh against the spirit.

This is not to say the flesh is intrinsically bad or that the passions are evil in themselves. It basically means that our minds and wills, informed by faith and strengthened by grace, must keep the passions under control. We must redirect these potentially self-destructive energies to more positive and virtuous goals.

Baptism purifies us from all our sins, but the effects of original sin remain. Our minds find it hard to know the truth. Our wills are weak. Our passions are strong. This is why we must pray for the gift and virtue of purity that helps us love God with an undivided heart and treat others with reverence for their personhood, never treating them as objects, always as persons.

God's grace will give us a purity of intention by which we see clearly what God has planned for us and take the means to achieve the goal which God intends for us. We must learn to pray for purity and see it as a gift just as St. Augustine did. "I thought that continence arose from one's own powers, which I did not recognize in myself. I was foolish enough not to know . . . that no one can be continent unless you grant it. For you would surely have granted it if my inner groaning had reached your ears and I with firm faith had cast my cares upon you" (*Confessions*, 6, 11, 20).

It has always been known that modesty is needed to be pure. Modesty is a form of the virtue of temperance or self-restraint. This is the very opposite of the worldly axiom, "Let it all hang out." The modest person refuses to reveal what should be hidden. The current fashions tease and torment and seduce, the very opposite of what a modest dress code would be like. Modesty also includes how we look at one another with our eyes, how we touch each other, how we act.

Modesty protects the mystery of the human person so that we do not exploit one another. Such an attitude introduces patience and reserve in our approach to each other. There is neither an unbecoming stripping of ourselves nor of the other. It becomes mutually understood that we are committed to the conditions of intimacy that are laid down by our very natures due to God's natural law implanted in our hearts as well as the principles of sexual activity laid out in Revelation — in other words, the absolute connection between sexual behavior and the marital state.

The ideal of modesty is sorely challenged in a culture which has become so sexualized that it soon is taken for granted that is the way it should be. The thousands of sexual stimulants bombarding everyone each day in the ads in the papers and magazines, the visuals on TV, the movies, and on the Internet assail the spiritual and moral sensibilities of every living person. This environment of indecency challenges all men and women of faith and good will to choose modesty, and to undertake the purification of a culture gone mad.

The permissive culture is based on a false premise of human freedom. It says we are free to do what we want. It should say we are free only to do what we should. We must not be discouraged. The Gospel was first preached to a permissive culture and won the day. The Gospel can renew and purify our decadent culture and remove what increases the attraction of sin. We must reassert the Gospel by word and witness so that we may elevate the morality of our culture and take the potential virtues in the human heart and make them blossom by restoring them to Christ.

Catechism Reflection

1. What does the ninth commandment require?

"The ninth commandment warns against lust or carnal concupiscence" (*CCC* 2529).

2. How shall we struggle against carnal lust?

"The struggle against carnal lust involves purifying the heart and practicing temperance" (*CCC* 2530).

3. What does purity of heart need?

"Purification of heart demands prayer, the practice of chastity, purity of intention and of vision. Purity of heart requires the modesty which is patience, decency, and discretion. Modesty protects the intimate center of the person" (*CCC* 2532-33).

Connecting to Our Family

Advertising gives all of us three thousand "shots" a day. A large number of these appeals use sex to sell the product. The social climate for raising a family is toxic. The moral antibiotic is modesty, purity, and discipline. The more that like-minded families band together to create a chaste counterculture, the healthier our children are going to be. Here are a few pointers that every family can practice to create the chaste counterculture:

(1) Thou shalt dress modestly. There is a way to remain fashionable and modest at the same time. People speak of the "classic cut" which survives amid all the vagaries of fashion. Hence this suggestion is not meant to make family members look like "Miss Early America of 1912." Clothing makes a statement. If our clothes are intentionally seductive, then a wrong signal is being given. If they are quietly modest, whether formal or informal, then the signal is, "I respect you; I respect myself."

(2) Thou shalt speak with imagination. Virtually every young person is getting a relatively good education today; a great many even obtain college degrees. The potential for speaking good, appealing English is greater than ever. It takes imagination to find new words and fresh expressions to say what we want to say. The experience delights the speaker and listener. The habit precludes reliance on vulgarity, sexual curses, and other refuges into degrading what should be a noble future in marriage.

(3) Thou shalt listen to good music. This can include pop music and modern musical forms as well as the classics. Music sends powerful emotional messages. Why not listen to that which enhances love without immediate sexual gratification; music that inspires us to treat each other as persons and not objects of violence and degradation; music that is romantic without bullying the young into premature relationships?

(4) Thou shalt acquire "visual literacy." This refers to movies, TV, and the Internet. If young people banded together and formed a civil rights movement for youth and issued a statement that they would no longer support the trash (in both violence and sex) that is fed to them by the popular media, it would not take long for the producers to get the point. There was a time when films were both entertaining and modest. It's not an impossible ideal. It is a dream that can be recaptured.

(5) Thou shalt save sex for marriage. Virginal purity in both men and women is an attainable ideal. It was done by cultures for centuries. It can be done again. There is nothing so new about our culture that it automatically demands the breakdown of morality. Cultural changes have occurred time and time again. Permissiveness has often accompanied such changes in the past, but people came to their senses and returned to the classical religious and moral virtues. We are not helpless. We are simply being sold a bill of goods that we do not have to buy.

1. How is modesty practiced in your household? What expectations do you have about clothing, music, language, TV, movies, and the Internet? What success stories from other families have been helpful to you?

2. If you were able to create a neighborhood that supports your family values, what would you require? What help in this matter do you expect from your parish family? How can the Church be your partner in producing a chaste culture?

3. What is the greatest obstacle to chastity that you see today? What is the relationship between chastity and marriage?

Family Prayer

Jesus most pure, bring to our family the gift of chastity and modesty. Help us to resist the allurements of lust that comes to us from so many parts of the culture. Help us also to overcome the rebellion of our inner passions. Draw us to meditate on your example, that of your Blessed Mother, and all the saints. Open us to realize that your divine assistance is essential for our self-conquest.

Glossary

Chastity: Bodily chastity means abstaining from sex outside of marriage. For spouses it means no sex with anyone else. Chastity of heart means overcoming sexual lust for anyone because lust degrades, dehumanizes, and exploits the other for one's own selfish pleasure. Married and unmarried people (priestly and religious celibates, singles, widows, and widowers) should have chastity of heart.

Lesson 28

Stop Taking and Start Giving: The Tenth Commandment

Resource: *CCC* paragraphs 2534-2557

If I were a rich man, da, da, da . . . . If I were a wealthy man.
— Fiddler on the Roof

What's a Rich Man to Do?

In Matthew, chapter nineteen, a rich young man comes to Jesus to discuss eternal life.

"Teacher, what good must I do to gain eternal life?"

"Why do you ask me about the good? If you wish to enter eternal life, keep the commandments."

"Which ones?"

"Don't kill. Don't commit adultery. Don't steal. Honor your parents. Love your neighbor as you love yourself."

"I keep these commandments. What else do I need?"

"If you want to be perfect, sell your possessions and give the money to the poor. Then come and follow me."

The young man is a spiritual seeker. He knows there is a connection between moral goodness and a fulfilling spirituality. He knew the commandments and kept them, but he needed to be in touch with someone who could witness and reveal their fuller meaning. He is attracted by Jesus and presents him with the perennial questions about good and evil.

Jesus first points the young man to God, the source and model of all goodness. The eternal God is one who loves and gives. To have eternal life, the young man must do more than keep the commandments in a mechanical way. He should adopt the inner attitudes and virtues that are embodied in the commandments. He must identify with God and be totally committed to Christ. To be perfect, he must sell all and follow Jesus.

He is unable to do that. Confronted with the challenge to be as generous as God, he realizes how tied he is to his wealth. He refused Christ's challenge because he had great possessions. He loved things more than he loved people. He loved himself more than he loved others. Trapped by these choices, he could not give himself to Jesus. "He went away sad, for he had many possessions" (Mt 19:22).

Not Anything That Belongs to Your Neighbor

The rich young man exemplifies the reason for having the tenth commandment. Every human being faces the choice either to be greedy or to have a generous heart. Money is not the root of all evils. "The *love* of money is the root of all evils. . ." [emphasis added] (1 Tm 6:10). The seventh commandment deals with the external acts of stealing, envy, and injustice. The tenth commandment deals with the inner attitudes of greed and envy on the one hand and of generosity and giving on the other.

Our sinful inclinations lead us to envy what others have and to give in to an unrestrained desire to amass material goods. We are born with a legitimate desire to obtain what we need to survive and take care of our families. But here we deal with a disordered expansion of such a desire. It has gotten out of hand. The greedy person will violate all laws of reason or justice to get money or property. Worse yet, such a person will then sin further to keep what has been gained and may use money and possessions to commit other kinds of sins.

The *Catechism* establishes a close connection between greed and envy. Envy is an act of sadness at the sight of others' goods and can result in a disordered desire to acquire them for oneself, even if unjust means are necessary to do so. It is a tightening of the heart and a refusal of love. Baptized people should counter envy with a spirit of detachment and greed with a habit of generosity.

The tenth commandment needs the light of the first Beatitude about poverty of spirit for its proper practice. The poor in spirit have learned that the ultimate and most worthy end of human desire should be God. The first Beatitude calls us to be poor in spirit and preserves us from the dangers of riches, worldly honor, and useless vanity.

Catechism Reflection

1. What is forbidden by the tenth commandment?

"The tenth commandment forbids avarice arising from a passion for riches and their attendant power" (*CCC* 2552).

2. What is envy?

"Envy is sadness at the sight of another's goods and the immoderate desire to have them for oneself. It is a capital sin. The baptized person combats envy through good-will, humility, and abandonment to the providence of God" (*CCC* 2553-54).

3. What should be our attitude to wealth?

"Detachment from riches is necessary for entering the Kingdom of heaven" (*CCC* 2556).

Connecting to Our Family

In his book *Small is Beautiful*, E. F. Schumacher has this to say about the problems generated by greed and envy:

I suggest that the foundations of peace cannot be laid by universal prosperity, in the modern sense, because such prosperity, if attainable at all, is attainable only by cultivating such drives as greed and envy, which destroy intelligence, happiness, serenity, the peaceableness of man. It could well be that rich people treasure peace more highly than poor people, but only if they feel utterly secure — and this is a contradiction in terms. Their wealth depends on making inordinately large demands on limited world resources and thus puts them on an unavoidable collision course — not primarily with the poor (who are weak and defenseless) but with other rich people.

No one is really working for peace unless he is working primarily for the restoration of wisdom.

In our study of the commandments we have stressed repeatedly that they hold up for us a virtue to acquire as well as a vice to avoid. Within the family there is the opportunity to learn a healthy freedom regarding material goods. When there is a generous spirit of sharing, there is a corresponding decline in envy. When a giving attitude prevails, then the members cease to think about taking. When family members find true enjoyment in one another, the hunger for things is less frantic. The consumer culture will keep breeding greed, but a Christian family ethic of sharing and giving is a powerful defense against this and a positive contribution to society.

1. If envy were out of control in your home, what would you do to turn the situation around? What family rules do you have to contain a greedy and avaricious attitude? How do you cope with our consumer culture?

2. What experiences have you had of families that were ruined by a gross attachment to material possessions? What families do you admire for their simple lifestyle? How did they achieve it?

3. How successful is your family in giving of their time, talent and treasure to others in need? How do you think people come to know the "joy" of giving? What does the prayer of St. Francis mean when it says, "It is in giving that we receive"?

Family Prayer

Generous God, you have poured your abundance into creation for our benefit. You have given each of us the potential for happiness so long as we use your gifts for the purpose you had in mind. Help our family to put aside all envy and greed and replace these attitudes with those of generosity and selfless giving. Save us from the materialism of our culture and raise us on the food of higher virtues. Teach us to practice the maxim that it is in giving that we receive.

Glossary

Covetousness: Another name for greed. Usually refers to a selfish and unrestrained desire and effort to acquire material wealth and the power that comes with it.

Love of Money: Money alone does not corrupt us. It is the *love* of money that generates envy and greed which leads to power and domination over others.

Chapter Four

Christian Prayer

Virtues
— by Raphael

Lesson 29

Real Prayer Arises From Our Hearts

Resource: *CCC* paragraphs 2558-2758

It is not a carol of joy or glee, but a prayer that he sends forth from his heart's core. I know why the caged bird sings.

— Paul Laurence Dunbar

I Learned From A Wildflower

One day, while walking in early spring in a remote part of the woods, I stopped to pick a wildflower. As I gazed at its delicate beauty, a quiet awe filled my soul. I found myself saying, "You are so beautiful, and yet no one would have appreciated you if I did not notice you." As I dropped the flower, a thought crossed my mind, "You never stopped to admire a flower before and certainly never talked to a flower." Still, that quiet awe continued to bring a delicate joy to my being. I found myself humming a tune.

Some weeks later I was involved in a time of reflective prayer. I asked the question, "Lord, when were you trying to speak to me this past month?" I reviewed my calendar and reflected on the many ways God had touched me. I listed forty items. None of them struck me as the key moment.

Then I remembered the moment with the flower. The Lord spoke, "That quiet awe was Me. I was trying to tell you, 'It's all right to be a flower in the woods.' "

I am a bishop. I have a schedule full of activities — work for the Church, for the Lord. I was not accustomed to think of myself as a flower in the woods. I seldom regard myself as one of his masterpieces. To the contrary, I acted as if I needed to earn God's love.

Now, like sunshine breaking through the clouds. God's light broke the shadows of my spiritual blindness. I realized that God is pleased with me just the way I am because He loves all of His creation, especially humans. We have the glory of reflecting his image and likeness. Before that moment, I could usually point to some activity every day that I thought pleased God. Now I saw that my activity does not make me beautiful. God makes me beautiful. This has made a colossal difference in my life — including my prayer life.

Reflective moments like that are common in my life now. I try to pray this way at least twenty minutes each day. For the past nine years I have kept a daily record of my reflections.

— Bishop Joseph McKinney

God Calls Us to Prayer

What is prayer?

In prayer we raise our minds and hearts to God and ask for the good things we need.

Our prayer is Trinitarian. The One God calls us to prayer. The Father gives us renewed life in our prayer. The Son advances our salvation. The Spirit increases our holiness.

Our prayer should arise from the *heart*. The word *heart* appears one thousand times in the Bible. What does this mean? The *Catechism* lists seven qualities of heart prayer. It happens where I live in the deepest part of myself. It is beyond reason, though not opposed to it. Prayer is more than thinking deep and inspiring thoughts. Such prayer is known by the Spirit whose "ear" rests next to my heart. Heart prayer occurs where we make our decisions that direct our futures. This prayer is beyond our psychic drives, hence pious emotions and feelings are not the same thing as heart prayer. Emotion is useful, but we must pray even when we don't feel like it. The heart beats whether we are feeling emotional or are just washed out. Heart prayer arises at the center where we experience God's truth. Finally, heart prayer is the holy ground where we encounter God.

Scripture is filled with stories of prayer. The *Catechism* calls this the "Revelation of Prayer." God starts prayer by calling each of us to a conversation with him. We all know that God called Abraham to have faith and the patriarch responded with humble belief and trust. God called Moses to be a savior of Israel and Moses thus led his people to freedom. God called David to write the greatest prayers ever written, the Psalms, which are sung every day all over the world. God called Mary to say "yes" to having the divine child who would save the world. Her "yes" was the most important prayer response ever made.

Prayer can be seen in the whole history of salvation. It is always an event in which God calls and the person responds — and even receives the grace needed to respond. Prayer is a uniquely divine-human event, with the divine graces calling us and helping us to answer.

Jesus gave us the Holy Spirit to teach the Church and its members what Jesus wanted us to know, remember, and practice. The Spirit is our chief prayer teacher. From the Spirit we learn how to praise God for every single blessing we have. The Spirit moves us to ask God for what we need, not because God doesn't know our needs, but because we need to express and realize what is necessary for our lives. The Spirit creates a lifeline between us and Mary and the saints, who have a powerful place of intercession in the heavenly court. The prayer of intercession puts constantly on our lips the words "Pray for us."

There is never a moment in which we are not the beneficiary of divine gifts — our life, family, friends, food, material benefits, etc. Hence our mouths should always be filled with "Thank You! Thank You! Thank You!" All we own we owe to God. A grateful heart is a prayerful heart. Because God blesses our hearts, they have the intrinsic skill needed to bless God in return.

The Tradition of Prayer

The Spirit manifested the Church at Pentecost and continues to sustain and nourish the Church, especially the Church's prayer life. Our prayer will be authentic when it is fed from the richest possible sources: Scripture, the Church's liturgy, and the practice of the virtues of faith, hope, and love. When trained by these sources we quickly learn that prayer is primarily addressed to the Father, from whom all blessings flow.

Various schools of spirituality have arisen throughout Church history which have stayed in constant and productive touch with the Church's living tradition of prayer. These schools offer us incomparable guidance for our spiritual life. To cite a few of these approaches, we mention the *lectio divina* (the divine reading — meditative reading of the liturgical texts and Scripture) of the Benedictine and Trappist tradition, the contemplative wisdom of the Carmelite school, and the Jesuit Exercises of St. Ignatius. But no school can replace the family, which is the domestic church and the first place we learn to pray.

The Life of Prayer

In the name of God, the Church calls us to prayer every day. We should not wait until we feel the "urge" to pray. It matters little what we feel. It's the call that counts and that is given to us always. The "ear" of the Spirit is always next to our heart waiting to hear our cry. The Church trains us in prayer by instructing us to begin and end our days with personal prayers. The Church invites us also to daily Eucharist and the Liturgy of the Hours — especially Morning and Evening Prayer. For this latter prayer, consider using "The Prayer of Christians," which contains the morning and evening Liturgy of the Hours.

When our prayer flows from the liturgy (including the feasts of the liturgical year), we are put in touch with the whole Body of Christ. Our minds and hearts are shaped by the universal prayer of Christ praying in the heart of the Church. "Pray in us, Jesus, as head of the Church. Pray for us as our priest. We adore you as our God." The daily training and practice we receive from liturgical prayer establishes the rock upon which our meditative prayer can rest securely. In liturgical prayer we learn directly from the Holy Spirit how to pray and why we must never tire of praying.

The Three Expressions of Prayer

The three ways to pray may be captured in this prayer: May the Lord be in my mind (meditation), on my lips (vocal prayer), and in my heart (contemplation). These three forms of prayer always are connected to the "heart prayer" mentioned above.

• Vocal Prayer — Lips. It is not unusual that prayer should be associated with something physical, such as our voices. After all, the Word became flesh to speak to us. Our words "become flesh" in prayer. Jesus prayed out loud in the Temple, the Upper Room, at Gethsemane, and on the Cross. If Jesus did it, so can we. We are body and spirit. We need to translate our inner feelings and thoughts externally. Nonetheless, all vocal prayer should be accompanied by the presence of our heart, so that our words are more than mere idle chatter.

• Meditation — Mind. The mind needs to understand what God wants of us. This is not easy to do. Books help us, especially the Bible, the writings of the Fathers, and the great masters of the spiritual life. We can also learn from the "books" of creation and history. Meditative writings help us to pass from our thoughts to the reality of our lives. They train us to be reflective in an atmosphere of grace. There are many meditation methods. A method is a means to an end, which is an encounter with Jesus. Let the Spirit guide you along this path. Meditation mobilizes thoughts, imaginations, feelings, and desires to one purpose — meeting Christ.

• Contemplation — Heart. In an excellent section on this topic (*CCC* 2709-19), the *Catechism* offers the following suggestions for contemplation prayers.

(1) Take time to be alone with Christ. Choose a regular time every day for this. Gather up your whole self to enter the presence of Jesus who awaits you. Pray with the humble childlikeness of a forgiven sinner, aided by the Spirit. Recall that contemplative prayer is always a gift which we should accept with humility and a recognition of our poverty.

(2) Surrender to the "intensity" of this prayer so that you will be grounded in love. Gaze with faith upon Jesus. You will learn that Christ in turn gazes on you with affection and with a look that is purifying. Listen to God's word with the obedience of faith (Rom 16:26). Sink from this divine word into the silence of God. Learn that your contact with the mystery of Christ in contemplation enriches your encounter with Jesus in the Eucharist. All prayer must cope with distraction and dryness. It will not always be easy. Hence, be ready to abide in the "night of faith" of Jesus at Gethsemane, the tomb, and the Easter vigil for the sake of the Church.

Catechism Reflection

1. What is the "Revelation" of prayer?

"God tirelessly calls each person to this mysterious encounter with Himself. Prayer unfolds throughout the whole history of salvation as a reciprocal call between God and man" (*CCC* 2591).

2. What is the Holy Spirit's role in prayer?

"The Holy Spirit who teaches the Church and recalls to her all that Jesus

said also instructs her in the life of prayer, inspiring new expressions of the same basic forms of prayer: blessing, petition, intercession, thanksgiving, and praise" (*CCC* 2644). "By a living transmission — Tradition — the Holy Spirit in the Church teaches the children of God to pray" (*CCC* 2661).
3. How often should we pray?

The Church must " 'pray constantly' (*1 Thess* 5:17) It is always possible. It is even a vital necessity. Prayer and the Christian life are inseparable" (*CCC* 2757).

Connecting to Our Family

I always begin my prayer in silence, for it is in the silence of the heart that God speaks. God is the friend of silence — we need to listen to God because it's not what we say but what He says to us and through us that matters. Prayer feeds the soul — as blood is to the body, prayer is to the soul — and it brings you closer to God. It also gives you a clean and pure heart. A clean heart can see God, speak to God, and can see the love of God in others.

— Mother Teresa in *A Simple Path*

The Christian home is the best school for learning to pray and acquiring the habit of prayer. Morning and evening prayers and meal prayers can be learned very early in life. Every child should be able to pray the Our Father, Hail Mary, Glory be to the Father, and the Apostles' Creed as well as a meal prayer. Because a child's memory is so agile and impressionable, these prayers can be memorized quite easily.

Then there should be room for other prayers to Mary and the saints. Along with this, children can learn how to talk to God as to a friend. They don't need much training in this so much as encouragement. God is very real to children. Lead them to share their lives with Jesus, the Father, the Spirit, Mary, and the saints. You will smile at what they say and you will recover your own simplicity as you listen to their childlike conversations with God.

Set aside a regular time for family silent prayer, a few minutes in which all members open their hearts and hands to the voice of the Lord. Sing hymns at home. *Sing* a prayer and you pray twice. Mount symbols and pictures that go with the liturgical year — purple art for Advent and Lent, white and gold for Christmas and Easter, red for Pentecost. Collect pictures or icons of the saints to be put at your family shrine for their feast days. We cover our walls and tables with family pictures and secular art — can we not also make room for images that draw our attention to the world of the spiritual?

1. What have you been doing to deepen the prayer life of your family? How can you involve all the members in making prayer a time of love for

God and an act of praise? How do you draw your family to pray for the needs of others?

2. How could you create a meditation corner in your home where silence makes it possible for some meditation? What are some books and articles you have read which motivate you to pray? What do you find is the best time to pray?

3. Who are people you admire for their prayer lives? What could you learn from them? What are some prayers God has answered for you? How do the liturgy and Scripture help you to pray?

Family Prayer

Father, you call us to prayer constantly. You also provide us with the graces to respond. Help us to be aware of your invitations to pray and of the presence of the Holy Spirit who helps us meet you in prayer. May we learn that prayer is our lifeline to you and the food of our souls. We know the Spirit places his "ear" to our hearts to hear our response. In your kindness prompt us to join you in this communion of love which is the act of prayer.

Glossary

Prayer: Prayer is the raising of one's mind and heart to God or the requesting of good things from God.

Lesson 30

How Did the Lord Teach Us to Pray?

Resource: *CCC* paragraphs 2803-2865

For me, prayer is a surge of the heart; it is a simple look toward heaven,
it is a cry of recognition and of love, embracing both trial and joy.
— St. Thérèse of Lisieux

The Many Ways I Pray

How do I pray now?

"I pray as I did as a child, knowing now that the infinite variety and
beauty that enthralled me as a child is a reflection of God, His wisdom,
mercy, and love for us. Every day, snowflakes, a hilltop of trees, sunsets
and sunrises, even dandelions, inspire prayers of thanksgiving, often word-
less, sometimes (to my children's horror) sung.

"I pray as I did as a new convert, with the Mass, morning and evening
prayers, the observance of feast days, and devotions, not with the fear that
God will reject me if I do wrong, but with gladness. I pray knowing now
that God created His Church and its rituals for His children, as parents
create routines to guide and discipline their family.

"I pray as a wife and mother, loving and serving God through my
family, knowing now that their soft cheeks and sleepy breath are gifts from
God. If the wonderful intricacies of a leaf are a reflection of God's splendor, how much more splendid is God's creation of a child! I pray with hugs
and cookies, with the Rosary and special intentions, with seeing into their
hearts and praying for their futures.

"I pray as an adult woman, both silently and out loud, knowing now
that how I pray is not as important as the fact that I do pray. I pray throughout the day knowing now that when I pray is not as important as remembering that who I pray to is always listening" (Catherine Fournier, *How I
Pray Now* p. 71).

The Seven Petitions of the Our Father

The Gospels show Jesus praying many times, both in public as well as
alone all night on a mountain. Christ's witness of prayer so impressed the
Apostles that they asked him to teach them how to pray. Christ replied by
teaching them the Our Father. The *Catechism* devotes its final section to a
meditation on the seven petitions of the Our Father. Here we look at the
highlights of the *Catechism's* treatment of the Lord's Prayer.

Jesus began with the words, "Our Father." Jesus tells us that he wants us to meet his Father and to know what he is like. By his saving work in the paschal mystery of his death and Resurrection, Jesus can bring us to the Father as an adopted son and daughter. That is why we are able to say "Our" because we have become the Father's children in the adoption of grace. We are in communion with Jesus and the Church and thus have drawn away from any individualism which isolates us from others. We are indeed unique persons, but always in communion with one another and the members of the Trinity.

Hallowed Be Thy Name

We first heard the name of God when it was revealed to Moses at the burning bush. God said, "I AM." God therefore was not a thing, not the moon worshiped by the Babylonians, nor the sun adored by the Egyptians, nor a star worshiped by the Assyrians. God is a person who can know and love us and save us from our sins and follies. Philosophy can know God from reason, but such a god is hardly more than an idea, an abstraction that leaves us cold. God revealed himself as a person to Moses and the prophets.

Then Jesus came and showed us that God is a Father who has begotten a Son, both of whom sent us the Spirit. The Name of God is Trinity, a loving community of persons — loving each other and loving us with infinite, compassionate, and forgiving affection. God's name is holy because the Father is divine and beyond us, yet through love as near to us as our hearts. The infinite God is both "mighty Father" and intimate, an affectionate Hebrew term for "daddy" — *Abba*.

Thy Kingdom Come

Jesus preached the Kingdom of God during his ministry in Galilee and Judea. Jesus said that his Gospel and his very self embodied this kingdom, already present, yet still to come in us and the Church in all its fullness. The kingdom exists, but we pray that the kingdom will take possession of us so that we may live and witness it in the world.

What is this kingdom? It is the appearance of God's rule in the world, a rule that establishes love, justice, and mercy. It is a divine, transcendent, supernatural kingdom that by the Father's power penetrates the world through the Church and its members. This kingdom is only partially realized on earth. We will experience its fullness in heaven.

Though it sounds like a political term, the reality of the kingdom is never the same as a state, a government, or a social arrangement. True, it has the quality of a dream, of an ideal human system that leads some thinkers to imagine a "utopia" on earth. But the kingdom is resolutely a divine reality that does indeed have an impact on politics and society, though it is meant to move us all beyond the present age to the world to come.

We beg the Father to make his kingdom come more effectively in our lives, our Church, and the world. We are basically praying for Christ's love, justice, and mercy to take hold of all of us more deeply.

Thy Will Be Done

The human heart is the fundamental battleground in the world. All external conflicts are reflections on this interior war we experience within ourselves. Reduced to its simplest components, this war is between God's will and ours. Our song is usually, "I'll do it my way." That was the fatal lyric of Adam and Eve — as well as of the devil and his fallen angels. God declares his will. We are faced with the choice of his will or ours. We can choose the obedience of faith or the disobedience of pride. We should say this prayer often and with great fervor, "Thy will be done."

Why do we act otherwise? Why is it hard to follow God's will? We are born in the state of original sin, the result of the disobedience of our first parents. By Baptism we are delivered from this state and restored to original holiness and justice. Christ's saving act on the Cross and in the Resurrection made this possible.

But we retain what St. Thomas Aquinas calls the "wounds" of original sin. They are: (1) Ignorance in the mind, which makes it hard to know the truth or even to believe knowledge of truth is possible and is why relativism is so popular today; (2) malice in the heart, a movement that replaces the heart's instinctive wish to love with a spiteful approach to others; (3) emotionalism, which should be at the service of reason, but is rebellious, advocating an independence of the passions; and (4) weakness in the will, which ought to be submitting to God's will, but tends to prefer one's own wishes to those of God.

Our problematic wills cause us the most trouble and activate the other three wounds to push us away from God. It's no mistake that abortionists use the expression "pro-choice," a celebration of a sinful will. We should reverse this misuse of the will by praying with all our hearts that God's will be done.

Give Us This Day Our Daily Bread

St. Augustine says we pray, not to let God know our needs, but to remind ourselves of our needs. After all, God does know what we need, but until we are aware of what those needs are, God cannot give us what we don't think we should have. God never forces himself on us. He respects our freedom and urges us to use it productively.

Above all, the Eucharist is our daily bread. The Eucharist is the summit and source of our holiness and salvation. Every spiritual gift that we need is contained in the Eucharist. Just as we need physical food for daily nourishment, so we need supernatural food to minister to the hunger of our souls.

We should not be too proud to beg. We ought not be like the biblical man who said he was too weak to dig and too ashamed to beg. There is dignity in begging for graces we cannot obtain unless we ask for them. The fictional woman Auntie Mame, said "Life is a banquet and all you fools are starving!" What she said about worldly pleasures is also true of spiritual ones. Why starve when our Father has an armload of Bread for us, if only we would ask?

Forgive Us Our Trespasses As We Forgive Those Who Trespass Against Us

The best way to obtain mercy is to be merciful. The measure of forgiveness that we hope will come our way is proportionate to our willingness to forgive others. Failure to forgive others is one of the greatest of all human problems. Holding grudges against others is as common as the air we breathe. Families, neighborhoods, and countries are routinely torn apart by failures to forgive.

Read and meditate on Psalm thirty-seven. Fret not. Be still before the Lord. Wait in patience. Calm your anger and forget your rage. God does not accept the sacrifices of the sowers of disunity. We celebrate the Eucharist of forgiveness. We must practice it too. God practices fore-giveness, not after-giveness. Forgiveness causes repentance and makes reconciliation possible. After-giveness is too pompous because it means we withhold our forgiveness until the other grovels and apologizes before us. We want to humiliate, not forgive. We want to exact our pound of flesh before we give mercy.

By offering forgiveness, we receive the forgiveness we need and open other's hearts to the repentance that leads to reconciliation.

Lead Us Not Into Temptation

Temptations help us see what our moral weaknesses are and motivate us to correct our character flaws. The Holy Spirit helps us distinguish between challenges that develop our moral character and temptations that lead us into sin. Our response to temptation is a decision of the heart. Jesus endured temptations in the desert at the beginning of his public ministry and at Gethsemane at the end of his ministry. Jesus resisted temptations, exposed the lies of the tempter, and submitted to the Father's will instead.

No temptations need overcome us. "God is faithful and will not let you be tried beyond your strength; but with the trial he will also provide a way out, so you may be able to bear it" (1Cor 10:13). A life of prayer is essential for overcoming temptations. A solid spiritual life is the best guarantee for having the strength to resist temptations to sin.

But Deliver Us From Evil

We live in a world where good and evil live side by side. We cannot escape the presence of evil around us. But we can be delivered from its power to corrupt and damn us. We pray to God for the practical application of the salvation we receive and experience as members of the Church, participants in the sacraments, and practitioners of the virtues. We are always in the process of being saved, which is another way of saying we need a lifelong purification from sin and its effects as well as growth in union with Christ and the practice of virtues. A saint is a sinner making progress toward holiness.

The *Catechism* in this section highlights the reality of Satan as a source of evil temptations. This is to say that evil is more than an abstraction; it is embodied in a person. Satan was a "murderer from the beginning. . . . When he tells a lie, he speaks in character, because he is a liar and the father of lies" (Jn 8:44). We are engaged in a spiritual warfare. We struggle against the principalities and powers of evil.

But we do not fight alone. Christ fights with us. The Spirit and the Church are our helpers. We must remember that God is more powerful than evil. Grace is stronger than sin. Hence there is no reason for pessimism or defeatism. We have won the victory over evil through the work of Christ. With him, in him, and through him we shall prevail. Christian tradition, with a surge of gratitude for this teaching on prayer, has added, "for the kingdom, the power, and the glory are yours now and forever." This exclamation of praise is found in many passages of the Book of Revelation, one text of which we cite here.

Doxology
"Worthy is the Lamb that was slain
to receive power and riches,
wisdom and strength,
honor and glory and blessing" (Rev 5:11).

Catechism Reflection
1. What does the Lord's Prayer summarize?

"'The Lord's Prayer is truly the summary of the whole Gospel' [Tertullian, *De Orat.* 1: *PL* 1, 1251-1255]" (*CCC* 2774). "[It] is the quintessential prayer of the Church" (*CCC* 2776).

2. Why can we call God Father?

"We can invoke God as 'Father' because the Son of God made man has revealed him to us. . . . The Lord's Prayer brings us into communion with the Father and with his Son, Jesus Christ" (*CCC* 2798-99).

3. What are the purposes of the seven petitions of the Lord's Prayer?

"In the Our Father, the object of the first three petitions is the glory of the Father: the sanctification of his name, the coming of the kingdom, and the fulfillment of his will. The four others present our wants to him: they ask that our lives to be nourished, healed of sin, and made victorious in the struggle of good over evil" (*CCC* 2857).

Connecting to Our Family

Once upon a time there was a little girl who believed strongly in the power of prayer. She was bothered by her brother's building a trap to catch birds. She prayed to God that her brother's plan would fail. She confided her thoughts to a neighbor who was also a bird lover. One day she had a radiant smile on her face. Her neighbor noticed this. "You look unusually cheerful. You must be sure God is going to hear your prayer." "Oh yes, I am certain my prayers will be answered. Yesterday, I kicked my brother's trap to pieces."

In her simple way the little girl discovered an old spiritual principle. "Pray as if everything depended on God. Act as if everything depended on you." The seven petitions of the Our Father present to your family the seven guidelines for how to pray. We have already mentioned that it is a good idea for all members to memorize the Lord's Prayer — along with other prayers. Now we must spend a lifetime probing the meaning of the Our Father and see how it applies to our lives.

As we come to the end of this book, it may be clearer to you that the Our Father is best lived by observing the commandments, celebrating the liturgy, and mastering our understanding of the creed. In a way, the whole *Catechism* is condensed in the Our Father. As you unwrap the words you will hear sounds of thoughts from every part of the *Catechism* — and indeed of the Gospel itself. No one ever prayed more deeply or beautifully than Jesus. No one has ever been a greater teacher of prayer. The Lord's Prayer is the best of all.

1. What prayers has your family memorized? Which ones should still be added to your memory? What is the value of a memorized prayer? Why is it important to know and probe the meaning of memorized prayers?

2. What are some prayer stories from your family you would like to share with others? What prayer stories from other families have you heard which have inspired you?

3. What has convinced you to believe in the power of prayer? Why do you think some people stop praying? What are examples of prayer converting people who otherwise would have seemed impossible cases?

Family Prayer

Lord Jesus, thank you for giving us the Our Father to show us both how to pray and what to pray for. Each time we say the Our Father, be with us to say the words from our hearts and with the same attitude you brought to the prayer. Show us how to avoid being mechanical in our praying. Fill us with the patience and peace that makes profound praying so settling for our souls and so beneficial for those for whom we pray.

Glossary

Hallowed: Old English word for holy. In the Our Father we sound as if we are saying that God's name should become holy. But God's name is already holy. Our petition both reminds us of God's holiness and our responsibility to reverence the holiness of God.

Trespass: Our sins, especially those sins of failure to forgive. We ask for forgiveness of our sins in the measure of our willingness to forgive others' offenses against us.

Appendices

Prayers Every Catholic Should Know

The Sign of the Cross
In the name of the Father, and of the Son, and of the Holy Spirit. Amen.

Our Father (Lord's Prayer)
Our Father who art in heaven, hallowed be thy name; thy kingdom come; thy will be done on earth as it is in heaven. Give us this day our daily bread; and forgive us our trespasses as we forgive those who trespass against us; and lead us not into temptation, but deliver us from evil. (For thine is the kingdom and the power and the glory forever.) Amen.

Hail Mary
Hail Mary, full of grace. The Lord is with you. Blessed are you among women, and blessed is the fruit of your womb, Jesus. Holy Mary, Mother of God, pray for us sinners, now and at the hour of our death. Amen.

Prayer of Praise
Glory be to the Father, and to the Son, and to the Holy Spirit: as it was in the beginning, is now, and will be forever. Amen.

Prayer to the Holy Spirit
Come Holy Spirit, fill the hearts of your faithful, and enkindle in us the fire of your divine love. Send forth your spirit and we shall be created, and you shall renew the face of the earth.
O God who instructed the hearts of the faithful by the light of your divine Spirit, grant us by that same spirit to be truly wise and to rejoice in your holy consolation through the same Christ, our Lord. Amen.

Act of Contrition
O my God, I am heartily sorry for having offended thee, and I detest all my sins because of thy just punishments. But most of all because they offend thee my God who art all good and deserving of all my love. I firmly resolve, with the help of thy grace, to confess my sins, to do penance, and to amend my life. Amen.

Apostles' Creed

I believe in God the Father Almighty, Creator of heaven and earth; and in Jesus Christ, his only Son, our Lord. He was conceived by the power of the Holy Spirit, and born of the Virgin Mary. He suffered under Pontius Pilate, was crucified, died, and was buried. He descended to the dead. On the third day he arose again. He ascended into heaven, and is seated at the right hand of the Father. He will come again to judge the living and the dead. I believe in the Holy Spirit, the holy Catholic Church, the Communion of Saints, the forgiveness of sins, the resurrection of the body, and life everlasting. Amen.

Act of Faith

O my God, I firmly believe that you are one God in three divine persons, Father, Son and Holy Spirit; I believe that your Divine Son became man and died for our sins, and that he will come to judge the living and the dead. I believe these and all the truths which the holy Catholic Church teaches, because you revealed them, who can neither deceive nor be deceived. Amen.

Act of Hope

O my God, relying on your infinite goodness and promises, I hope to obtain pardon of my sins, the help of your grace, and life everlasting, through the merits of Jesus Christ, my Lord and Redeemer. Amen.

Act of Love

O my God, I love you above all things, with my whole heart and soul, because you are all good and worthy of all love. I love my neighbor as myself for the love of you. I forgive all who have injured me, and I ask pardon of all whom I have injured. Amen.

The Rosary

The rosary is an important prayer in Catholic Tradition. It involves vocal prayers (Apostles' Creed, Our Father, Hail Mary, Prayer of Praise), meditative prayer (on the mysteries of the rosary), and usually the use of rosary beads as a person or a group of people say the rosary.

Mysteries of the Rosary

Joyful Mysteries — events surrounding the birth and early life of Jesus
Annunciation
Visitation
Birth of Jesus
Presentation in the Temple
Finding the Child Jesus in the Temple

Sorrowful Mysteries — events surrounding the passion and death of Jesus
Agony in the Garden
Scourging at the Pillar
Crowning with Thorns
Jesus Carries His Cross
Death of Jesus on the Cross

Glorious Mysteries — events and faith of the early Church's experience
Resurrection of Jesus from the Tomb
Ascension into Heaven
Descent of the Holy Spirit upon the Apostles
Assumption of Mary into Heaven
Coronation of Mary as Queen of Heaven and Earth

Seven Sacraments in the Catholic Church

Baptism
Confirmation
Eucharist (Communion)
Reconciliation (Penance, Confession)
Marriage
Holy Orders
Anointing of the Sick (formerly called Extreme Unction)

Seven Capital Sins

Pride
Covetousness
Lust
Anger
Gluttony
Envy
Sloth

Order of Mass

Gathering and Entrance Procession
Greeting
Opening Prayer
Prayer of Praise
Penitential Rite

Liturgy of the Word

First Reading (usually from the Old Testament)
Psalm Response
Second Reading (usually from an epistle in the New Testament)
Gospel
Homily
Creed
Prayer of the Faithful

Liturgy of the Eucharist

Preparation and Offering of the Gifts of Bread and Wine
Preface Prayer of Praise and Thanksgiving
Eucharistic Prayer (including words of consecration and concluding with
    the community's great AMEN)
Communion Rite: Lord's Prayer, Sign of Peace, Communion, Meditation
Concluding Prayer
Blessing
Dismissal

Rite of Reconciliation for Individuals

(Penance, Confession)

Greeting from the Priest

Sign of the Cross

Scripture Passage

Confession of Sin

> Here, honestly confess the sins that have been part of your life. All serious matter should be included, as well as less serious things that are troublesome in your life with the Lord.

Advice and Spiritual Counseling

Penance

> The prayer or good work that you will be asked to take on is a sign of your sincere repentance.

Prayer of Sorrow or Contrition

Absolution

> The Priest places his hands on your head (or extends his right hand toward you) and prays these words of forgiveness:
>
> God, the Father of mercies, through the death and resurrection of his Son has reconciled the world to himself and sent the Holy Spirit among us for the forgiveness of sins; through the ministry of the Church may God give you pardon and peace, and I absolve you from your sins in the name of the Father, and of the Son, and of the Holy Spirit.

Prayer of Praise, such as:

> Priest: Give thanks to the Lord, for he is good.
>
> Response: His mercy endures forever.

Dismissal, such as:

> The Lord has freed you from your sins. Go in peace.

Responsibilities for Catholics

The Great Commandment

"You shall love the Lord your God with all your heart, with all your soul, and with all your mind. You shall love your neighbor as yourself" (Mt 22:37-39).

The Ten Commandments

(cf. Ex 20; Chapter 15 of Invitation)

1. I am the Lord your God. You shall honor no other god but me.
2. You shall not misuse the name of the Lord, your God.
3. You shall keep holy the Sabbath.
4. You shall honor your father and mother.
5. You shall not kill.
6. You shall not commit adultery.
7. You shall not steal.
8. You shall not bear false witness against your neighbor.
9. You shall not covet your neighbor's wife.
10. You shall not covet your neighbor's goods.

The Beatitudes

(cf. Mt 5; Chapter 15 of Invitation)

1. Blessed are the poor in spirit; the reign of God is theirs.
2. Blessed are the sorrowing; they shall be consoled.
3. Blessed are the lowly; they shall inherit the land.
4. Blessed are they who hunger and thirst for holiness; they shall have their fill.
5. Blessed are they who show mercy; mercy shall be theirs.
6. Blessed are the single-hearted; they shall see God.
7. Blessed are the peacemakers; they shall be called sons of God.
8. Blessed are those persecuted for holiness sake; the reign of God is theirs.

Spiritual Works of Mercy

To admonish the sinner
To instruct the ignorant
To counsel the doubtful
To comfort the sorrowful
To bear wrongs patiently
To forgive all injuries
To pray for the living and the dead

Corporal Works of Mercy

To feed the hungry
To give drink to the thirsty
To clothe the naked
To visit the imprisoned
To shelter the homeless
To visit the sick
To bury the dead

Laws of the Church

Use the text from the new *Catechism* paragraphs 2041 to 2043

Holy Days of Obligation (in the United States)

January 1 — Solemnity of Mary Our Queen
Ascension Thursday — 40 Days after Easter
August 15 — Feast of the Assumption
November 1 — All Saints' Day
December 8 — Feast of the Immaculate Conception
December 25 — Christmas Day

Regulations for Fast and Abstinence

Fasting means giving up food, or some kinds of food, for a specified period of time. In Church regulations, abstinence means giving up meat for certain times. (For many years, abstinence was required of Catholics every Friday, as a communal way of observing Friday as a day for special penance. Catholics are no longer required to abstain from meat each Friday, although they are expected to exercise some form of penance on that day, in remembrance of Jesus' death for us.) Catholics are expected to fast from food and liquids (other than water and medicine) for one hour before receiving Holy Communion.

Certain days are also set aside as days of fast and abstinence for Catholics, when adults are expected to eat only minimum amounts of food, no meat, and nothing between meals at all. In the United States, Ash Wednesday and Good Friday are such days of fast and abstinence.

Index

Our Sunday Visitor...
Your Source for Discovering the Riches of the Catholic Faith

Our Sunday Visitor has an extensive line of materials for young children, teens, and adults. Our books, Bibles, booklets, CD-ROMs, audios, and videos are available in bookstores worldwide.

To receive a FREE full-line catalog or for more information, call **Our Sunday Visitor** at **1-800-348-2440**. Or write, **Our Sunday Visitor /** 200 Noll Plaza / Huntington, IN 46750.

Please send me: __ A catalog
Please send me materials on:
    __ Apologetics and catechetics   __ Reference works
    __ Prayer books   __ Heritage and the saints
    __ The family   __ The parish

Name_____
Address_____Apt._____
City_____State ____Zip_____
Telephone (   ) _____

                                                       A73BBABP

Please send a friend: __ A catalog
Please send a friend materials on:
    __ Apologetics and catechetics   __ Reference works
    __ Prayer books   __ Heritage and the saints
    __ The family   __ The parish

Name_____
Address_____Apt._____
City_____State ____Zip_____
Telephone (   ) _____

                                                       A73BBABP

OUR SUNDAY VISITOR BOOKS **Our Sunday Visitor**
200 Noll Plaza
Huntington, IN 46750
1-800-348-2440
OSVSALES@AOL.COM

Your Source for Discovering the Riches of the Catholic Faith